CONTE

To David,
Emer and Karen

ACKNOWLEDGEMENTS

Many people helped in the writing of this book, most importantly those who gave their time and thoughts and the many others whose observations down the years are looted from notes and memory. I would like to thank all of them, and I hope none of them will think their trust has been abused.

The generosity of the Joseph Rowntree Charitable Trust lifted financial worries and Stephen Pittam offered unfailingly cheerful moral support; Rowntree have a way of making it seem as though grant recipients are doing them a favour. Duncan Campbell-Smith and Daniel Franklin of *The Economist* tolerated with kindness a distracted writer in Belfast. The Blackstaff Press gave such care and encouragement, it was hard to believe they had other books to worry about. As always, and as he has for so many, David McKittrick, in the middle of his own busy life, provided advice, information, reassurance and jokes when they were most needed: I owe him.

Family and friends put up with a lot and helped in many ways – especially Caitriona, my Aunt Margaret, Emer and Karen, who repaid neglect with treats and hugs, Brigid, my parents – and above all David, who read, reread, listened, gave honest opinions, ran the household and kept me going.

INTRODUCTION

Sense of identity is something people imagine they will be embarrassed to talk about, until they start. The fifty people I interviewed as the core of this book, even those for whom being interviewed is a routine business, visibly considered and reconsidered their answers. There were moments at which each one said, 'Wait a minute, hold on now, I've never thought about *this* before.' Almost all of them said they enjoyed the discussion in part because they found themselves stopping for the first time to consider attitudes habitually produced as a reflex – some were none the less uncomfortable with their own conclusions.

Their opinions either illustrate or counterpoint an analysis that also draws on my twenty-five years' adult life as a Northern Catholic, and on the views of many others, noted in the course of twenty years' reporting. Few of those who agreed to be interviewed would accept in total the arguments their words now enliven – a considerable number might object strongly. I hope I have not hurt any of them.

The Catholic community in Northern Ireland is a community with a high level of political awareness and a widespread consciousness of the factors that go to make up 'identity', though the word itself was not used widely or unselfconsciously until fairly recently. Some think the slogans and beliefs their parents lived by are long overdue for an overhaul; others regard any examination of terms like 'Irishness' or 'Northern nationalist' as in itself threatening a sense of communal identity; many are somewhere in the middle. But even those who most resist self-questioning have to admit that they can no longer presume too much about Catholics on the simple basis of origin, and that even self-description as 'nationalist' now needs more explanation. Repeated academic surveys through the years have of course attempted to measure feelings about nationality and preferences on government: suspicion that a set number of prefabricated answers cannot adequately reflect the fluid state of many people's opinions is borne out by the twists and turns of conversation.

'Nationalist' and 'nationalism', like 'republican' and 'republicanism', are to some contemporary Northern Catholics interchangeable, and to others terms of bitterly charged mutual opposition. The second, I think, would not have been true for many twenty-five years ago, when the most pacific of people – although well aware that the few IRA members of the time also claimed the name – often casually described themselves as 'republican' to suggest a more radical and anti-clerical turn of mind than that of the Nationalist Party. But 'nationalist' then as now was also a general term which the bulk of the Catholic population accepted as a basic political description. There were 'Nationalist' councillors and Stormont MPs, and a mass of 'small n' nationalist people, many contemptuous of the Nationalist politicians who at least nominally represented them. Some still insist that they are not themselves 'nationalist' largely because they so disliked the Nationalists of the past. For various reasons it seemed better to take 'Northern Catholic' as an inclusive term – to cover all those born into Catholic families, if nothing more.

Perhaps the greatest difficulty in attempting to pin a slippery idea like identity on a page is knowing when the job is done, especially in a combination of direct quotation, reporting and analysis. Early on it sank in that to make transcription from tapes possible in a reasonable time, I would have to limit interviews to fifty – and if those were to give any kind of roughly representative flavour, then all the interviewees must be Catholic. Beyond an effort to produce a range of backgrounds there was no great science in their selection. About one-third chose themselves, as people with known and controversial views on identity: a greater number I had never met, several suggested by others who knew them in various capacities but did not know their views.

Though there are obvious gaps in this range of voices, I do not believe any significant strand of opinion is missing. Plainly, however, Catholic ideas about identity are influenced by Protestant behaviour and attitudes, past and present. But Protestant ideas about Catholics is another book, for someone else to struggle with.

The bulk of the interviews was taped in lengthy conversations during 1992, a few in 1993. I went back to some people a second and third time – former Sinn Féin director of publicity Danny Morrison answered questions in a series of letters from jail.

In terms of quotation, and incidental to descriptions of attitudes, this is a Catholic version of events and developments during the Troubles (itself a term Catholics use more readily than Protestants). There are, however, no prolonged accounts of suffering at the hands of loyalist paramilitaries, British soldiers, the predominantly Protestant Royal Ulster Constabulary or the almost totally Protestant Ulster Defence Regiment (now merged in the Royal Irish Regiment). Three women coincidentally described to me a phase of their lives at the same period in the same area in August 1969: two are still to some degree influenced by their impressions then of violence by Protestant civilians and by the state, the third was more affected then and since by the violence of Catholics. But the attitudes of all three have clearly been as much shaped by character, opportunity and subsequent experience.

I did not go in search of Catholics with tragic histories to interview, from a mixture, maybe even a muddle, of motives: in part because there was to be no comparable Protestant account of pain and loss, partly because it always seems such a disproportionate intrusion to ask someone to relive pain and sadness for the sake of a journalistic account. In addition, over the past twenty years I have listened to spontaneous descriptions from scores of people – Protestant and Catholic – damaged in numerous ways by the violence of the Troubles, and in general their attitudes do not seem altered because of what has happened to them in a way that is distinctly different from the changes in attitudes of others around them.

Perhaps the decisive factor was that though a considerable number of those I interviewed certainly believe Catholics have suffered more from Protestants than the other way around, none told a tale of personal tragedy or loss as explanation of the current state of their own identity.

Agonising about bias and balance – in addition to asking others to reveal their own attitudes – probably demands some personal details. I was born in Belfast, brought up in a large family in Tyrone, south Armagh, Antrim and Belfast again by devout Irish-language-loving parents, went to school in Kilkeel, County Down, and Ballymena, County Antrim, met my first Protestant friend at fourteen, stopped believing in Catholicism as a teenager: the last two details are entirely unconnected. I am married to a Northern Protestant. We send our children to integrated schools, one of which we helped start. In 1970 I went to work in Dublin and discovered with dismay that the rest of the sundered Irish nation was foreign to me: it later sank in that Dublin is not the sum total of Ireland. Once I marched for civil rights and called myself socialist and pacifist. I am certainly neither British nor unionist, but for years my sense of Irishness has been at least as confused as that of many people I talked to. The only ism I could now declare wholehearted allegiance to is feminism, and that as a principle rather than a set of dogmas.

Three final technical points. Many of those who allowed me to interview them did not want to be identified, most often out of a simple desire for anonymity, occasionally out of fear that something they said would attract loyalist paramilitary attention, or because they voiced anti-republican views and were afraid of the IRA or of their own family's disapproval. Where a first name appears in capital letters, it is a pseudonym, and the background details given – birthplace, occupation etcetera – are fictional but comparable to the real ones. Throughout, the quoted opinions of those named come from interviews with me unless otherwise specified.

The book deals in turn with attitudes to class, political allegiance, the IRA, Protestants, Britain, the South, and the Church, in the belief that together these constitute a picture of Northern Catholic identity. No one I interviewed pointed out any serious omission.

1

'I remember . . .'

ARDOYNE

Three women, three stories. All Catholics brought up in Ardoyne, a sprawl of working-class housing in north Belfast running up to bigger and better houses on the Crumlin Road. MARY MCALEESE is forty-two now, successful, well-known, the Director of Professional Legal Studies at Queen's University Belfast. In August 1969, the date usually recognised as the beginning of the Troubles, she was an eighteen-year-old schoolgirl.

'From the first day of the Troubles, I turned my face away from taking any part. I watched the B Specials walk up the Crumlin Road with a Protestant crowd intent on burning out Catholic homes. And having seen these forces of law and order behaving in an extraordinary, totally unacceptable way, I turned my face against that and set out to become a lawyer, not a revolutionary – more important, set out to try and find my way through the Church and through Christ. I struggled with that, couldn't sleep over it. But that was the decision I made – to go with the Christian view, not the way of violent revolution.' She was explaining why she found it galling, working in Dublin later, to be written off as a 'maniacal nationalist, an ultra-republican, a Provo, because I was an Ardoyne Catholic and I told them we had suffered'.

ANN was younger at the time, thirteen. She lived in the middle of Ardoyne. Her father was unemployed and sick for most of her childhood. Her first Troubles memories are of standing with her parents watching the houses burn on the Crumlin Road. Later she heard her father argue with her brother about joining the IRA. 'He said you haven't a chance, because you've got the British government against you, you've got the RUC and the Irish government against you, and what chance have you when you haven't unity in your struggle? And if you're going to win at any point, the Free State's going to step in and put the hammer on it. I think he believed all that, but also he was afraid for him. The result was my brother never did get to the stage where he joined.'

JEAN was eleven. She lived immediately behind the Crumlin Road, 'in the older houses, with a toilet outside'. The family was better off than most – her father was a docker. Jean's early memories run into each other.

'When the soldiers came, I remember taking trays of tea to them, and gunmen running about on the street.' Soldiers raided her house, and when she and her sister came home from school they had to tidy up. 'I never felt any hatred for them. They were sent for, they arrived – I was just angry because there were bootmarks on the sheets. They were strangers coming into areas where people ran taking them tea and then turned against them, and they really didn't know who would say hallo to them, and you were afraid to speak for fear of other people in the area threatening you.' On another occasion the soldiers arrived in the middle of the night. 'We had a bed in one corner, my ma and da slept in it, and us three girls were in the other, and my da shook us and said, "It's the soldiers." And you sort of woke up out of your sleep. I was all embarrassed, at that teenage stage, but I went down the stairs and ended up making them all cups of tea even though they were in raiding the house.'

Jean lives in Carrickfergus now. She is married to a Protestant; they have two sons who go to a Protestant school. She and her husband are unemployed. 'I hate going back to Ardoyne. Going into those areas I'm watching and I'm looking and you know people look at you and they know you're a stranger. He's only been up a few times.

'I have a cousin doing life, he was involved in killing an old man. The one who pulled the trigger, he's in Monaghan – *I'd* have given his name. What's he doing life for?

'I just always stood back. I had a boyfriend, I used to say to him, "You ever get involved with the IRA, that's me and you quits." But this night he was in a dance hall, Toby's Hall. He was given a leaflet and he tore it up. When we went to the hall the following Sunday night he was taken into the toilets, a couple of fellas, they put a gun to his head and says to him, "You were seen tearing one of our leaflets up – what did you tear it up for?" And that guy had to stand there and say, "I didn't want the soldiers reading it." He never got involved – I wondered was that anything to do with me, because it's so easy in those areas to get involved.

'Maybe I was more observant. I went to school with a girl, very Provo-minded. Coming home from school one day, her young sister was about three, I saw her coming up firing stones at the army and calling them all the *b*s of the day. We can all swear – but a three-year-old? And I thought, imagine your kid doing that!'

Jean did not remember Bloody Sunday in January 1972 when soldiers shot and killed fourteen unarmed demonstrators – part of most Northern Catholics' mental file on the Troubles. 'But I'll tell you what I do remember: the three young Scottish soldiers – ah my God.' They were among the first soldiers to be shot by the IRA, in March 1971 – off-duty, two of them teenage brothers, shot by IRA men who had spent the evening drinking with them in a downtown bar. 'And I remember a young fella, lived in Elmfield Street, the same age as me. He was dark, I remember him going by in the street. He was fifteen, cleaning a gun in his own house, shot himself . . . '

Mary McAleese is now a prominent lay Catholic, married with three children. She lived in Dublin for some years with her husband after both their families had lost their homes and businesses through the Troubles. 'We lived on the Crumlin Road itself. My brother, who is deaf, was very badly beaten by a bunch of thugs at our own front door. That was the first indication we'd been marked out for any special treatment because we were Catholics. Then they shot our neighbour, Gerry Kelly, in his shop. We used to put up these screens on the windows from five o'clock on, thinking we might get petrol-bombed. But in fact they emptied the contents of two machine guns through the windows. It was just God's mercy none of us was killed. This was 1971.

'In 1972, my father had two pubs, one off the Falls, the Long Bar, and the Red Barn downtown. It was burned to the ground and the Long Bar was bombed [by Protestant, loyalist paramilitaries]. A young woman, a sister of a friend of mine, was killed – a mother of young children. It was a crazy thing: the bomb exploded, it didn't do all that much damage. But the keys to the car struck her and broke her neck. She'd run across the street to grab her little girl. My father took it very badly, he couldn't believe she was dead, he thought she'd just fainted . . . he felt responsible and he was very ill for a couple of years thereafter.

'We left Ardoyne and went to live in Andersonstown, rented a house off nuns. That was another joke. It was a big old house in Fruithill Park, a lot of land – I suppose to kids who didn't know any better it would have looked like we had buckets of money. The day we moved in a crowd of teenagers broke nineteen windows. On the next day, the army came into the house and searched the garden and found the tail fin of a rocket launcher. Thanks be to God they found it before some of our kids did – but unfortunately they had their photographs taken holding the tail fin. It exploded, one of them was killed and the other lost his sight.

'My husband's family – they lived on the Albertbridge Road. In the loyalist workers' strike, they were put out on the street. They went to live in Rathcoole. Their first week there, their youngest son was coming home from school and a shower of bad boys scraped UVF with glass on his arm. Then we went to Dublin, and working for RTE [Radio Telefís Éireann] I met this coldness and "Don't tell *me*, your story is the story of a Provo." Merciful God!'

Ann married a Provo. When their eldest was three and their twins a year old, he was charged with the murder of a soldier four years earlier. She had their fourth baby a few months after her husband was arrested; he was in jail for the next thirteen years. They live in Craigavon, County Armagh. Ann works with travellers and is doing a degree, like her husband. Her schooling was disrupted by an incident when she was fifteen.

'I was in Toby's Hall and a British foot patrol came in – one soldier opened fire in the hall and shot a fella dead. This would have been late 1970. I wasn't allowed to go there but I went to meet a fella. I was sitting with a few friends and this patrol came in. A normal occurrence: they'd have harassed a few people, shoved a few around, anything to upset your night's entertainment.

'This night they appeared to be kind of drunk and they demanded drink. And of course, being a republican area, obviously they weren't given any. A few people started banging bottles of beer on the tables and shouting "Out out out" and then one person threw an empty glass and it smashed on the floor beside them. Well, one soldier lost his nerve – how I know, the true story came later from one of the other soldiers, he deserted and went to Dublin and gave a press conference. But all we could see was one of the soldiers, he turned full circle and opened fire while he was turning. There were soldiers outside as well and when they heard shooting inside, they started shooting from outside in.

'It was only a prefabricated hut, you know. I can't believe there wasn't a massacre. People just shoved everybody down on to the ground and lay there – and it seemed as if there was a million bullets flying around. I remember thinking, when I look up everybody's going to be dead. Not far above my head to the ceiling was all smoke. The soldiers had left and everybody was shouting and crying – pandemonium. And there was a fella lying dead – but we thought he was just wounded. The fellas, fair play to them, they were trying to keep everyone calm, and they surrounded him and tried to cope and look after the girls.

'Somebody got up and started to sing an old hymn which was well-known in Ardoyne, "Faith of Our Fathers". I think it was to calm people down. Everybody stood and started singing it. When I think of it now, what did the soldiers outside in the dark think? "Faith of Our Fathers", inside this hut. It seemed like ages, no ambulance, nothing. I was just in shock. Then a priest came along, he must have been giving the young fella the last rites, and we were all being taken out one by one. When I opened the door, there were the soldiers, all lined up, down on their hunkers with their rifles pointed towards the door. And I thought, they're going to shoot us one by one. They had to practically pull me out of the place.

'They couldn't get me settled. The doctor wouldn't come

out when they said it was Ardoyne. "Have you any nerve tablets? Have the neighbours any? Give her one," he said, "and if that doesn't work, give her two." So I was on six Roche 5 a day, and I was fifteen. I was on them for two years till we moved out of Belfast, and then a doctor stopped me cold. My parents thought, this place is destroying their lives, we'll have to get out. I left school because of it, lost tons of weight, my hair started falling out. There was a lot of loss: some of my friends left and went to England, others emigrated, my very best friend went to Australia.

'Half, three-quarters of Ardoyne was on nerve tablets, they were dished out like Smarties. It was sad leaving Ardoyne, though – and part of you never leaves.'

2

'Two very different lifestyles'

CLASS

Introduce the idea of class and its effects on identity to Catholics of varied backgrounds, and most assume instantly that what you want to talk about is the emergence and increasing prominence of a bigger and more influential group of middle-class Catholics than ever before. Only a few of those I interviewed focused instead on the striking divisions that now exist inside what was once a relatively coherent community. There is a general realisation that some have been remarkably successful, and that major shifts in lifestyles have happened very fast indeed. But it is equally plain – and universally admitted, though with varying degrees of concern – that the last twenty years have meant dramatically differing experiences for whole subsections of the community. The effects are not so easily summarised.

'There's a sizeable Catholic middle class for the first time, and I don't think we've seen the full impact of that yet,' said a prominent churchman. 'I think it's having a powerful influence on Catholics' sense of identity. But that's still very much in genesis. In fifteen to twenty years the results will be more visible.'

Across a wide middle band, neither rich nor poor, the impact of direct rule of Northern Ireland by the British government – and a steady rise in the number of Catholics obtaining third-level education – has meant increased access to jobs in the public sector, the civil service, health, education and housing administration. For most, moving into Northern Ireland's middle class does not mean great affluence. But the history of discrimination against Catholics during the decades of Unionist rule means that it does, however, often signify the first pensionable, secure job or jobs a family may ever have had and the realisation that promotion is now a possibility, with all that entails in expectations about lifestyle and attitudes towards participation in society in general. The implications for political attitudes are becoming clearer: having a stake in society is as powerful an influence towards moderation and conservatism in Northern Ireland as anywhere else. But the question of identity is also affected by internal community tensions caused by this rapid transition – and by Protestant reactions to visible Catholic success, affluence and influence.

The reactions seem largely caused by visibility, where before there was none. Even thirty years ago the Catholic middle class was comparatively insignificant, consisting in the main of those who serviced their own community: builders, solicitors, publicans, shopkeepers, teachers, priests. In 1975 the Catholic social profile was summed up by the American Edmund A. Aunger, in what has been called a 'path-breaking study':

While a clerk may be a Catholic, it is more likely that the office manager will be a Protestant; while a skilled craftsman may be a Catholic, it is more likely that the supervisor will be a Protestant; and while the nurse may be a Catholic, it is more likely that the doctor will be a Protestant.

('Religion and occupational class in Northern Ireland', *Economic and Social Review*, vol. 7, no. 1, 1975)

The most recent research shows that Catholics are still under-represented in many high-status, well-paid jobs. Large areas of business and commercial life are still very substantially Protestant. But a growing number of economists, statisticians, scientists and engineers – and journalists – are Catholic. The law is an increasingly Catholic profession, topped up by about 60 per cent of the yearly intake of trainee solicitors and barristers. The judges' bench, once almost exclusively Protestant, has become more representative of the population balance. (Though there has been dispute about the proportion of Catholics to Protestants, consensus of expert analysis on the 1991 census is that Catholics now form 42 per cent of the population of just under 1.6 million.) Studies show that Catholics make up about 30 per cent of managers and administrators in both the private and the much bigger public sector.

The civil service, Northern Ireland's biggest employer and once a byword amongst Catholics for discrimination, is now 35 per cent Catholic at management level. In the last two years promotions have made an even more striking impact: of the ten people at the most senior, permanent secretary grade, three are Catholic. In December 1992 the Northern Ireland Office announced that the government had set a 'goal' of 25 per cent Catholic representation in the top 'policy-related posts', to be achieved by the end of 1996. Only ten years ago, senior civil servants tried to delay the publication of a damaging Fair Employment Agency report showing that there were only two Catholics among the top forty-three officials, and that promotion patterns had not substantially changed since British direct rule replaced the Stormont parliament.

Perhaps the most significant change is in the student body at Queen's, the North's main university. More than 70 per cent Protestant at the beginning of the Troubles, it is now more than 50 per cent Catholic, with a Catholic majority in several faculties. The growing trend for young Protestants to emigrate as third-level students and not return means that Catholics increasingly make up a larger proportion of the graduate pool – which in turn ensures that the Catholic middle class will continue to grow.

The speed with which Catholic lawyers, doctors, accountants, and entrepreneurs of various kinds have developed access to political decision-making, and made their way into an economic mainstream once largely closed to them, has left nerves jangling inside the Catholic community and beyond it. In such a small society, and because the public face of Northern Ireland was formerly Protestant to such a degree, economically successful Catholics – often with distinctively Irish, Catholic names – make an impression disproportionate to their numbers. Clustered in the comfortable suburbs, particularly in Derry, Dungannon, Newry and Belfast, the newly arrived have in addition developed a reputation as free-spending, confident and optimistic, an image that increases their impact.

Nationalist politicians wonder what growing affluence and an increased stake in Northern Ireland society have already done to traditional political expectations. But when people try to assess the consequences in terms of Catholic identity, they find a tension between the confidence born of success and increased wealth, and the depression of the long-term unemployed and low-paid who have few hopes for their children.

The pattern of advance is by no means universal. Even the significant improvement in educational opportunity and achievement has not altered a fundamental gap. In June 1993 the Fair Employment Commission published a breakdown of the latest census data, which showed that 'Catholics are in the majority in the student population and are as likely to have educational qualifications as Protestants – but Catholic unemployment rates for men and women are higher than those of Protestants for each level of qualification'. While thousands of Catholics have done conspicuously well, for the substantial section of those who are either unemployed or in low-paid jobs, the past two decades have been years not of progress but of increasing disadvantage. Perspective on the extent of change is provided, and the disparity that still exists is underlined by the judicious John Whyte, whose *Interpreting Northern Ireland* (Oxford, 1990) digested more than 500 pieces of research on the developments of the last twenty years. Commenting on a 1980 study (*Northern Ireland: Between Civil Rights and Civil War,* by Liam O'Dowd, Bill Rolston and Mike Tomlinson), he concluded that it 'showed direct rule had made remarkably little difference to the structure of power in Northern Ireland . . . and that Catholics were still systematically the underdogs in every sphere . . . [an analysis] largely vindicated by subsequent research into the economic gap between the communities'.

The fact that some Catholics have prospered as others have fallen behind, their conditions actually worsening while cousins and in some cases sisters and brothers forge ahead, causes all the usual resentment of unequal fortunes – but in this case heightened by a sense of political betrayal. Twenty-five years ago the central demand of the civil rights movement was for an end to discrimination against Catholics. The altered Catholic social class profile is due to a combination of direct rule administration, fair employment legislation, expanded employment in education, health and welfare, and increased educational opportunity. It is widely accepted that barriers to Catholic advancement have fallen, to a great extent because of the reforms eventually initiated and administered by British politicians –

although it has taken steady Irish-American lobbying to toughen the legislation and quicken the pace. Fair employment legislation, however, has had patchy effects in helping to provide equal opportunity, while economic recession has hurt the most vulnerable Catholics in greater proportion than Protestants.

Not surprisingly, the perception that British direct rulers have none of the discriminatory instincts of Unionist government is more enthusiastically expressed among Catholic civil servants and lawyers than it is in unemployment blackspots like Strabane, Creggan or Ballymurphy. Unemployment, running at a much higher level than before the Troubles, continues to hit Catholics disproportionately: the Catholic rate of joblessness remains over twice as high as that for Protestants. The unskilled once found work in the building trade, now squeezed by recession: Protestants, who dominated manufacturing employment, have found a substitute in the ranks of the Royal Ulster Constabulary (RUC) and the Royal Irish Regiment (RIR), not an option for most Catholics – either because they regard the state's forces as tainted or because joining would expose them to IRA attack, community disapproval and ostracism. The security forces provide about 25,000 jobs.

The greatest concentration of unemployment, as of poverty, ill-health and a number of other social problems, is in the urban areas of strongest support for Sinn Féin, and for the IRA – Creggan and Brandywell in Derry, Whiterock, New Lodge and Ardoyne in Belfast. Those are, of course, also the areas where army and police checkpoints, searches and patrols are concentrated. Surveys regularly show that more than one-third of Sinn Féin voters are unemployed, compared to about 13 per cent of Social Democratic and Labour Party (SDLP) supporters. Nationalism is a powerful force, but by their own accounts, people in the most deprived parts of Derry, Strabane, Newry, Lurgan,

Portadown and Belfast support Sinn Féin and the IRA from a mixture of motives: in part as a protest against the circumstances of their lives, but also as a gesture of defiance and rebuke to the more middle-class, and therefore more conformist, supporters of the SDLP. They know they are not alone in believing that it has taken the pressure of IRA violence on top of civil rights agitation to push Britain towards substantial reform. Some SDLP supporters, and non-voters, have unwillingly reached the same conclusion.

'There was a sense of togetherness among Catholics – that's been lost,' says JIM, a retired academic in County Down. 'There's a painful and an angry division now between those educated, mobile, skilled and in work, and those who are not. Sure, Dublin's a much more divided society, but here the division's on top of other forms of disaffection.' It is all the more painful and intrusive in such a small society. Among the fifty people I talked to, several spoke of the striking disparity in incomes, and in political attitudes, that now existed inside their own extended families. One described a common situation: 'There are sixty-five in my generation of the family, between different batches of cousins, and they represent the whole social range and nearly the complete spectrum of political views as well. There are those who've done well, those who've not done so well, people who manage fairly comfortably, people on the dole and some in highly paid professional jobs – and you've politics that run from Alliance right the way through to Sinn Féin... there's an obvious link between not doing well and support for Sinn Féin.'

Many families manage to maintain a closeness in spite of new class differences, but many of those I talked to described difficult scenes and considerable tension when clashing lifestyles were matched by conflicting political views. The clashes are most dramatic when one branch of the family remains in a deprived

area that more prosperous members have left, and when those
who stay express strong republican views. In Derry, and even
more so in Belfast, those who have moved out in the past ten
years can be touchy and defensive, those they leave behind
rough-tongued. 'The break is not that significant yet in Derry,'
said Bishop EDWARD DALY, 'but there's some degree of hurt
among the people left behind – there's definitely a growing
middle class that wants to move away from where they were
born and create a little bit of distance . . . we're getting jokes in
Derry now about the Culmore Road, which is the Malone Road
of Derry.' (The Malone Road is the old-money, formerly
mainly Protestant part of south Belfast.)

Imprisonment for IRA offences can cause open rifts. In sharp
contrast to the many families who become more overtly and
staunchly republican when a relative is imprisoned, others allow
contacts to wither. Some relatives never acknowledge the imprisonment and certainly never write to or visit the prisoner.
Prisoners' families react with considerable bitterness, usually expressed as a conviction that, as one woman put it, 'Of course,
they couldn't admit they'd an IRA man in the family, with the
fancy neighbours they have now.' A number of those I interviewed insisted that snobbery, as much as principled objection
to republicanism, dictated attitudes.

Drawing parallels with the experience of other countries is a
dubious exercise, but a number of people who had spent time
in the USA described how struck they were by the similarity of
the gulf between poor and newly rich blacks. They recognised
the disaffection of those left in the ghetto who now see
themselves as victims twice over – in Northern Ireland first,
discriminated against by the Unionist state, and next abandoned,
and then criticised, by people whose rise they believe is largely
a result of a campaign of protest about disadvantage they
themselves still suffer.

THE GAP

In Belfast, Derry, Newry and other towns where a very short geographical distance – sometimes less than a mile – can mean an entirely different daily experience of the Troubles, it is far from fanciful to suppose that attitudes can be affected by where people live. A number of those I interviewed had moved some years ago to a better-off district, or were about to. Some were highly conscious of what this had meant for others and insisted that their own attitudes had not changed and would not change. SHEILA is forty-three, a dental technician who went back to school after she had her two children. She is now three-quarters of the way through a second degree. She and her husband, a printer, live in Andersonstown. They are thinking of buying a house on the fringe of comfortable south Belfast, but they know they will face some criticism for 'selling out' if they do, which bothers Sheila. Her father always called himself a socialist. She grew up proud to be working-class.

'Growing up in Ballymurphy in the fifties, what the middle class was to me was a group of people that I would have seen as having a bit of money and being involved with the Catholic Church – I would have associated them I suppose with the *Gaeilgeoirí* [people who are keen on the Irish language] and clean faces . . . small shopkeepers, say, on the Falls Road whose kids went to the same school as me, the "respectable" people. Certainly the important people in the Church were the respectable ones. Respectability and the Church, certain things seemed to go together. And the Irish culture in some ways, Irish dancing and stuff like that.

'I suppose those people weren't really middle-class – maybe we were aware of them because living in Ballymurphy set you apart. The estate had enormous problems right from the word go. It was something to be ashamed about, living there. And being treated differently in the school as well. Children from the red-brick houses, God help us, they were the cream ... I'm embarrassed now by memories of meeting boys in the town and telling them I lived in Whiterock instead of Ballymurphy – and being left home on occasions to Whiterock, no more than a quarter of a mile from home, because it was outside the estate.'

The association in Sheila's memory of money, 'respectability', and closeness to local clergy was made by many others – from small towns and the countryside as well as from urban areas – when they tried to recall how they first defined a Catholic middle class. They also remembered linking this group with 'Irish culture', a connection few would make any longer.

'The new middle class now, I don't have much contact with them – maybe one doctor and one lawyer. Most of the people that I would know would be people from my own background, people who are first-generation educated,' says Sheila.

'There's a gap, and there's a real tension as well, between the Catholic middle class and where I think it sees the Catholic working class. There's guilt, I think – a feeling that they've made it on the shoulders of the poor. And there's also the practicalities: the middle classes have an interest in the stability of the state, right? So what do you do about this instability, which is located in the Catholic working class who vote Sinn Féin and, however reluctantly, nevertheless support arms in some way?

'What some do is they ghettoise it. Talking all the time about Catholic, nationalist west Belfast as problematic is something that should be looked at quite critically. I want to say, hold on, it's not that easy.'

Sheila's view of what she took to be a new class was expressed with all the sharp edges of a recent perception, and in a more consciously political way than by most others. But the theme of guilt about profiting during the Troubles, 'making it on the shoulders of the poor', came up in varying forms from a whole range of people, from the wealthiest and least apologetic to those who view that wealth with some misgivings, or with anger. For more than a decade BRIAN FEENEY has been a prominent SDLP politician and frequently a broadcast commentator on political and social affairs. He is scathing about the new Catholic middle class 'climbing out of the ghetto and kicking the ladder away, slamming the door behind them as they leave', and he speaks of those professionals who each day work in west Belfast as teachers, doctors, lawyers as 'driving into the area in the morning and home to more comfortable, affluent, peaceful north and south Belfast at 5 p.m.'. It is in many ways a self-portrait. He grew up in west Belfast himself, works as a lecturer in the Catholic teacher training college in the area, but no longer lives there: he too lives in comfortable north Belfast. But those he criticises are the people with a degree of financial comfort who 'put nothing back', essentially by refusing to become involved in politics or community work.

Feeney admits instantly that his was a middle-class upbringing, pointing out as others often do that west Belfast then was a community with a complete class structure of its own. 'Doctors, a big fruit importer, accountants, dentists, solicitors – it was a heterogeneous society. That counted. You felt you were as good as anybody else. You didn't feel you were in a ghetto because you had a complete mix right the whole way down – As, Bs, Cs.'

Many Catholics pick out the eleven-plus examination, the selection procedure which for decades decided which children won scholarships from primary to grammar schools, as the first stage in the development of their community's assertiveness. (When Labour government reforms gave Britain a largely comprehensive secondary system in the sixties, Northern Ireland retained a strong grammar school sector and selective secondary education, now modified but in principle unchanged.) JOHN

HUME passed the exam in its first year in 1947, his success a personal milestone he still uses regularly to illustrate the narrative of his own career, and of Northern nationalist resurgence. Research in Northern Ireland several years ago showed the exam to have been consistently weighted against girls: education reformers long ago damned it as socially divisive, concluding that as a narrowly based test of academic aptitude it unfairly favoured children from more literate, middle-class homes. Hume still will not have that. 'There's no education system in the world that'll put brains into someone who hasn't got them,' he says. 'Selection means that people of ability, no matter what their social level, can break through.'

Several generations of working-class Catholics saw the eleven-plus, and were encouraged by their schools and many of their parents to see it, as their best chance of progress in an unequal society. Northern Ireland's fee-paying grammar schools had always been the route to third-level education and so to the middle class, but it took the education reforms of the forties to provide at least the chance of free second-level education for all. Catholic folk wisdom knew that poor Protestants had the pick of unskilled labour and could hope for apprenticeships in the shipyard: if poor Catholics had 'the brains for it', education should instead be their salvation. It became a doctrine, and marks the upwardly mobile of today no less than their predecessors.

Intensive teaching methods boosted or substituted for natural aptitude. 'We didn't do Irish history,' Brian Feeney remembers, 'we did the eleven-plus.' More brutally direct than most, his first comment on the exam is that it was the 'determiner of future class'. He remembered the teacher who 'pounded stuff into you'. 'He used to recite to us: "You're doing the eleven-plus now, and this is your big chance. If you pass the eleven-plus you'll go on to St Malachy's or St Mary's. If you don't pass the eleven-plus, you're going out at fourteen to dig sheughs." The guys who didn't pass and stayed on at primary school – because there was no secondary school for them to go to in Andersonstown then – they ended up weeding the parish priest's garden and mowing the lawn or whatever. Primary Nines, they were called. I think I might have met three or four of them in the rest of my life. A couple of them joined the British army, which is what you did in 1962–63 when you got to be sixteen or seventeen. They just went into a different stream of existence. You went to Mass in the same church, but you came out and you went home, you had different friends and you went to school in another part of Belfast, and you had no contact whatsoever unless you met them at a match or some sporting event. But you tended not to, because sport was also a middle-class thing. The teams we played for were nearly always all grammar-school boys. Digging sheughs, you were wrecked at night.'

Awareness of the separation Brian Feeney highlights comes up in conversation all over the North – a phenomenon no less marked among Protestants, where the selective school system has created exactly the same social divide. But the extra dimension for Catholics is the particular political significance grammar-school education has had for them. Many in the more prosperous Protestant community had always been able to pay for places in grammar schools as their passport to middle-class jobs. It was the arrival of free second-level education and the selective filter of the eleven-plus that straightened the path for the Catholic community. The process has steadily produced those who have gone on to become prominent in business, teaching, law and politics. In 1973, 63 per cent of the SDLP Assembly members at Stormont described their occupational status as professional: 57 per cent were university-educated.

Statistics consistently show a high percentage of A level passes in Catholic grammar schools. They also show that the highest proportion of school leavers with low qualifications or none at all is among boys leaving Catholic secondary schools. In the most deprived urban districts, there is keen awareness that a place in a grammar school sets not just a child but potentially the whole family on a different path.

GUILT

'Guilt is the essence,' a lawyer told me, 'it's all you need to know.' He announced this as soon as I said I wondered what effect new affluence and status in Northern Ireland had on Catholics. But soon it became clear that he was talking about a very small group of super-earners, perhaps thirty of them – more an upper class than a middle class, mostly lawyers, some doctors, making £300,000 to £400,000 a year. Most of this group, he estimated, was produced by the Troubles, and the rest by political reform. 'It's on the back of the Troubles and the reverse discrimination that came with it.'

Much of the lawyers' money, he said, came from legal aid for the lengthy trials of 'scheduled offences' – defending republican and loyalist paramilitaries – and from handling insurance claims for property damaged by IRA bombs. The doctors had private practices and hospital consultancies; they made extra money as medical advisers for the government, effectively arbitrating on the compensation claims of people injured in violence. 'I wish the Troubles were over, I really do – but I know if they ended tomorrow our earnings would be divided by ten,' the lawyer said. Others suggest this is an exaggeration of the contribution of the Troubles to super-earners' incomes.

Guilt among his fellows – all men – emerged, he said, 'in drink, that's when we admit it to each other'. He laughed. 'You couldn't say it to anyone else, could you? And what can you do about it? Everybody can't afford to be missionaries like Joe Hendron and Alasdair McDonnell.' (Hendron and McDonnell are both GPs and SDLP politicians.)

The lawyer supposed the guilt came out of a suspicion that he and his fellows were profiting to an exorbitant degree from violence and misery, and ultimately from a conflict they felt no connection with. In his case, guilt expressed itself as rage, apparently on behalf of Catholic judges and crown prosecutors whose lives were now at risk from the IRA – or as he put it, 'those wee bastards trying to kill them'. (The IRA have killed five legal figures during the Troubles, three of them Catholic.)

Lawyers now in danger from the IRA, he said, included several who had 'marched for civil rights, for equality for Catholics, saying we don't get a fair crack of the whip'. He reeled off names, though he was unable to substantiate the point that these had in fact been civil rights supporters. 'They've climbed to the top, taken posts, responsibility and service, not power. They did it to serve their people. I know those guys. They felt honour bound to take responsibility when it was offered to them, though it meant a big drop in earnings – and what happens? Those wee bastards . . . '

He was certain that super-earners in general felt no pangs about the Catholics still in the ghetto. 'They find themselves under attack from their own community, the community they've left – the unemployables. Most of us made it on our own. No family money, just ability and a lot of hard work. We had no connections, no advantages. Twenty, thirty years ago, we were just like you . . . exactly like you: first-generation university, no money in the family. If we could do it, why can't they? They'd rather moan about discrimination, wouldn't they? I get it all the time. What do you work at? I say. "Ach, I couldn't get a job," they say, "I went for one forty years ago, and I got turned down. Where's the point in trying? You know what it's like for Catholics." . . . It makes me sick.' It clearly did.

But in the main the most affluent and those on the next few

rungs down have neither opted for posts that would expose them to IRA attack, nor offered any criticism of the system in which they prosper. Emergency legislation has repeatedly tinkered with conditions of arrest, powers to detain, conduct of trials. The new wave of Catholics in the legal profession, like most of their predecessors, have with very few exceptions been content to work the system in silence.

HUGH is a 59-year-old businessman from the Tyrone-Monaghan border who now lives in the next south Belfast avenue to the angry lawyer. His attitude is very different. He made money by finding and selling a product no one else had marketed with any energy, dealing resolutely on both sides of the border at the same time. Catholics are born entrepreneurs, he says – an assessment he insists is not meant as a slur on Protestants. Seeking out ways to make money, and risk-taking, were forced on people with no foothold in traditional finance, 'and then we developed a flair for it'. But he thinks confidence is an essential quality and a recent development. His own assurance was the result, he reckons, of having been brought up in a mainly Catholic environment. He works voluntarily through various schemes to develop job training and to bring investment to the most deprived areas. Watching communal confidence grow in recent years has pleased him. But he is not impressed by many of the attitudes he sees – nor by the affluence in one broad band of Northern Ireland society.

'I think at the moment to keep the standard of living going, it's essential that violence continues. That's an awful thing to say, I know that. But look at it – look at the employment the violence causes. You've got racketeering; next level up, security firms; then the police earning £30,000 to £50,000 a year; then lawyers, accountants, builders, glaziers. Bombs in the centre of Belfast, they keep I'd say in excess of a hundred legal firms going for a year or more. And all that money's going out into

restaurants, pubs, car sales, concert sales, good holidays. A
society with lots of money washing around, and it's a society
that's not producing anything that anybody wants.'

Catholics who have moved into the Malone Road in the last
ten years tend now to refer to it familiarly as 'the Road', the
same phrase people use to refer to the working-class Catholic
Falls Road. Often, of course, they are the same people. Hugh
enjoys life and is happy to have given his children a 'good start',
but he thinks life on 'the Road' has its drawbacks, and some of
his new neighbours, though he admires them, will be more
pleasant when they mature.

'A huge percentage of the people who have moved in here
came from Andersonstown, west Belfast, and life's much more
pleasant here in many ways. But it's lonely. We twinned the
parish with Twinbrook at one stage, two parishes in the same
diocese, in the same city, but wildly different. The one thing
Twinbrook scored over Malone on was companionship and
community. You don't rap your neighbour's door and go in for
a yarn, and you don't hang around your newspaper shop and get
all the gossip. There isn't a newspaper shop, for a start.

'And people are on this upward spiral that leads to selfishness.
They're achieving that much that they don't have time to
wonder about who they've left behind. It's a luxury to have
time to think, like I have now. There isn't the time to listen to
music, to read. That non-stop climb destroys the quality of life.
But you couldn't tell anyone that. The difficulty is having the
confidence to stop, the confidence that comes from continuing
wealth. We haven't got that. Because you're a self-starter, you
only know one way to go – you don't know what these plateaus
that you can drop off contain. Catholics I know who've gone
to Dublin, they made it by clearing out, they went as emigrants
and they've boomed as well, because instead of stopping at six
they worked on until ten or eleven, weren't into the society bit,

the golf clubs. And the same thing is true here. You meet
solicitors who think nothing of working seventy or eighty hours
a week. They aren't in clubs, the Ulster Orchestra committee.
They're only in one thing – their own business.

'I think it will change as people learn to enjoy the fruits of
their labour. I hope it does. I think those who try to put
something back now are limited in number. All the time they
have this awful fear, that they have to keep working, they don't
know how long the business is going to last.'

For the moment, however, upwardly mobile Northern
Catholics – like much of the rest of the Northern middle class
– seem to have been cushioned from the effects of the recession
in Britain. It is clear that, while many parts of Britain experienced decline, areas in south Belfast, in Newry, Dungannon,
Derry and elsewhere, have profited over the same period from
a stable and, in some cases, buoyant property market.

'OUR PLACE TOO'

For anyone under forty who barely remembers pre-Troubles
Northern Ireland, it can be difficult to appreciate how dramatic
the change has been in the public profile of Catholics. Thirty
years ago in Dungannon, County Tyrone, PATRICIA and CONN
MCCLUSKEY started the Campaign for Social Justice (CSJ), the
group that made the first systematic attempt to quantify
discrimination against Catholics, by working out the sectarian
balance in local public sector employment. Now in their late
seventies, the McCluskeys live in Dublin. Conn was a doctor,
Patricia a social worker – they belonged to a middle class that
was small and passive, protecting its own privileges by keeping
quiet. On visits back to Dungannon, the McCluskeys are amazed at what seems to them a transformation – economical, social,
political, and perhaps even psychological.

Patricia McCluskey remembers the wealthy Catholics in

Portadown where she grew up. 'The people my parents mixed
with, they all packed up and went south when partition came.
The people that were left had no inclination to lift their head
above the parapet.' Conn is sure the considerable number
involved in the CSJ who had been educated in the South, like
him, had more confidence. 'The ones who went to St
Malachy's, in Belfast, they were very inhibited compared to us.
They felt inferior. Well, we did too, but less so. Now it's completely changed. Once, recently, I was in Armagh, in this
Protestant-owned shop: very up-market draper, austere sort of
crowd. In the old days it was nearly like going into a church,
it was so respectful and restrained. This last time I was in, it was
full of young Catholic girls, shouting and talking and laughing
as equals.'

When the McCluskeys began to organise, they had difficulty
finding support. 'In Dungannon, like everywhere else then, the
senior jobs were held by Protestants – and we were definitely,
fearfully, second-class citizens, that was the aim,' says Patricia.
'Catholics kept their heads down. When we started to look for
comparable people to ourselves in every town to gather figures,
they weren't there, or if they were, they didn't want to know.
We worked terribly hard, writing to Whitehall, getting these
endless letters back from people like Alec Douglas-Home. They
didn't even read the letters they signed, and sometimes I felt all
our work was going to be for naught. It hasn't been for naught.
You've only got to go to Dungannon now to see the prosperity.
Actually, the Catholics are taking over. Doctors, accountants
. . . All the big Protestant shops are being sold to Catholics.
Protestants are beginning to move out.'

Conn McCluskey adds, 'It's becoming a Catholic town, and
Derry is the same . . . and the confidence everywhere, it's completely changed. You're beginning to see slightly chancy but
clever opportunism and entrepreneurism coming to the surface,

and it's all Catholic. There aren't the same number of new Protestant businesses.'

Hugh agrees: it is a subject he came back to when talking
about relationships now between Catholics and Protestants. He
thought a recent but now established confidence was the key to
the political attitudes he saw evolving around him. 'This is a
middle class here with a standard of living that's not available
anywhere else, because their wages are related to British wages
and their mortgages and expenses are Belfast expenses, a lot
smaller. There are wonderful opportunities to get on here, and
Catholics have grabbed them. They're fearless in their purchas-
ing of houses and in the improvement of their businesses. The
march is on and is unstoppable.

'The Catholic community are confident in their own success
– it has come through most in the legal profession – and their
kids are confident. They're confident in their culture, and in
their Irishness. I know they're integrating into society up here,
on their own terms. And when it isn't on their terms – like
when there's a toast to the Queen at the end of some function,
the dinner of a professional association, say – they can say to
themselves, my father would turn over in his grave if he knew
I was doing this, but I'll do it for good manners and in that way
draw the sting.

'Although I remember being in Balmoral Golf Club on a
Saturday night when there was a dance and then they played
"God Save the Queen". Looking around, I realised, God, 60 per
cent of the people here are Catholic: who's insisting on this?

'In my generation we knew there was no future here. You'd
succeed in limited ways, you'd get by, there was always a hope
things would become equal – but eventually there was one
solution, and that solution, some time, was a united Ireland,
which each generation passed on.

'But they're not seeking that. The generation after me

haven't got the same desire for a united Ireland. They have a desire for their Irishness – but they wouldn't take the Republic as they find it at the moment. What I see is, among those my children's age and people like me who've got this far in their lives, we do want to be part of Ireland, to say we're Irish – but we're not going to let anything go on up here that we're not part of. This is our place too, and it's taken us long enough to get this far.'

Hugh expressed with exactness, perhaps especially when he sounded most unclear, the mixture of emotions their new-found status caused a number of middle-class Catholics. His account of the mental gymnastics performed in the time it takes to drink a toast or stand for the British national anthem rang true for many others. Few Catholics feel neutral about such rites: few believe the rites themselves are neutral observances. The end of the night in a golf club, after a good dinner, is not the time for self-examination. There is embarrassment because this is in public, exasperation that something their parents complained of and that seems to them archaic should still be happening. There is above all an acute awareness of being inside a club they were brought up to think of as excluding them – and then discovering that although they are now welcome to pay membership fees, the rules still have the flavour of exclusiveness. Formality softens the irritation. The more formal the occasion, the easier it is to regard toasts and anthems as extra knives and forks. 'I'll do it for good manners' is the usual conclusion, but it leaves a bad taste. Younger people seem more blithe about it, apparently taking the view that these rituals are all nonsense, already out of date, and bound to be abandoned very soon. But a number of those I talked to, all in their fifties or older, prefer to stay away from professional society dinners rather than be 'put in that position'.

Hugh's mention of the 'Irishness' of the newly affluent

Catholic is also intriguing. In what was largely a poor community for many years, wealth naturally tended to be associated with the unionist ruling class. Awareness of the existence of poor Protestants did nothing to diminish the popular conviction that big houses, land, and possessions were unlikely to be in Catholic ownership. Where they were, instant qualifications were made: 'He came from a well-off family,' a woman in her seventies remembered, talking about a man who is best-known for his republican views. 'Big publicans, owned a string of pubs in the city – but he's a good Irishman, none better.' The 'but' was an essential element of the description. Once, achieving wealth meant attracting the automatic suspicion that you were now more likely to be seduced into participation in the alien state, to 'sell out', become a 'Castle Catholic' (as in Dublin Castle, seat of British rule until Irish independence) and 'pro-British' – since Catholic society offered few satisfactory middle-class status symbols.

The old curse words still have some force, but increasingly sound dated and inadequate. The members of the class Hugh describes have little of the sense of vulnerability of their Catholic predecessors, largely because it is becoming more difficult to depict the society they increasingly participate in as alien and unionist, apart from leftover rituals.

British, yes, but what does 'British' mean now? Direct rule by secretaries of state with plummy English accents is unmistakably British rule, but it is not seen as discriminatory against Catholics: or at least, it is not seen in that light by those who have done well out of the reforms of the past decade. On the contrary, an important factor in the new Catholic middle-class self-assurance is the conviction that the British rulers in Stormont and Hillsborough find them more congenial than Northern Protestants.

Many in this rising middle class see the SDLP as accurately

reflecting their hopes and concerns. They are particularly aware that they owe their access to government to the policies of John Hume and his party, whose successful cooperation with the Dublin government produced in the Anglo-Irish Agreement of 1985 the framework of a joint approach by the British and Irish governments. That arrangement satisfies the desires of a growing number, the people Hugh talks of who 'aren't going to let anything go on up here that they're not part of'.

Since the Anglo-Irish Agreement, the most tangible signs of Catholic middle-class access to government and increased influence have been jobs and promotions across a wide range: from sensitive posts to a whole raft of nominations for membership of advisory and consultative bodies. Lists of names come from the SDLP through the Irish government to the Northern Ireland Office, with Dublin's Department of Foreign Affairs adding a number of nominations of its own. Some are examples of straightforward patronage, designed to reward the party faithful; others are an attempt to represent Catholic opinion beyond the ranks of recognised SDLP support. Even for the most trivial appointments, there are sensitivities, principally fear of Unionist anger. The libel laws make it unwise to give examples of bodies to which such appointments have been made. A new judgeship some years ago led to an expensive damages settlement when a journalist reported that colleagues thought the appointee inadequate and foisted upon them by Irish pressure. (The judge in question was subsequently killed by the IRA.)

But there is less sensitivity now about criticism from other Catholics. Hugh uses the old slur 'Castle Catholic' against some whom he believes 'compromise themselves by never saying what they think – and it's stupid as well as cowardly because there's no need for that any more'. These were almost all people in unimportant posts, however. He thought the most prominent

were above any such criticism, naming one as 'the complete opposite of a Castle Catholic – he's had to be accepted because of
his ability, not to make up the numbers, not because "we must
have 33 per cent Catholics"'.

But among the less prosperous, the unemployed and the low-
paid, some reckon the middle class's terms for integrating into
Northern Ireland society are completely unrelated to their own
very different concerns. For years BRENDAN helped to train
teenagers and the long-term jobless in basic skills in Belfast's and
Derry's worst areas of unemployment. He sees a basic lack of
sympathy across what he believes is now a divide in both class
and political terms. He hears the Catholic middle class, in the
form of the Catholic Church and the SDLP, 'berating' the Sinn-
Féin-voting poor 'from above, from a great height – endless
statements about what we should do and should not do, from
people who live different lives . . .

'There are only so many people you can involve in the structure of things – it's possible if you could give jobs to everybody
and produce a much better standard of living, you wouldn't
solve the problem overnight but you'd make a change. A good
wage, maybe two, a nice house, holidays – you can insulate
yourself. The people that Hume is accommodating, that's what
happens to them. They're protected. But Hume can't accommodate all of us. The lives of the people who are still living in
Creggan or Ardoyne or Turf Lodge are terrible. By anybody's
standards it is a poor way to live, culturally, spiritually, it's
rotten. And increasingly what a lot of people are feeling –
they're contained, they've been contained. The whole place
could be sealed off in ten minutes flat. As long as the problem
is kept in there, then really they feel a lot of other people have
just abandoned them or abandoned worrying about them.

'That's why sometimes you see in the nicest people – who
I don't think would blow anybody up – a sort of almost repressed

glee when golf clubs get blown up or fancy city-centre stores. There's a feeling of, at least it's not all up here. You could see elements of a class war about that in some ways: "They're sitting up in Fortwilliam Golf Club there ... " '

CLASS POLITICS

The theme that the better-off have now abandoned the poor, socially and politically – by fleeing the areas they once shared and adopting a less dogmatic form of politics – was voiced in various ways by a number of people. Some, like the retired academic in Newcastle, County Down, who thinks the 'sense of togetherness' Catholics once had has been replaced by painful division, see the sense of betrayal on one side matched now by fear on the other. 'In 1969 a lot of people came from the worst bits of Belfast to Newcastle and Cushendall, Downpatrick, Portaferry, places like that – Catholic, peaceful – and the locals took them in and welcomed them. Now they're afraid of the new estates on the outskirts of their towns. They think, they're all Provos, they'll seduce our youngsters. If Belfast went up in flames the same way again, I don't think there'd be the same welcome.'

With occasional exceptions, Sinn Féin leaders try to soft-pedal class divisions among nationalists. GERRY ADAMS, for example, emphasised that nationalism is not the prerogative of the unemployed and, referring to the 1981 republican prisoners' hunger strike, remarked on the surprise of Belfast youths, bussed in for funerals, at the imposing rural houses some hunger strikers had lived in. 'They couldn't believe these were Catholics' houses,' he said. 'They thought all republicans lived the same way as themselves.' Some of his senior urban colleagues less diplomatically admit their first sight of hacienda-style republican homes in the countryside gave them the same culture shock as 'the wee lads'. Leading republicans are aware of middle-class

nervousness of the kind the Newcastle man described, and in
turn have their own anxieties about the political priorities of the
upwardly mobile – specifically about the prospect of increased
participation in the Northern Ireland state further weakening
traditional Northern nationalism.

MITCHEL MCLAUGHLIN, a 47-year-old Derryman, is Sinn
Féin's Northern chairman. He describes himself as being from
a 'respectable Catholic middle-class background'. Before he
became a full-time republican, he was an electrical engineer,
and he likes to suggest, jokingly, that if he had so chosen he too
could have had a comfortable lifestyle. In Derry, he says, the
new social divide between Catholics is glaringly obvious.

'There are two very different lifestyles. There's those who
still live in the ghetto, who would have a working-class
experience and view of the world. In the nationalist six counties
that can mean overwhelming depression and oppression – I'm
not just talking about British security policies but male
unemployment in the upper eighties, endemic for generations.
And then you can have, in a small town like Derry, in a suburb
out the Culmore Road, Catholics now living in £100,000
houses, driving two cars, two or three holidays a year.

'You meet them on the street: these are people maybe that
you know, sometimes people you went to school with,
sometimes relatives, and they've got their suntans – the effects
of that in terms of a wee bit of world travel and a different
perspective ...

'These are people for whom the whole civil rights movement
is now a distant and confusing memory. They've forgotten
already that eighteen years ago they couldn't get into the
Chamber of Commerce and weren't allowed near the Chamber
of Trade. Now they're into wearing the gold chains and they're
the appointed spokespersons, particularly in the event of an IRA
bombing or operation.

'They're now in the high streets and some of them are doing very well indeed... there are a number of Catholics in very senior civil service positions. That has to translate into political confidence – their ability to pull strings, to address particular issues. It focuses the question of where their interest now lies. Maybe more often than not, they're into a working alliance with those they would have regarded as the people who were oppressing them just a short time ago: Unionists, Protestant businessmen.

'That's reflected in the politics you hear coming through from the Catholic Church or the SDLP. A clear class division is starting to develop within the nationalist/Catholic community. They're not voting Unionist, no. But it has affected attitudes towards nationalism, a united Ireland, the viability of the six-county state.' He smiles. 'There's a blurring of what used to be clear perceptions of where *mañana* was to be found.'

The accusation of short political memories and the suggestion that those in least need profited most from civil rights agitation is familiar: republicans often make the point. But there is a reluctance – at least among the republican leadership – to go further and denounce the newly comfortable as traitors, collaborators with an altered but still undeniably British regime. The words are not used. This is partly because republicans know their supporters have a limited appetite for abuse of other Catholics: the community is simply too small, family links too strong. In what was once a predominantly poor community, and in spite of reservations and political resentment, there is also a pervasive pride at some of the successes. It is no coincidence that by and large these are not posts that are politically sensitive: only a couple of dozen at most through the years have become judges, magistrates or prosecutors, for example.

There is another reason for downplaying criticism of those who participate in the structures of the state. Even the least-reconciled traditionalist is forced to admit that Northern Ireland now is not quite Northern Ireland as it was before the Troubles.

'Of course there have been gains,' Mitchel McLaughlin says impatiently, 'real changes, it's nonsense to say there haven't. Houses are better, some Catholics are in real jobs now, they have real shops they didn't own before. Of course that's significant – but the things that bring real progress have not changed, like the British government's attitude. You could argue that they have enlisted the Catholic middle class and the Dublin government into their 'project'. It is clear, however, that republicans have lost their old, seamless certainty about the selfish bad-mindedness of that British 'project'. At least some sections of their leadership can now see pragmatism in others where once they saw only the worst motives: imperialist greed on the part of the British, self-interest and subservience among 'Castle Catholics'. Indeed, pragmatism was once an irredeemably dirty word.

'Even if those people ended up voting Unionist,' Mitchel McLaughlin says now of the new middle class, 'it wouldn't be legitimate to call them collaborators. They're acting in their own class interests, they're voting in a fairly pragmatic way.'

The uncomfortable truth is that republicans are not sure where the SDLP-supporting new middle class is heading politically – and although SDLP leaders will not admit it, nor are they. This is a group with its own dynamics, several of which are novel, in an unfamiliar political setting. 'I *think* they'll stay solid SDLP,' said one senior party figure privately, 'but their children mightn't.' He had been talking about his belief that although the newly affluent feel less alienation from the Northern Ireland state than do their parents, they will not support any settlement that returns them to a purely British jurisdiction, that has no Irish government element to legitimise their sense of Irishness.

Presumably a considerable number of Catholics who now live in the most expensive and once largely Protestant parts of Northern Ireland would find this discussion of their possible political attitudes bizarre, Catholics who do not vote and are not interested in those around them who do. I failed to meet any – but others denounced them to me. SEAMUS MALLON, the SDLP's deputy leader, said those he despised were 'the people who milked the advances of the civil rights movement dry, and put nothing back into it. They would tell you they never had anything to do with politics, as if that's some kind of virtue. They're not representative of nationalism – but they're invited to dinners in Hillsborough Castle and Stormont House and they're the people the Northern Ireland Office quotes when it talks about ordinary nationalists and unionists saying politicians aren't representing people's desire for compromise. They're like leeches – and it's equally applicable to affluent Protestants. It's remarkable how easily people are moulded by flattery.'

It was an angrier description than that of any Sinn Féiner. Others echo Hugh's accusations of selfishness and self-centredness, but point out that this is an evolutionary stage. 'It's probably an emergent politics as yet,' says a Southerner who for several years has been living in one comfortable Northern area and working in another. 'Some accuse this new class of being hedonistic, not fired with any strong ethos, much more materialistic than anything else. They are very much partici-pators in the good life – and that doesn't make for radicals.'

In several interviews people made similar suggestions, some more censorious than others, about 'the showiness of a lot of this spending, a really greedy pursuit of pleasure', several half-admiring of a 'Catholic lack of guilt about enjoying themselves', as one put it. 'Go into the best of the restaurants and look around: I'll bet you'll find the majority any night of the week are Catholics, cheerfully spending £80 a couple – and they're enjoying it all the more because they weren't brought up to it, it's a new experience.'

Many touched on another theme: that these people have considerable flexibility and openness about their political future, a quality not common in Northern Ireland. Academic lawyer MARY MCALEESE thought this was now a characteristic among Catholics generally: 'A willingness not to define too sharply the shape of what's to come – I think it's visionary and creative.' She thought members of the new middle class, because of their social and economic advantages, had more freedom to explore and express this openness. She is also sure they have a 'bottom line' – which happens to coincide with the SDLP's declared preferences.

'It's very hard to pin people down as to what they want for the future. Most have a vision of an Ireland without borders, where the country will develop as one unit – but the people I would socialise with don't come at the problem with a hard-and-fast view, and I find that tremendous. There's a tremendous sense of Europeanism, people talking about a united states of Europe: it's certainly not the language of "wrap the green flag round me" any more. There's a more modernistic idea of what an all-Ireland state might be, they'd argue much more strongly for pluralism. But people are not prescriptive. Their idea is, let's leave it to the constitutional politicians, and if they're prepared to settle . . . I think they've a great respect for the likes of John Hume as an international statesman.

'But I think there's a bottom line, and it's, "No thank you very much, we're not going back into any kind of power-sharing in Stormont – we've already had that and it didn't work." There's no belief in power-sharing. One of the things that can't be sold to the Catholic population – whether middle-class or working-class – would be going back into a Unionist-dominated local assembly. We've moved on.

'For Catholics, direct rule has been the best form of government we've had, with a number of direct effects, for example in fair employment. We'd still be waiting for a local assembly to introduce fair employment legislation. But we have it, it's up, it's operating, slow enough in some places but on the way... And the relationship between Catholics, nationalist politicians and Westminster – that they have direct access and a good profile in the world at large – these things have come about, in all honesty, as a result of direct rule as well as much greater organisation among Catholics, and very good leadership.

'There has been a growth here into a sophistication that one can be very proud of. I thought at first that the Anglo-Irish Agreement was an awful fudge of a document, but it's what people think it says that matters, and it *did* grow. The agreement, and direct rule – between them, they've offered people a way of living.'

3

'Shifting, complex and ambiguous'
POLITICAL ALLEGIANCE

In the face of a united unionism that controlled the Northern Ireland state, nationalism before the Troubles was above all disorganised, and Northern Catholics were by and large politically helpless, hopeless and cynical. One man remembers the politicians of his youth 'whingeing on the sidelines', their policy no more than wishing the state away. Now it is unionism that is fragmented and demoralised, while Catholics, although still divided, increasingly show a confidence many Protestants struggle to come to terms with, and which the old Nationalists would scarcely believe. For some it comes from a belief that they have made clear their disaffection from the Northern Ireland state so violently through the IRA, that they can never be ignored again. 'The Croppies won't ever lie down now,' Sinn Féin president GERRY ADAMS says, invoking rebels of two hundred years ago – derided in a contemporary loyalist song – to suggest the unchanged defiance of republicans. For others, represented by the SDLP, confidence is born of an altogether modern satisfaction at the new status they or their children enjoy or have a chance to enjoy, and the conviction that their political leadership will build on this. 'We're not going back to *their* wee Northern Ireland,' a delegate told the SDLP annual conference in 1992 to delighted applause.

Self-assertiveness does not always mean a clear-cut and conscious sense of political allegiance. There are many non-voters who are either too cynical about all the existing parties to give them support or who believe party politics has no answer to Northern problems. But otherwise the pattern of Northern Catholic voting throughout the Troubles is clear. Apart from a period when the Alliance Party looked attractive to middle-class Catholics, votes for unionist or left-wing parties have been insignificant. Since there has been a choice, a steady two out of three Catholic voters have chosen the SDLP, one out of three Sinn Féin. The SDLP originally brought in people involved in the civil rights movement and inherited voters from the old Nationalist Party; Sinn Féin attracted those who habitually opposed any participation in the Northern Ireland state and withheld their support from the Nationalists, as well as a younger generation shaped by the Troubles. The divide, however, is far from exact, and masks the unhappiness of those who think that in effect they have no choice, and the reservations and even unease many feel about the political parties their votes support. DANNY MORRISON, in jail since 1990 but formerly Sinn Féin's director of publicity, says republicans are well aware of this. 'Support can't always be taken for granted. Some agnostic Catholics who are working-class and unemployed, who have experienced Brit harassment and suffered perhaps even the violent death of a loved one, will still have a moral problem with the armed struggle; whilst some middle-class SDLP supporters I know were severely disappointed that the IRA missed Thatcher at Brighton, and were quite emotional and angry about the hunger strike. And when John Hume (as sometimes he does) meets a British government minister

head-on and genuinely stands his ground – the tendency I think
would be for republicans to privately applaud him.'

As a teenager in south Derry MICHAEL FARRELL remembers
thinking of the whole Northern nationalist community as 'lacking in self-respect, desperately looking for the South to rescue
them', a judgement John Hume and Gerry Adams would
second. A quarter of a century into the Troubles, self-respect
still dictates many political allegiances – and, in essence, that
now means a determination that the state of Northern Ireland
must change to reflect two identities, Irish as well as British. As
Northern Catholics have become more confident about expressing a sense of Irish identity, forms of politics that ignore or
downplay that conviction have steadily become more and more
irrelevant.

The Alliance Party was an early victim. OLIVER NAPIER is
fifty-eight, knighted by the Queen for 'political services' in
1985; he helped found the party and was its first leader. He is
a Catholic unionist, but he was brought up to think 'the ideal
was the unity of Catholic, Protestant and Dissenter'.

'Then I asked myself, how do you achieve such unity? And
I realised the Protestant and the Dissenter were damned if they
were ever going to be united with the South. Some time
around the end of the IRA campaign [December 1956–February
1962], I appreciated that the only progress that could be made
was going to be made in the context of the Union.

'When the civil rights thing broke out I said, this is disaster.
I was totally in favour of what they were trying to do – it was
methods I was very concerned about. If you bring people onto
the streets, they're going to appear threatening and therefore
will be divisive. I didn't blame the people who were marching
– they had a case which was totally unanswerable. Nothing had
been done about it. I didn't join because I thought it meant
confrontation and if you want to reconcile and create ideas of

common identity, you don't operate that way...Though I don't blame those who thought this was the only way to produce anything in the short term. And they probably were right. Unfortunately my political thinking has always been in the longer term, and in the period 1968–69 in the Catholic community there was deep resentment of what the Unionists were failing to do – and probably, therefore, a greater bitterness against somebody like me, who was seen not to be kicking them where they should be kicked, in fact trying to reason and produce another concept. Yes, it was quite bitter.

'I believed there would be an explosion from the Catholic population in the sixties, I saw it coming. They weren't quiet years, as people sometimes say. There were expectations, growing all the time...I believed then and I still do that the only hope for a peaceful and happy Northern Ireland was to have cooperation between different sections of the population. In other words people had to work together, not against each other. I joined the Ulster Liberal Party, then four Liberals formed the New Ulster Movement, putting forward the idea that the people of Northern Ireland have far more in common with each other than with anybody in the South or in Great Britain. In due course the Alliance Party was formed.

'My views were that any party which did not accept the constitutional position in Northern Ireland was not going to be listened to by anybody in the majority – if you were threatening their identity, that's what it amounted to. If you threaten the Protestant population with an eventual united Ireland you bring up the laager mentality and that is going to resist all change, good and bad.'

But overriding concern not to antagonise unionist opinion is an unpopular political tack among Northern Catholics, commonly described as an 'apologetic' attitude. Alliance's message of non-sectarianism, cooperation and togetherness once sounded plausible and progressive to some in the middle class. But a steadily more assertive sense of Irishness has led the new expanded middle class instead into the SDLP, a party they believe has helped them rise and which now perfectly reflects their aspirations.

HUME

People support the SDLP or they support Sinn Féin because the image their chosen party presents is how they want to see themselves: or because they cannot bear to be seen as supporters of the other party. For many in both groups, the figure of John Hume, the SDLP's leader since 1979, is highly significant. Northern Catholics say that they hear him redefining their sense of nationalism realistically, in language that strikes them as modern, intelligent and reasonable – all of which matters to Northern Catholics to an extraordinary degree. The long years of sullen submission, when this community saw itself represented by the inept and the impotent, their politics no more than wishing the state away, have left a lasting mark. It is remarkable how many early campaigners for civil rights still recall their frustration at a television performance, in the early sixties, by a Nationalist MP who was 'shown up' by the then Minister of Commerce in Terence O'Neill's government, the highly articulate Brian Faulkner. In contrast, twenty-five years after Hume's first appearances on local television to make an impassioned, eloquent and reasonable case for Northern Catholics, a particular pride in Hume's ability is still widespread.

To people who inherited the suspicion that their second-rate status perhaps meant they were indeed second-raters, the way he outshines Unionist politicians still counts. The compliments come from both ends of the political spectrum as well as from SDLP voters, and from non-voters. A former Alliance member described him as 'probably the greatest politician in these islands, indeed in Western Europe, a man of rare skills'. A senior republican thought he was merely the 'man in the best position to deliver a new image, Nationalism Modernised, when the old Nationalist Party lost its grip' – but he conceded that Hume had 'political genius'. In what seemed a remarkable admission of dependence on an avowed political rival, a Derry Sinn Féin representative said it was 'no wonder Hume looked depressed all through the inter-party talks in 1992 – he was carrying the weight of republican hopes as well as of his own supporters'.

Given this kind of acclaim over a prolonged period, even saints would have difficulty in retaining a sense of their own limitations. John Hume is a politician, not a saint. He resents criticism and answers it sharply, a habit partly responsible for the SDLP's chronic lack of internal debate. Though there is a journalistic predisposition to give him extensive and usually favourable coverage as the leading anti-IRA Northern Catholic voice, the media gets a similarly thin-skinned response. One seasoned observer thinks that the very different public reactions to Hume and to Gerry Adams have had a considerable effect on both men. 'Hume is cocooned from criticism and swathed in flattery. Unlike his earlier, innovative days, he scarcely stands back any more to look at the direction and effect of his policies. Self-criticism's become unthinkable because he gets so little. Adams on the other hand is barraged, and as a result you can almost hear him digging in and only moving cautiously when he moves at all.'

But largely thanks to Hume's cultivation of links with politicians elsewhere, the SDLP has status and considerable clout in the Republic, with Britain and abroad. Although it contains other people of ability – and deputy leader Seamus Mallon has a different kind of appeal – in the eyes of friends and foes alike the party depends to an alarming degree on the 57-year-old leader's energy and political resilience. Readiness to delegate is not among his talents. Even among veterans, there is considerable scepticism about the fragility of the party's organisation and a tradition of often derisive criticism, though it is rarely voiced directly to the leader.

'All the SDLP's about is non-violence,' says one. 'Count the branches that put down motions for any party conference now,' says a former official. 'Ten years ago we had a hundred – in theory anyhow, maybe sixty-five active. Now it's more like twenty, with two or three activists apiece and five years' work at the most in each of them.'

'Just an election machine,' another says. 'There's an executive of muppets, and the four SDLP MPs [Hume, Mallon, Hendron and Eddie McGrady] are their own authority. They're barons, they run their own wee fiefs.'

'Forget any ideas about socialism because of the "Socialist" in the name,' says a former executive member. 'It's able to articulate what the grassroots would like to say about unionism, that's what the SDLP's about. And it allows people to be confidently Irish. Hume's never here, and when he is, who does he talk to?'

All these people still canvass during elections, several hold or have held party office, and all of them have represented the SDLP in public with considerable prominence and apparent conviction. Begrudging and backbiting is in part tribute to rare skills, and in part inevitable because so few have the opportunity to deploy any political skill of their own. The party is in many respects a broad front, a range of local and small-scale networks unified only by Hume's talent for presentation and the need to voice a constitutional alternative to the IRA.

An early civil rights campaigner who says his politics are still 'left-wing, but I've no one to vote for', long ago decided John Hume was 'essentially a social conservative' and sees him intent on furthering an essentially undemocratic arrangement by which 'the British, Irish and maybe even the American governments get together and decide things and then say to people, this is what you get'. Republicans may reluctantly recognise Hume's ability – but that only means they have more reason to fear his achievement of a compromise, an accommodation of shifting nationalist aspirations that will condemn their purist demands once more to oblivion. One veteran of pre-Troubles nationalist politics, 'driven with some discomfort towards Sinn Féin', wonders 'how many of the thousands of wee men around the country who put on their caps and their wellington boots and march down the mountain and stick the ticket in for John and the boys really know that it's not a nationalist party at all. I honestly don't think most people in the SDLP know *what* the party's about. They think that John Hume's a nationalist.'

MARY-ROSE, on the other hand, has no doubt that Hume is a nationalist in the same way she is. Aged thirty-two, from a small farm in hilly south Armagh and living now in a comfortable home on the affluent outskirts of Newry, she thinks the SDLP and its leader perfectly suit the aspirations of many contemporary Northern Catholics, particularly in the new class she believes she is part of – and about which she has no illusions.

'I've heard it said in south Belfast that the Provos are the insurance policy: it's good that they're there. The bulk would find the Provos alien but a lingering number are happy to see them in existence. They say, we don't want them over here, of course, but it's good that they're there in case there's a pogrom, Doomsday. These are people who've dropped out of society in terms of making a contribution. They're not going to join political parties like the SDLP, Alliance. I think they don't vote at all.

'But the majority of new educated Catholics feel that it's John Hume who symbolises them – the intelligence dormant for years in the heads of their parents, with no way of emerging because they were so far down the social ladder and had no money and no driving force. Hume might be getting tired, but he still does them proud. He catches exactly what they want . . . what we want. Symbolism will do, because money's taken the edge off the grievance. Status, I suppose. We're still Irish, we're not British. But a united Ireland's not on the cards for a long time, is it?

'The Anglo-Irish Agreement meant a lot to me. And it means a lot to others like me. We want fair play and equality, that's all we're after – and a recognition that this place is ours too, it's not all British. I don't want any kind of devolution – where'd be the point in going back to that carry-on? There's got to be something a bit grander than that.'

HUGH, the businessman born on a small farm in County Tyrone who now lives in the most exclusive part of Belfast's affluent Malone Road, supports the SDLP, as do many of his neighbours. Once, though, he says, they voted Alliance.

'That was when they moved here first. They hadn't the confidence then that they have now, and they thought of Alliance as a nicer kind of political allegiance, more polite. Now it's respectable to say you're Irish – that's a change. And I give Hume full credit for that, it's what the Anglo-Irish Agreement has done. That, and directing us towards Europe. He realises the day of a united Ireland on the old model is gone so he's moving along. He is the one politician there's been – and it creates a fear among unionists that's almost irrational, because they equate him almost with terrorism, a terrorism of the intellect. You can almost hear them thinking, he's taking us on, and he's winning. He should be admired cross-community, and he's not – he's an unacceptable Catholic because he takes them on.'

From the comments of these people – and from others who were less affluent – it seems that Hume's vision, and his method, exactly suit the interests of many SDLP supporters. He does not want a British government withdrawal from Northern Ireland for some time – if ever - and nor do they, because they fear it would mean greater loyalist violence and more general instability in Ireland. He does not promise them a united Ireland because (a) it is unattainable in the old sense of a unitary state delivered in the foreseeable future, and (b) he is acutely aware of the depth of Southern aversion to any such idea. Much of this Hume will not state too starkly; nor will his supporters. 'Where the problem lies is in using the right language to spell it out, so that you don't provoke an emotional reaction,' he admits. The unconverted find the 'right language' foggy and repetitious, apparently chosen to obscure rather than define.

But approval of Hume's 'moving on', in Hugh's phrase, and praise for the way he has relegated the old-model united Ireland, is widespread. Hume's prescription for an enthusiastic Europeanism to 'transcend' a 'narrow, sterile and outdated nationalism' suggests a cosmopolitan identity and an intellectual approach that are particularly attractive to many in the new middle class. '"Transcend": what genius thought that one up?' one longtime Hume-watcher remarked, drawing out the sound of the word to invest it with maximum pomposity. Hume's invocation of modernity also has a general appeal to people who have always been keen to convince the world outside that the tag 'narrow, sterile and outdated' is properly applied to Northern Protestants, not to them. As for the rest of Ireland, which Northern Catholics once reflexively applied to be merged with, Hume is perceived as having built a practical link with Southern governments into the mechanism of the Anglo-Irish Agreement – unlike the insecure and humiliating relationship with the South of pre-Troubles days.

WHOSE NATIONALISM? WHAT NATIONALISM?

The Anglo-Irish Agreement, and the SDLP's promotion of it, can impress people but still leave them unpersuaded to vote.

Deputy leader SEAMUS MALLON, whose redefinition of traditional loyalties has always been more circumspect than Hume's, makes an analysis of Catholic political allegiance and identity that traces shifts in attitudes during the Troubles but is emphatic about the centrality of nationalism. 'There are different elements of Northern nationalism. The first's a fairly loose nationalist position that can accommodate, because of class, social position, intellectual disposition, a Northern Ireland context – they describe themselves as nationalists but are within the Alliance position. Some vote for us, for localised and personalised reasons.

'Second's the broad spectrum of nationalism – very deep-rooted in history, politically defensive of the nationalist position and which has accepted that the route to obtaining nationalist objectives can only be obtained through the political process. As a result of the last twenty-odd years, these people have realised that the route through the political process is not a straight line: it will move in various directions, but inexorably along the one line. Those people will not settle for a six-county arrangement. They do not want a nod in the direction of nationalism, lip service. They want their position to be an inherent, intrinsic part of the solution to this problem. Those are the vast majority of the nationalists in Northern Ireland – and the vast majority of *them* vote for us.

'The third element I won't define as being Provo or Sinn Féin, although many of them are – part of the legacy of the fifty years before '68, which had a womb comfort in being absolutist in their position and haven't moved away from the position where if you say a thing, it will happen. The reality is that it can only be done through the physical force method or the political method.

'A number are caught in a no-man's-land between those two positions – again for historical reasons, or because they've got the wrong end of the stick from security forces operations. Many are thinking their way out of that position, but haven't got to the stage where it's formalised in their voting pattern.'

But this is the analysis of a full-time politician. TONY is a 38-year-old Derry-born academic, who thinks political views need to change 'from the bottom up', through people forming community groups rather than through party politics. He has 'no time for most of the politicians' and says he knows lots of others with similar views.

'I've never actually voted. The constitutionality of Northern Ireland is not uppermost in my mind.' He laughs. 'The only political development that's involved me for years was the Anglo-Irish Agreement. When that was announced live at Hillsborough I remember it reverberating right through my whole body, that I would never ever apologise again for where I was coming from. And I've found myself defending it ever since. I remember Tom King saying there are *de facto* two traditions in Northern Ireland, and our role is to acknowledge the validity of both. Whether it's because I was thirty that year, I'd come to a stage in my life where I wanted to hear that, but it actually meant a lot to me.

'The actual framework, what Garret FitzGerald and Margaret Thatcher did – I don't for one moment think the Brits or the Irish took it all seriously. I don't think they worked it, and I think they were only expedient in what they put their energies into. But it still meant that acknowledgement to me, something never done before – and that's so important, recognising that there are two traditions here, as important as each other.'

BEN CARAHER, like Seamus Mallon, dislikes people who are dismissive of politics and politicians: 'That's just a cop-out.' A former vice-chairman of the SDLP, he is a backroom boy rather than a would-be elected politician, who in the early days helped work out the policy ideas that John Hume has largely operated on ever since.

Now fifty-five, Caraher was brought up in Crossmaglen, County Armagh, and despite years teaching in Belfast still thinks of himself primarily as a native of south Armagh – which was 'Irish' to his mind rather than 'nationalist', marooned on the very edge of an alien state. In the fifties, approaching adulthood, like many in his generation Ben Caraher saw the IRA campaign of 1956–62 and the nationalist politics of the time as equally futile, and unionism as totally alien. Like many others, he says his earliest political interest lay outside Ireland.

'In so far as I was interested in politics, I was indignant at Suez, I was a big Labour Party supporter – and later I remember rejoicing at the Labour victory of 1964. If you'd asked me about politics then, that's what I would have meant – Labour politics in England. What went on here to me, it just wasn't a political entity that operated in a real way or that greatly engaged me. I would have described myself as a nationalist, but I thought the physical force programme was mad and the Nationalist Party were silly. In retrospect, I suppose it's unfair to blame the actual people involved. What could they do?

'You had the Unionists firmly in control here – they could afford to laugh. All *they* had to worry about really was if they drew attention to themselves from London. But apart from that, they could despise the Nationalists, as they did – almost as much as the nationalist population who voted for them despised them. It was because of the pointlessness of their political programme: they had none, except to say that in an ideal world this state wouldn't exist. But they had no programme to bring about this ideal world, no function other than to protest.

'There was nothing the Nationalists could do. The political tradition out of which they grew did not have anything useful to say about the North.'

After involvement in the Queen's University New Ireland Society, Caraher helped found the National Democratic Party, a forerunner of the SDLP which merged wholesale with the new party. He sees considerable progress from the dead politics of his youth and the confusion of the civil rights days to the SDLP's present position, and is inclined to dismiss debate about the party's nationalism as a distraction from the central question about political allegiance.

'The problem here is one of legitimacy, constructing institutions where people who are ruled by them recognise their right to rule. Even in the fifties, when the Southern state was a ramshackle affair, nothing to be admired, the state in Northern Ireland still lacked legitimacy. There was no emotional identification with it. And you ultimately didn't recognise its right to tell you what to do. You obeyed the law – a quite wise thing, to obey the law – but that sort of commitment was not there, and still is not there, in the mildest of nationalists.

'The problem is, is the very fact that you construct institutions that would have the support of nationalists, does that very fact make them insupportable to unionists? If it does, then there is no solution – if the very fact that they're acceptable to one means *ipso facto* they're unacceptable to the other, which might well be the case. But you presume that it isn't, and you still search for ways of squaring these circles, basically to find a way of running the place, to construct institutions. That's the major problem now, rather than the assertion of national identity.

'It's why I've always felt at home in the SDLP, that it's less a nationalist party than a party which takes account of national identity. It recognises nationalism as something that has to be accommodated in Northern Ireland. But nationalism hasn't the status of a religious belief, it isn't a belief system. There isn't a party definition of it. The party doesn't even think it is "a good thing". It's there, it has to be accommodated.

'I have never called myself a "nationalist", except in shorthand terms. I don't believe that the government of national

units is the be-all and end-all of human existence. I don't think
that at all.'

For Ben Caraher, the SDLP's first and most lasting achievement was to 'think about it all and work out a new approach'.
He thinks there can be no doubt that John Hume has
dominated the political scene ever since. 'It's surely a measure
of the SDLP's success that everyone now, including the British
government and the Provos, is using the language that we have
been using for years.'

Many are similarly pleased that there is now general recognition of what they regard as an updated and rational formulation
of nationalist demands by Hume and the SDLP. Others resent
media emphasis on, and overt approval for, the 'Hume line'. In
the course of preparing this book I came in for a blast of anti-
media rage from two people who refused to be interviewed as
a gesture of their disgust: Bernadette McAliskey and Father Des
Wilson. After she had given me about six hours' worth of interview, a similar anger boiled over in SHEILA, a Ballymurphy
woman.

'Journalists all take the SDLP line on nationalism. That's the
orthodoxy, to praise John Hume, to think he's great. I bet *you*
think he's great. And the result is people don't feel they're being
heard. They're turned off. You can see why. The range of
voices the media presents is very narrow, isn't it? Look at it,
listen to it: BBC, RTE, the Dublin papers, the *Irish News* – how
many journalists have opposed the broadcasting ban [British
government restrictions on broadcast interviews with Sinn Féin
and others], for instance? It means there's no real discussion, and
it just heightens the mistrust.

'When it comes down to it, people don't trust the SDLP. In
talks, there's the fear, the belief, they'll go into an internal settlement. And if you tell me they won't, that's not what they're
about now, I don't believe you.'

Beyond that, and a suggestion that she does not vote, Sheila did not voice her own political preferences. But her suspicion that the SDLP would agree to go 'into an internal settlement' is familiar. Leading Sinn Féin people concede that in the 1992 inter-party talks John Hume eventually made clear his determination not to be part of another devolved government at Stormont (on the model of the 1973 power-sharing experiment) by insisting, against Unionist and Northern Ireland Office pressure, on Irish government involvement in any future arrangement. Others remain unconvinced.

The distrust Sheila has for the SDLP is common, but she emphasised that even in the republican stronghold of west Belfast, the district she knows best, this distrust does not automatically translate into votes for Sinn Féin. Political allegiance, she says, is 'shifting, complex and ambiguous – not a simple pro- or anti-IRA decision by any means. It's a problem for a lot of people.' Of the considerable number who described such arguments with themselves, MÁIRÉAD was the most open, and the most coherent. She is a forty-year-old community worker in west Belfast, who lives in north Belfast. She thinks from talking to Catholic friends that her confusion and doubts about how to vote are common to many.

'I always use my vote. Sometimes I've done eccentric things, like voting for Paddy Devlin.' She laughs. 'But now I vote for the SDLP although I'm very sceptical about them – I think I'm probably one of the many, many people from whom the SDLP regularly gets votes but who are half-hearted about them. Working in west Belfast, you hear people joking: "Somebody in west Belfast votes SDLP – who is it?" Everybody laughs, no one owns up. But obviously a whole lot of us do.

'It means in my case I wish to register my vote for people who are to some extent acceptable to me – and I don't support the continuation of armed struggle. Nevertheless in my case it would be wrong to read my vote, that I have no sympathy whatsoever for the political attitudes of republicanism. I find it still very difficult. Every election is something to be thought about, and it isn't an easy kind of choice.

'As the campaign against Sinn Féin has increased, the use of censorship, and even more so the loyalist killings, I'm struck by some of the things that Gerry Adams says about the demonisation of people who support Sinn Féin. My inclination is increasingly to support their right to exist and to be voted for, to say that it's not a terrible or immoral thing to vote for them. They're a political organisation. And when I look at what happens to people in west Belfast, at their everyday lives, I know why they're voting for Sinn Féin, I can't see that as something they should be punished for.

'Having said that, I would find it difficult to vote for Sinn Féin myself. Partly because I don't like so many things on their programme, but also because of the morality of it. Not that I think anyone here has clean hands. A government that bombed Iraq talking about the morality of supporting violence is a joke. But people generally should think about what it is they're doing when they uphold a point of view. A voter for the Democratic Unionist Party has got as big a moral problem as somebody voting for Sinn Féin. I don't vote Sinn Féin because I don't want to give sanction to an armed struggle. I want the Provos to stop, completely.

'I vote SDLP because I don't want to be alienated from the political structure, and they're the best I can do. Ten to fifteen years ago I would have voted for the Workers' Party, but not now. Not only because of the hand-washing of the most useless kind they do but also because when you run up against them at ground level in west Belfast, when you see how they behave – how they can preach to anyone else gets me . . .

'The Alliance Party is not an option at all. You get nice polite people coming to the door and saying we all want peace. But I have to at least vote for somebody who sees that this is a political problem and the sorting out of it has to be in terms of meeting some of the nationalist demands.

'So people like me vote for the SDLP – not because they're clearly anti-Provo, anti-Sinn Féin – they might have ambiguous attitudes to the whole Provo thing – but because they don't support the continuation of an armed struggle. They don't think, though, that the way to differentiate themselves from that is to wear a badge saying "I WANT A CEASEFIRE". There are a lot in that position. We don't support the IRA. We vote SDLP – but that doesn't mean we're saying, can we just have an internal solution, a wee bit of reform, the Anglo-Irish Agreement, and that'll be enough.'

One of the most interesting points that Máiréad made was her observation that she knew why west Belfast people voted for Sinn Féin. There was not the slightest mention of republicanism, nationalism, a desire for a united Ireland. Clearly she believed their choice of party was coloured at least partially, and perhaps to a great extent, by their circumstances, by poverty and the presence of the British army – 'what happens to people . . . their everyday lives'. In other words, it was a protest vote, which naturally went to Sinn Féin.

Her own vote for the SDLP, on the other hand, seemed to be nothing more than a protest against the IRA: though she went on to express some admiration for John Hume, it was in a way that suggested she thought of him and his party as separate entities.

TO STEPHEN, a former priest who now lives in London, less than wholehearted support for Sinn Féin and simultaneous suspicion of the SDLP are familiar emotions. He met both among his parishioners in mid-Ulster. Being in the community but not of it, which is how he saw the experience of being a

priest, led him to weigh and judge the political options for
Catholics with some detachment. From the distance of England
now, he sees a community that has lost coherence and a unified
sense of political identity.

'I don't think there's that great sense of grievance any more
– that was what we all had in common, wasn't it? We were anti-
Stormont, we knew we were being discriminated against. The
SDLP's not a party of grievance. It's a party that's arrived, its
time has come. It's gained great advances for the people, it's got
a respectable, respected leader. The only people carrying the
grievance now are Sinn Féin.'

Like many others, Stephen believes republicans' growing
sense of isolation is heightened by an awareness that SDLP supporters are relatively content. There is an argument that the way
the SDLP and John Hume have translated and then tackled nationalist grievance has in one sense merely added a new layer
of anger. The most aggrieved – and people have no self-
consciousness about using the word – now also feel shut out of
the consensus Hume and the SDLP have built. It is a form of
double alienation, all the sharper because the aggrieved know
that their anger, christened 'alienation' for the purpose, was
used by the Irish government and the SDLP – though Hume
steered clear of using the word – as pressure on the British, the
promise of their eventual reconciliation dangled as the carrot to
produce the Anglo-Irish Agreement. And the symbolism and
drift of the agreement has to a great extent accommodated the
much less pressing grievance felt by SDLP supporters.

One SDLP theory suggests that the Sinn Féin vote is now
holding steady only in the centres of urban deprivation: Derry,
Newry, west Belfast above all. There is talk of an 'underclass',
bitter and anarchic because disadvantaged by poverty, not
peculiar to Northern Ireland though with an extra layer of disaffection because of partition, similar in many ways to the USA's

and even Britain's poor inner-city blacks. The idea offers the SDLP the comfort of explaining in global terms its own failure to dent Sinn Féin's hold on this poor urban vote: which stood at a total of 28,000 in greater Belfast in both the 1987 and 1992 general elections, more than the entire Sinn Féin vote in the Republic. And in the 1993 local government elections, Sinn Féin became the largest party in terms of first-preference votes in Belfast city council.

WEST BELFAST

When at the 1992 general election the SDLP captured Sinn Féin's greatest electoral prize, the West Belfast parliamentary seat – courtesy of Protestant tactical voters out to dislodge Gerry Adams – there was at least an awareness that the Adams vote had stayed solid, and some care not to gloat. Joe Hendron, the new MP, having for nine years been the contender, has at last put in place a local office with young local staff. It remains to be seen whether grassroots organisation will follow.

Party politics in West Belfast have to contend first with apathy and depression: a steady one in four in the constituency does not vote, with the lowest turnout among those living at subsistence levels. The SDLP vote seems to have settled at around 15,000: substantial enough, given that the party struggles to find candidates and workers in each local election. But Sinn Féin appeals strongly to young voters, and more than half the population is aged under twenty-five – as is the case in all the working-class Catholic areas of Belfast and Derry.

Gerry Fitt and Paddy Devlin, the big West Belfast political names of the past, famously maintained their local government votes, and Fitt his Westminster seat, on little more than their own charisma and the tirelessness of their wives as phone answerers and constituent-soothers. When Fitt finally departed, the SDLP salvaged part of his personal vote, but no machine.

The seamless takeover of the old Nationalist Party vote in rural areas had no parallel in early-Troubles Belfast. 'In 1970 you weren't relevant in Ardoyne or up the Falls unless you were giving out flame-throwers,' growls Paddy Devlin. While republicanism was still split and bereft of anything resembling political organisation, in Belfast's Catholic enclaves the kind of people who began to support the new SDLP elsewhere were in many cases joining the Citizens' Defence Committees, which were to be swiftly taken over by the Church. The times did not favour the organisation of traditional political parties: the huge movement of people displaced by intimidation and the burnings of 1969 went on shifting, settling and resettling throughout much of the seventies. Several of the youngest people I talked to had moved two and three times in their first few years, sometimes with a period in makeshifts such as prefabs, a story common to thousands. (In 1974 a Community Relations Commission report said that firm evidence existed of 8,180 families forced to evacuate their homes in the greater Belfast area between August 1969 and February 1973, 80 per cent of which they estimated to be Catholic.)

While the SDLP undoubtedly is an 'all-class alliance', as a Derry Sinn Féiner put it ruefully, it has had a particular attraction for the upwardly mobile of the past two decades. The Belfast MPs who helped form the new party, the urban 'republican socialists' Fitt and Devlin, were always uncomfortable in what they felt from the start was an organisation dominated by rural conservatives. A helper in the Fitt campaigns of old remembers asking him how he was getting on with his new colleagues. 'I'm up to my arse in fucking teachers,' the present Lord Fitt replied.

But in the end it was the increased militancy and republicanism of their working-class voters that drove Fitt and Devlin out of nationalist politics, and the SDLP. Both increasingly condemned

the IRA and suffered in the process: their homes attacked, Paddy
and Theresa Devlin's younger children abused and insulted at
school and in the street. Fitt took a much-ridiculed title and
now holds court in the House of Lords, his speciality being
denunciation of nationalism as espoused by both the Provos and
the SDLP, the party he once led; he makes little distinction
between them. PADDY DEVLIN, now sixty-eight, helped to form
the United Labour Party in 1978, and the Labour Party of
Northern Ireland in 1985: both collapsed. He is a founder of the
Peace Train organisation, formed to lobby against IRA attacks
on the North/South rail link.

'I split with the SDLP essentially because of their closeness to
the Catholic Church and their lack of socialism. The second
wave into the party after we founded it was all Catholic
schoolmasters, principals mostly – and I always suspected
Cardinal Conway encouraged a lot of them to join up. The
shape of the party was clear after that. . . You add up the votes
now, there's only about two votes out of eleven in favour of
getting rid of the border. The full nationalist vote, nor anything
like it, isn't coming out for the Provos and the SDLP together.
I reckon there's a possible Labour vote there – at least there's
a possibility they're looking for Labour. They might be too
fatigued with all the parties at the minute.

'The Provos stop a lot of people coming out to vote, just by
their presence on the streets on polling day. Because the one
thing they have done, which is very effective, is that they've
kept a register of those people who're voting for them and those
people who vote against them.

'There's other things more important to me now than
politics: I love rugby, I'm on the Boxing Board of Control, I'm
the President of Immaculata Boxing Club, the vice-president of
all-Ireland boxing, I've just finished a play on the 1932 Outdoor
Relief Riots [when Protestant and Catholic strikers fought the

police together]. I don't bother with politics. People are thinking that I have changed my views and values, that I'm a government flunkey. It's not true, I'm a sterner critic of the system
than most people. I've criticised it all my life, I've fought it. *I'll
never be a lord because I wouldn't accept anything like that.*'

Throughout the Troubles, those who could afford it have
steadily moved to more peaceful places: up the Falls, into
Andersonstown – the drift that in the late eighties finally
became so evident and such a symbol as it fetched up in what
had once been solidly Protestant affluent south Belfast. Catholic
west Belfast is still much more varied socially than those who
steer well clear of it imagine, with a much-shrunken middle
class but still visible and sometimes striking differences in
lifestyles. The evidence, mainly anecdotal, suggests that it is
those who vote SDLP who have moved out in larger numbers.

During the seventies, trouble on the streets displaced most
other political activity. It took the H Block hunger strikes and
the emergence of Sinn Féin to set the scene for the clashes of
the past decade. A woman who arrived on the Falls as a community worker in 1980 saw the battle taking shape.

'The hunger strike brought a lot of people into the political
process and just sharpened it all up. You'd get these people
turning up at community meetings, for example about Divis
[the demolition of the hated Divis Flats], and you could see they
were going to fight it out for who'd get the political credit. The
Shinners [Sinn Féiners] then were a whole mixture of things.
Some got involved because of the hunger strike, who'd never
been involved at all before, some with notions of community
involvement wider than a purely party political approach. With
others it was, it's the movement that matters.

'The SDLP were essentially not at the match. If they had been
you wouldn't have had Cahal Daly sending out messages to the
middle class to get involved.'

It is widely believed in west Belfast that the Catholic Church, the British government through the Northern Ireland Office, and the SDLP have made common cause to push Sinn Féin into the political margins: common cause in the struggle – launched by Cahal Daly in his time in Belfast as Bishop of Down and Connor, and won by the Church – to control government-funded job schemes, and common cause during the repeated election battles to take the Westminster parliamentary seat from the Sinn Féin president, Gerry Adams. Even among senior clergy, the job scheme strategy from the start caused particular unease. 'Channelling British government money through the Church makes us look like an arm of pacification,' said one. A Sinn Féin councillor complains that no one in his party has ever been appointed to the board of governors of a Catholic school, though the SDLP is multiply represented. SDLP party workers are occasionally uncomfortable about the none-too-subtle help their always puny organisation in west Belfast is given by the powerful agencies of Church and state.

In the election court that adjudicated on a complaint that the SDLP victor, Joe Hendron, had spent more than the amount allowed in the 1992 campaign, the *Irish News* – founded by the bishops as an anti-Parnell organ and traditionally the voice of the conservative Catholic establishment – was asked to explain a considerable discount to Dr Hendron for advertisements, a favour not offered to other candidates. Few thought two senior judges likely to declare the election invalid and allow Gerry Adams another chance to retake West Belfast. But the court was widely expected at least to rebuke the SDLP election agent. Instead, agent and candidate alike were declared blameless – 'granted relief' in the court's language – and the complainants were told they must pay half the legal costs although the judges solemnly vindicated their right to take the case.

Off the record, several SDLP people described the judgment

as embarrassing. 'I blushed when Joe thanked the judges,' said one old campaigner.

There is a widespread perception of the party as detached from the concerns of an area with multiple problems, as an organisation essentially based elsewhere. A confidential survey carried out for the SDLP in advance of Joe Hendron's victorious 1992 campaign showed strong personal allegiance to Gerry Adams: 'strength of character and affinity for west Belfast' were deemed to be his key strengths among Sinn Féin voters. White-collar workers were three times more likely to have voted for the SDLP than for Sinn Féin; the unemployed and those at sub-sistence levels were twice as likely to have voted Sinn Féin.

Twenty-six-year-old SINÉAD, a nurse tutor who lives in 'posh' Andersonstown, focused on something many others mention. Her support for the IRA, untypical in her immediate district, and Sinn Féin – 'I think of them as the same thing,' she said – began with the hunger strikes, and originally came out of a desire to 'belong' to what she thought then was a unified west Belfast community. She now sees her vote for Sinn Féin as in a sense a protest against the SDLP's distance from the people. The SDLP MP Joe Hendron works as a GP in the area but lives in affluent south Belfast. Sinéad says he is someone she cannot take seriously.

'I vote Sinn Féin because I believe there is no politician who will actually stand up, and I think Sinn Féin is the nearest to it. We have to get behind something that will stand up for us, because the SDLP will always be happy with second-class citizenship and we need somebody who won't.

'The ideal would be somebody who'd say we're not prepared to be second-class and get together with Ian Paisley and sort it out. Whereas I believe the SDLP would be happy to be second fiddle to him. That's the thing about Catholics I don't under-stand – they tend to not mind, they won't stand up for themselves. The problem with Sinn Féin is people see them as Provies, not as politicians. We need politicians that aren't necessarily republicans, though I suppose if they aren't willing to be second-class, they'll be classed as republicans.

'Seamus Mallon I would see as a brilliant politician, and there's a few like him I would respect – but the others? Hume sits back a bit. When anything happens, what does he say? If Mallon was the head, I'd vote for the SDLP. Hume very rarely says anything, when there's an SAS shooting, say. Whereas Seamus Mallon will, which is almost a sign of a person who's saying, come on, we're not going to take this. He's maybe the only one of them, come to think of it.

'If we didn't have this problem, I wouldn't vote for Sinn Féin. It's just the person who's down will vote for the party they think represents them, people who have been brought up like them. Mothers etcetera in west Belfast vote for Sinn Féin because they think, this person's like me. That's a pity, because if somebody in the SDLP was strong enough they could...

'I think the Sinn Féin vote will go back up again. If there's something like the hunger strike. Every time anything happens in the areas, young people especially support them because they believe the others aren't any good. I don't think Sinn Féin will ever get anywhere. But that's not why people vote for them. They vote for them because they are the underdogs and because Sinn Féin are the underdogs – and because Gerry Adams will never give an inch.

'In a way that's sad that people like me should vote for him when I know he can't do anything. But I wouldn't vote for the SDLP – not because they won't get anywhere, but that they're not prepared to stand up for us. I'd hate to think *they* were representing *me*.'

Sinéad's comments raise several points. First, unlike other interviewees (including some Sinn Féiners) she clearly had little sense that the SDLP had made gains; or at least, she had no sense that any gains made had relevance to her or to people in her district. In common with many others, she was expressing an alienation apparently untouched by the Anglo-Irish Agreement. The agreement was said to be about lessening that feeling: for some, like Tony and Mary-Rose, it has, yet others' alienation seems to remain intact.

Sinéad's explanation of her support for Sinn Féin is also familiar from other accounts: as largely dependent on identification with the style and background of republican representatives rather than a belief that the party is making progress: as a protest against the situation of the people she lives among and the SDLP's response to that, rather than as an expression of ideological republicanism. Her admiration for Seamus Mallon appeared to be totally unconnected to her feelings generally about the party he helps to lead.

Like everyone else I spoke to from west Belfast, Sinéad's life and political views are powerfully influenced by her surroundings. But some with fewer options and fewer resources have much less interest in the political tensions around them. GEMMA is nineteen, has a baby and lives with her parents in Turf Lodge. Politics 'disgusts' her. All she wants is to get away.

'When the elections are on and people are saying vote Sinn Féin, vote Sinn Féin... you're living in a republican area and you say to yourself, I might as well. You've no choice and if you did vote anything else you wouldn't be wanted. Nobody hears what you vote for, I know, but you have to just go along with what everybody else says. And they'd know all right, unless you did a big act. So I don't vote. I did last year when I got the vote first, but I thought, not again. I don't believe in any of it. I just live here. I've no choice. I've nowhere else to go at the minute but I couldn't be annoyed with it.' She volunteered no opinion on the SDLP.

But Máiréad, who works with local young people, has strong feelings about the SDLP's behaviour and record in working-class Belfast – all the stronger because she feels she has no option but to vote for them because she is determined not to support the IRA.

'They're holier-than-thou towards republicanism. Joe Hendron's role in life seems to be to make statements that prove the SDLP is moral and the Provos aren't. You get it from others as well, like Brian Feeney: it's an "I'm going to sit up here and preach at you" attitude. What sort of relationship is that to have with the community? You can't act like God living here. Nobody's above it. I feel surges of irritation when I listen to SDLP men, though I know there's individuals who do good work. But they're afraid of people. Instead of believing that most are reasonably moral and trustworthy, a whole lot of SDLP representatives treat them as shifty, psychopathic even.

'It's something you really notice in places like west Belfast. Their attitude is never: "What's happened here? As your councillors, what do you think we should know?" Instead they say: "Oh we know what's going on, and these people are up to X, Y and Z – and they're all really Sinn Féiners anyway and what's the point in us going out to talk to them." I know it'd be a hard job going to talk to some people, but politics isn't easy. And they should have more confidence in what they stand for themselves and in what people are capable of thinking about and saying.'

Like many others in Northern Ireland, Máiréad feels particularly deprived of a secular, radical party to vote for, a party that would also in some way represent how she feels about the wider question of political identity. She is a feminist, and she and her husband chose an integrated school for their children rather than have them attend a Catholic school.

'In a general way, I don't like the SDLP's social policies. They say they're a social democratic party, but in European terms they appear to me to be more a Christian democratic party, weak on state intervention in the economy, for example, and very close to the Catholic Church. I would definitely want a party with a more secularist attitude. They're under a lot of pressure and I don't want to demean everything they do, but they don't stand for any real kind of pluralism. I suppose for me they're just too conservative. I want a society in which I can have the freedom to have an abortion, divorce – and not just the freedom, but that it's socially acceptable.'

In the end she laughs and gives an exasperated shrug. 'I think the SDLP must be nearly unique in European politics: if you could analyse the number of people who vote for it, feeling irritated every time they do. It must be a very unusual sort of phenomenon.'

'THE COUNTRY'

In the more conservative countryside, there is less sense of Sinn Féin versus a Catholic establishment than in the socially divided cities and towns. Rural republicanism is to some extent a different animal. When Cahal Daly moved from Belfast to become archbishop of Armagh, priests in his new diocese predicted that he would soon moderate the harshness of his anti-republican language, as in ways he has, when he discovered 'that he's not dealing with corner boys down here and some of the solidest Catholic families he has, pillars of the Church, are republicans'.

While Gerry Adams was insisting that 'republicanism is not the prerogative of any one social class' he remembered how during the hunger strikes and at other IRA funerals many city republicans were surprised to discover that IRA volunteers had come from 'what by Belfast standards would have been mansions in very lush pastureland – these were people who were, from hard work I have no doubt, relatively well off'.

Another leading Sinn Féiner, urban to the fingertips, said, 'The GAA [Gaelic Athletic Association] is a big conservative influence. That's who we're contending with for hearts and souls in the country, and we have to show respect as we do with the Church. You never arrange a meeting to clash with a match. I found out the hard way – there was outrage at the very idea. It's a more conservative world, no doubt about it.' He added, 'In the country the poverty doesn't seem the same. You'd get people suggesting a raffle with tickets costing £30 apiece – you wouldn't sell one in west Belfast at that price. And these wouldn't be rich country people.'

Increasingly, Sinn Féin votes in the countryside have been levered over to the SDLP, however, as in large measure they were in Armagh and Down and presumably will be progressively in Fermanagh–South Tyrone, by the time-honoured method of the sectarian head count. In the same 1992 election in which the SDLP was boasting of its cross-community drawing power in west Belfast (where off the record they admitted that they knew Protestants had voted tactically to get Gerry Adams out) and in Foyle (where John Hume claimed a Protestant personal vote) in Mid-Ulster Hume's senior aide, Denis Haughey, was appealing for votes on a strictly mathematical basis, calculating a narrow Catholic majority and reminding voters they had 'nothing to lose but Willie McCrea', the Reverend Ian Paisley's Westminster colleague.

The SDLP routinely professes to be 'pluralist', and spokespersons from time to time become exceedingly annoyed at the shorthand media description 'mainly Catholic party'. But appealing for every Catholic vote in order to unseat a Unionist is judged to be non-sectarian, strictly a tactical matter, legitimised by the ancient rules of Northern Ireland elections. In the course of an interview for this book, recalling the absence of any nationalist organisation and reliance on a simple head count in the fifties and sixties, John Hume remarked with what sounded like disapproval that 'every election called then was very similar to the ones we've returned to in Fermanagh and Mid-Ulster'. It was as though he was commenting on a phenomenon his party now views sadly from afar: a curious moment.

Sinn Féin's rural organisation is sketchy. Much like the situation in Derry and Belfast twenty years ago, it depends to an uncomfortable degree on the energy of individuals and on pockets of traditional loyalty in places like mid-Ulster. Some SDLP people in the country maintain that they have seen republicanism diminish in families in which someone has for the first time got a secure public service job. 'It fairly settles them down,' said one old farmer. The republican response, especially in the cities, is to suggest drily that 'the country' has never been entirely convinced about the wisdom of diverting energy and resources into political organisation and away from the IRA. But the more honest will admit that their own disorganisation has helped the SDLP to collect four Westminster seats.

In the border land of Fermanagh, in a county where a Catholic majority divided between 'constitutional' and 'physical force' nationalism has regularly delivered up its chance of political representation to unionism, there is a history of hotly disputed 'unity' candidates. Allegiance to modern political republicanism is fragile: BRIAN MCCAFFREY reflects that in the story of how his own views developed. He is thirty-six, a self-employed electrician, and a former Sinn Féin councillor in the small border town of Roslea.

'It was something I came to believe: our house wasn't political, there was no political connection anywhere in the family – I think my father might have been loosely connected one time to the Ancient Order of Hibernians! There was certainly no republican background. I probably wouldn't have really started to form any radical views myself until around the time of Bloody Sunday [30 January 1972]. The rest – the very bad housing, the B Specials, discrimination, the border between you and Clones where you went for the shopping at the weekend – that was all taken for granted. As a kid I never thought about it – even when the civil rights started, the bombing up in Belfast . . . You know the way when you're a kid it's only yourself matters?

'But Bloody Sunday, that made an awful impression on – not myself alone, but people I was at school with too. A lot of people I can remember knocking about with didn't want to know about Belfast, bombing. Their views just changed totally out of sheer shock. We were all about fifteen. There's a lot of them would still have the same politics as me. Some of them have been in jail, some are on the run. Within the school I went to, St Michael's in Enniskillen, it's peculiar to that year, and maybe the year ahead of us. Obviously, attitudes hardened all over the place and probably we were just a part of that.

'And then it was a natural progression for me towards Sinn Féin. I went through various stages without realising I was going through them. The guy I was working for got me to sit in a booth doing the register [checking the list of voters] for Frank McManus [Unity], then Frank Maguire [Independent]. But the civil rights movement was reasonable, the pressure from Frank McManus, Frank Maguire when they were MPs – and yet at the end of the day, while both did a good enough job of representing nationalists in the constituency who were downtrodden, highlighting it whenever it was appropriate, it never seemed to get anywhere.

'You just gradually thought, this doesn't work – you became more and more hardline. The major changes in housing only took place after the fall of Stormont. And even then in Fermanagh, for a rural area, we had an intolerably high waiting list. Nothing happened fast enough, and all the time we were

getting further into the situation where the UDR [Ulster
Defence Regiment] was formed, you ran into them, there was
constant hassle at roadblocks – where once it was the B men
[the part-time B Specials, a wholly Protestant force] . . . But they
were just the same, really.

'Once internment came, and the IRA activity in the aftermath of that, next thing people in the community started to get
arrested and you started realising the IRA was only ordinary
people. It was no longer three initials in a newspaper. It was
people you'd grown up with, that you knew were straightforward, ordinary, honest, decent people except they'd taken a
decision to go a step further. That had a big effect. The names
became known, you knew the families. People's perception was
those inside were innocent – and therefore it wasn't justified.
The whole thing snowballed from there. Bloody Sunday . . . the
aftermath, the cover-up . . . the realisation that at the end of the
day, no matter what happened, there wasn't going to be any
justice.

'I just thought to myself, well, you can't go on taking this,
and people shouldn't have to. You were generally driven to a
point where you couldn't hold any other viewpoint than where
I've arrived at: the conclusion that it was impossible to change
the system. At the end of the day the only option was to try to
remove it, to get rid of it.'

Brian McCaffrey makes no exaggerated claims about Sinn
Féin's base in the Fermanagh countryside. He is well aware that
republicans benefited, before they were ready to make the most
of the opportunity, from the fluke of Independent (Unity) MP
Frank Maguire's death during the surge of nationalist sympathy
for the prison hunger strikers of 1981. When IRA prisoner
Bobby Sands won the Fermanagh–South Tyrone Westminster
seat, it was not under a Sinn Féin banner: the ballot ticket read
'Sands, Bobby – Anti-H-Block/Armagh Political Prisoner'.

There was no SDLP candidate, nor had there been when Frank Maguire took the seat.

'Sinn Féin didn't exist in Fermanagh until the mid-seventies, and even then it was clandestine. You felt threatened – because of arrests and so on. It would have been something people shied away from. It straggled along until the hunger strikes, and there was a total change after that.

'Probably where we made a major mistake was in not contesting the local government elections immediately after Bobby Sands won the seat. A lot of us worked instead for the late Tommy Murray, the SDLP councillor who signed Sands's nomination papers. Tommy would have had connections in the fifties [in other words, someone related to him was in the IRA during the fifties campaign]. I think the hunger strike was more than he could take at the end of the day. [He was expelled from the SDLP, stood as an independent, then as a Sinn Féin candidate.] Definitely it was a major chance missed for us. It might have made a difference today – the vote we would have taken would have been well in advance of anything since, and Sinn Féin might have been taken more seriously. Fair enough, the effects of the hunger strike have made Sinn Féin what it is today, but we lost out to a certain extent.'

In 1987, on Remembrance Sunday, the IRA left a bomb at the Enniskillen war memorial. It exploded as the day's ceremony was about to start, collapsing the wall of a building onto the bystanders. Eleven local people died, a number of them elderly – many more were badly injured. The open sectarianism of the attack, on what is for Northern Ireland Protestants an important ritual, caused almost as much revulsion as the scale and nature of the deaths and injuries. In Dublin and Cork thousands queued to sign books of condolence. The then Cardinal Tomás Ó Fiaich, who had always condemned IRA killings while making his own brand of republicanism clear, made an emotional 'apology' on behalf of Catholics for the Enniskillen deaths.

Republicans realise that Remembrance Day finally put paid to their chances of improving the Sinn Féin vote in the South. Enniskillen also damaged Sinn Féin in Fermanagh, as Brian McCaffrey admits. The IRA claimed the bomb was intended for patrolling soldiers and was detonated prematurely by army equipment, a claim discredited by the subsequent discovery of a similar bomb at the war memorial in nearby Tullyhommon.

'Enniskillen was when we were really down,' Brian McCaffrey recalls. 'That was the final straw for me with the Church. It was as if they were saying that Enniskillen was intended, and weren't prepared to consider for one minute that it wasn't. It was the Church being nakedly political, to the same extent as the DUP virtually, and saying . . . these people, they're sinners, beyond redemption. When in fact if they'd taken into consideration what we'd said about it, they'd have seen we were as shocked as everybody else.

'There was just no way we would have wished Enniskillen to happen – it was as simple as that. It was one of the things that did do damage to Sinn Féin in this county, as well as the damage to the support for the IRA itself. Then we had eight Sinn Féin members on the council, now we have four. [Since then he has lost his own seat.] Probably at the end of the day, if it hadn't been for the fact that the media's endless condemnations flogged it to death, there would have been more damage done.'

Brian McCaffrey makes no attempt to attribute Sinn Féin support locally to factors other than those he described as influencing his own views. But he did say that he supposed he had 'generally left-wing, socialist sympathies', he thought Sinn Féin's support undoubtedly came from the poorer section of the community – and he had no doubt at all about the nature of SDLP support. He is also convinced that there is a gap between the SDLP leadership and the party's grassroots.

'The SDLP locally would always have been the middle class. I know all of them, but basically it's the relationship of somebody that's working-class with the professional person's family: the clergy, teachers, better-off farmers, bigger farmers.

'There's times I wonder are the SDLP nationalist at all, then I give them the benefit of the doubt. Hume might say he's not, but most of his support is, that's what he has to come to terms with. All that European stuff of his has very little relevance here to the ordinary Tom, Dick or Harry who's got a farm one side of the border and he's living the other. The European dimension doesn't come into it when you're sitting at a British army checkpoint for half an hour.'

The account Brian McCaffrey gives of developing republican sympathies from a non-republican background, influenced by the events of the early Troubles, has elements common to the accounts of many other people: Bloody Sunday, internment, the hunger strike and, in the end, the effects on the Sinn Féin vote of IRA violence. His sharp awareness of Sinn Féin's slowness in organising locally and the weakness that has caused is partly due, he says himself, to the experience of the 1992 general election when Sinn Féin 'held back' in the hope that another unity candidate in the mould of Frank Maguire might emerge – which in turn might have pushed the SDLP into a decision not to stand. 'We lost three weeks' campaigning time,' Brian McCaffey says, 'but we learned our lesson: we have to do it on our own.'

Much of the Fermanagh Sinn Féin story is peculiarly rural: intrigues over unity candidates, the intensity of feelings about 'splitting the vote'. But Brian McCaffrey's description of the local SDLP as much more middle-class than Sinn Féin supporters is almost word for word how republicans elsewhere see their more successful rivals for Catholic votes. The most prominent try hard to sound inclusive when they assess how their support and that of the SDLP differ on class lines: Danny Morrison insisting on the way lines blur, Gerry Adams affirming that no class has a 'monopoly' on Irishness. Less public figures are not so diplomatic.

From the one avowed IRA man I met, what came through was a strong dislike, compounded equally it seemed of resentment at the way some Catholics had prospered – and a frustration that it was their version of nationalism and nationalist grievance, the SDLP version, that monopolised political discussion and would inevitably dominate the historical record. A senior member of the organisation, he spoke with a sharpness about SDLP supporters and personalised the political divide in a style no leading Sinn Féin figures allow themselves.

'You feel an overwhelming sense within the whole community of its Irishness,' he began. What did he mean by 'the whole community'? I asked. 'Speaking from within Belfast – which is not the same as Feeny or Claudy – everyone has a very strong allegiance to nationalism, reunification. There's no clear division between Sinn Féin and the SDLP on those issues. There's also common denominators there: e.g. Britain's the ultimate problem.

'But there are clear differences. The SDLP bedrock vote is as committed as the Sinn Féin vote. These are people who would always have been uncomfortable with militant republicanism, ranging from diehard Catholics who'll always do what the Church says, to people who have a reluctance to confront anything – safe people, who play safe all the time.

'The Sinn Féin vote is massively committed, a different animal altogether, with a clear idea of where the solution would lie. You can see the differences best at elections, of course. SDLP voters will go and vote between seven and nine, then to Mass, the coffee house, off to be doctors, solicitors, a foreperson in

Marks and Spencer. Sinn Féin will work to get the vote out solidly all day, *en masse*.

'The other difference is that the SDLP accepts the traditional view of society, of those meant to occupy positions of power: doctor, priest, career politician. Republicanism is egalitarian, where the views of members are equal from the top down. It would be hard to imagine John Hume or Seamus Mallon fitting in, in the same way as Gerry Adams and Danny Morrison, with whatever needed to be done. Mark Durkan and Tom Kelly are younger, sure, but they still have very hierarchical views. Mark Durkan has a view of himself as a leader. He sees the community as his to lead.

'In republicanism there's a sense of where we're going as a movement, and Gerry Adams for all his abilities is no more important – though he is historically – than the volunteer out tonight or tomorrow night engaging the Brits, or the woman of sixty who sat in the polling booth all day long. I don't rate anyone more than the "minor figures" who sustain and carry us [in the IRA]. But it's your Mark Durkans who'll write the history books.'

The last reference was obviously intended as a bitter comment on the way the middle classes write history in their own image, the picture of doctors and solicitors idling in 'coffee houses' a weird distortion of the true SDLP voter profile in west Belfast and a parody of its more middle-class but still mixed support elsewhere. But again, as in Sinéad's explanation of her own vote and as in the way a number of people summed up their reasons for voting Sinn Féin, there was a final echo of defeatism: a recognition that history is written by those who end up most advantageously placed. In much the same tone, a dozen interviewees reckoned IRA violence had damaged Sinn Féin. It was always expressed the same way: not as a matter for resignation, but as a matter of fact, the way things are.

SINN FÉIN AND THE IRA

If Sinn Féin knows the IRA will always limit their vote, why do they not push for an end to the IRA campaign? The question so frequently put is based on a fundamental misunderstanding. Sinn Féin is not a separate and equal partner: the political party is the underling to 'the Army', as its members always call it. In its present form Sinn Féin was devised as an aide to the IRA campaign – with overlapping membership in sufficient numbers and at a senior enough level to give 'the Army' a controlling influence. The political party has changed out of all recognition from the scrappy pretence of 1970 through various phases: mere mouthpiece for IRA statements, enthusiastic collector of the votes generated by the republican prisoners' hunger strike, practitioner and for some time beneficiary of the 'Armalite and ballot box' dual strategy, claimant of a place on behalf of republicans in talks about the future of Northern Ireland.

A political voice developed to such a degree over so long a period has never existed before in republicanism's history, and there are bound to be unprecedented internal questions. But for observers, watching the interplay between what is clearly a close-knit and thoughtful group of leaders, scrutinising their statements for every scrap of significance much as China- and Kremlin-watchers used to do, forever on the outside of an organisation only a fraction of which is open to inspection, the temptation is to imagine tensions between two distinct groups. What has never changed, and in the nature of the relationship is incapable of change, is Sinn Féin's subordinate role. To suppose that there are leading Sinn Féiners who would like to alter that relationship is almost certainly to misunderstand how those people see themselves, and the nature of modern republicanism.

For years those presented as spokespersons for Sinn Féin raised no objection when it was described as the political voice, or

political wing, of the IRA. It was clear that the IRA had author-
ised an emphasis on electoral activity as a complement to their
campaign of violence. But although every conversation with
senior republicans about political developments continues to involve discussion of the IRA campaign, its intent and effects, the
official line now is that 'there are no organic links' between the
IRA and Sinn Féin.

This comes at a time when British ministers in Northern
Ireland have begun referring to the possibility of a debate inside
republicanism, and the encouragement of those who may seek
an end to the military campaign. It is possible that republicans
think maintaining a polite distance, if only verbal, from the IRA
might improve Sinn Féin's eligibility as negotiator should the
British ever decide to talk. But the denial of 'organic links' also
follows a period when the party's hopes of developing a vote
in the South finally collapsed, the Northern vote levelled off
and in some places began to decline, and when Sinn Féin
spokespersons became increasingly frustrated by being asked to
answer for IRA atrocities. Both Sinn Féin and the IRA now
admit that republican violence has alienated the South and cap-
ped the Northern vote – but far from this realisation prompting
a backing away from violence, some argue that it has had the
opposite effect.

The 1992 return of the car bomb to Belfast city centre and
elsewhere (in particular to a series of predominantly Protestant
towns and housing estates), concentration on a pattern of
bombings in Britain with a high risk and indeed repeated inci-
dence of civilian casualties, incidents like the Teebane workers'
bus ambush and the bombing in Musgrave Park Hospital: in that
none of these have left Sinn Féin any useful propaganda role
whatsoever, all seem evidence of a now-established switch to
unmitigated militarism. The twin-track strategy of Armalite and
ballot box, never a logical and coherent construct, appears to

have simply evaporated, its disappearance only recognisable by the aftermath.

A more useful question than 'Why doesn't Sinn Féin tell the IRA to stop?' might be 'What is the point of Sinn Féin now?' In this business of making sense retrospectively out of the doings of a movement dominated by a secret army, it is tempting to see significance in the conviction of the man who coined the 'Armalite and ballot box' slogan, Sinn Féin's former director of information Danny Morrison, for wrongful imprisonment of someone the prosecution claimed was about to be killed as an IRA informer.

'While I have been in jail,' Morrison writes, 'Sinn Féin has certainly distanced itself considerably from the IRA in comparison to former days. But the republican struggle as a whole still consists of a military campaign (the Armalite) and a political campaign (the ballot box). I have no problems whatsoever with the slogan being dumped because it is inappropriate and there is a different emphasis today.'

But in the comments of people who vote Sinn Féin while knowing little about its inner workings, there is no speculation on what the internal republican debate about a new emphasis might be, much less a discussion of where the party stands in relation to the IRA. It is simply taken for granted of the two supposedly separate organisations that 'they're the same thing'. The IRA man made it clear at the start that he would have nothing to say about IRA policy or the relationship with Sinn Féin: 'What relationship? There's no organic link,' he recited, with a trace of a smile. He was there as an individual to talk about his own sense of identity, he reminded me, not as a spokesman.

Other interviews suggested that if there is any distinct reason for voting Sinn Féin other than to show support for the IRA, it is as a form of protest against the SDLP, a marker: 'You may

settle, *you* may be accommodated, but not us, and despite
everything we're still here.' Sinn Féin officials on the other
hand tend to talk about their success in 'moving the SDLP
greenwards' – as though recognising that their role will never
be more than that of a pressure group. Occasionally, their
depression is unmistakable. Less than ten years ago, senior Sinn
Féin figures had visions of displacing the SDLP as the strongest
voice of nationalism.

GERRY ADAMS

The 23-year-old IRA leader released from detention and flown
to London in 1972 to negotiate a ceasefire with the then
secretary of state, Willie Whitelaw, is apparently, at forty-four,
Sinn Féin president until he chooses to retire. Writer of folksy
short stories, prison tales and memoirs of old Belfast, a pipe-
smoking thinker with impeccable manners and a slow, cautious,
intense way of answering questions, Gerry Adams has a public
image that reflects some of his private preoccupations and effectively disguises the rest. Losing the Westminster West Belfast
seat hit him hard. Being an MP, despite never attending Parliament, gave him extra status with foreign press and politicians.
At the count in Belfast's City Hall, when the SDLP's Joe
Hendron was declared elected, for once Adams's composure
slipped. He made a bad-tempered comment about the seat
being 'stolen' from the people of West Belfast, in one phrase a
declaration of religious and political sectarianism – denying the
equal right to be represented of the West Belfast Protestants
whose votes tipped the balance for Hendron and, as damagingly, the validity of the SDLP's 15,000 Catholic votes.

Adams's dignity has always been an important attribute in the
republican propaganda struggle to displace blood, death, misery
and the crude image of mindless 'Provos' – in particular, for example, the effect of television documentaries like the 1993 BBC

'Panorama' report that showed an IRA man turned double agent for the RUC talking about some of his colleagues as 'more blowy and shooty' than political.

Though republicans continue to insist that theirs is not a hierarchical movement, the Sinn Féin president has undoubtedly been awarded a special role: somewhere between policy-maker and father figure. To judge from the way he is presented on public occasions such as the annual ard-fheis (conference), his effectiveness is deemed to outweigh the disapproval of personality cults.

Speeches about the republican 'strategy for peace' – in essence laying out the conditions for an end to IRA violence – are made by a series of senior figures, not Adams alone: Martin McGuinness and Mitchel McLaughlin in Derry, Jim Gibney and Tom Hartley in Belfast. The substance is recycled, with occasional additions by one or other, which will then be rephrased in the next speech. Beyond this process, Adams clearly sees his particular public contribution as building self-esteem and a sense of republican communal pride in the poorest parts of Belfast and Derry where Sinn Féin and the IRA are strongest. But of all the best-known senior Sinn Féin figures, it is also Adams who in general works hardest at claiming a wider allegiance for republicanism.

Not for him the terminology of the imprisoned Danny Morrison: 'The SDLP versus Sinn Féin – in a sense it's the age-old split between O'Connell and the Young Irelanders, Parnell and the Fenians etcetera. A class analysis is helpful in that it provides something of a framework to explain the differences but, of course, it doesn't allow for the complexities and peculiarities of the situation. Regardless of the SDLP denying (with some truth) that it is mainly representing a middle-class ideal in its approach to and analysis of the conflict, there can be no doubting that in Sinn Féin's case we largely represent lumpen-nationalists and an alternative culture (our constituency being "a state within a state").'

No 'lumpen-nationalists' for Gerry Adams: instead he uses the words 'nationalism' and 'republicanism' interchangeably, keen to outline a unity among Northern Catholics which others believe no longer exists.

'There is, I think, something a friend of mine calls group Catholic thinking. About 80 per cent of Northern Catholics, after all, are only a generation away from the land or away from the ghetto and it doesn't take an awful lot to concretise their views...the hunger strikes, discrimination, the Queen's University member of staff who was called a "Fenian bastard" ...there's a tendency within this state for some aspects of life to remind you where you come from.

'There's a limit to accommodation and accommodationist politics – and it's the constitutional issue, because Protestants won't talk about it. It's the same thing as people making accommodations in their personal lives and then finding they come up against discrimination. Political accommodation in this state depends on the Unionists and British as much as anyone else. The Unionists have shown no great effort to accommodate, the British are not prepared to push the issue forward, and that brings people back to this group Catholic thinking. Maybe this will reinforce the Unionist paranoia that behind every Catholic, there's some sort of nationalist. I know that isn't the case. I'm trying to make the point that even when the SDLP were prepared to give under Sunningdale, the Unionists wouldn't let them, if you like. I don't think the SDLP any longer want to give. It has moved on, twenty years later. If the emergence of Sinn Féin means a slight radicalising of the non-unionist section of the community, so much the better.'

But having virtually suggested that Sinn Féin's effect on Catholic opinion had been minimal, Adams was less modest about the IRA. 'I think our history shows that progress has always been made around a hard edge of agitation. Demands were usually conceded to whoever the established constitutional politicians were – but that happened when there was unity of purpose or coincidence of objectives. The IRA is the catalyst for change. Britain I don't think would move otherwise. The SDLP know that: that isn't to say they welcome it, want it or appreciate it. But they know it's very difficult trying to persuade the British. Some say the IRA brought down Stormont – I think the whole resistance including the IRA brought down Stormont.

'There's a point people miss. A mass of people come through what's broadly called the republican movement – thousands here in west Belfast in the last twenty years. And I say to the people I work with, those people, although they're not active now, they are still republican. They may have hang-ups, they fell out with the leadership, don't like this or that, but basically what happened was they just couldn't go on. They got married, had kids, got older, couldn't take the pressure – but they still remain republicans. The march on the day Sean Downes was killed, it was just a normal march, a few thousand people. We called a march the following night and it was the biggest I saw on that road [the Falls], there were people there who you'd known in '69, '70, '71 or '72, in jail. They were there to fight, going up that road no matter what happened. Go round and ask those people now would they come out and do something and they won't do it. But when something happens that outrages them, like Sean Downes's death, like the hunger strikes, then all the reasons why they left vanish. They still have the aspiration. They're all there, they're still there.'

The intonation was unmistakable: 'I say to the people I work with . . . they're all there, they're still there . . . ' Authoritative, reassuring, like all effective leaders, Adams works hard at encouraging the troops. This far into the Troubles, however, he must hear the hollowness of his own reassurance that 'they still have the aspiration'. Gerry Adams knows that the lapsed republicans who marched when Sean Downes was killed by an RUC plastic bullet came out to protest at police violence, not because the 'aspiration' for a thirty-two-county socialist republic had reawakened in their hearts.

Adams hits a note with some resonance in the comments of others, however, when he maintains that a folk memory of shared disadvantage and awareness of continuing prejudice are still strong in many Catholics. Near the top of the social ladder, memory of disadvantage is fading, and often denied or muted – but I was surprised by repeated stories of prejudice encountered, and resented, at points late on in the climb.

ACCOMMODATION

John Hume manages to reassure many that discrimination is effectively a thing of the past, that the arrangements he envisages will remove what remains of their dissatisfaction with the state of Northern Ireland and will adequately reflect their political identity. Beyond that, no SDLP supporters I spoke to had much idea what the future shape of government should be.

PETER O'HAGAN is perhaps typical of the voter and supporter who is puzzled but still gratified by Hume's grand designs. He is an SDLP councillor in the Unionist-dominated Lisburn council, a retired secondary school head teacher. He has spent years asking for more RUC protection for Catholics against loyalist attacks, and charting the scarcity of Catholics in council employment. His first political involvement was in the Campaign for Social Justice in the early sixties, collecting statistics on discrimination that bolstered the civil rights agitation. He is sixty-two, one of the 'poor bloody infantry', in his own words, who has slogged through the Troubles at the SDLP's grassroots, and occasionally come close to despair.

One of those occasions was the famous moment during the negotiations that led to the Anglo-Irish Agreement when the then British prime minister Margaret Thatcher brutally and publicly dismissed the three constitutional models put forward shortly before by the New Ireland Forum: a unitary Irish state, joint British/Irish authority over Northern Ireland, and a confederation or federation.

'Give-up time was the '79 to '85 period,' Peter recalls. 'When Thatcher did her "out, out, out" bit, there were good people then saying "we're finished". The fortnight before the Anglo-Irish Agreement, '85, the party conference then – John made a speech about the rest of the world, he could have delivered it to the United Nations. I said if this doesn't come up with some kind of way forward, I'm going to pack it in.

'But I haven't, because the Anglo-Irish Agreement was unbelievable. It simply recognised the fact that the problem of Northern Ireland began a long time ago, was exacerbated by partition, it did not bring peace, stability or good government, to unionists even! For the first time in my lifetime somebody looked at it and said, let's begin to repair the damage. The two governments talking together . . . I said, this is worth giving a couple of heaves along the way.

'It's not that I can live with this state as it is, even with the changes with direct rule, the start of some kind of attempt to put discrimination right, and God knows there's still a long way to go. I can't live with it – but I've got to live with it, that's what I feel. Like thousands: we're trapped in this. All you can do is try to make a contribution.

'Withdrawal – that's an emotive word. But I do think the British have realised there's no future here. I'm not talking about abolishing this, abolishing that, or even the term "a united Ireland". I'm talking about getting together and working out a structure where the two parts of Ireland begin to work in harmony.'

Does this mean joint authority? How would joint authority work? Are we talking about a confederation of Britain and Ireland with a Unionist-dominated northern region?

In October 1992 Hume told BBC Radio Ulster that Northern Ireland was an 'abnormal entity' and that power-sharing in a devolved Northern Ireland administration – which Unionists continue to shy away from – would not be a solution. The Unionist furore this caused still reverberates. Hume had 'moved the goalposts' and made it clear for the first time, it was said, that the SDLP would not accept an 'internal solution' – meaning an arrangement in a purely British context. It is what Gerry Adams meant when he suggested Sinn Féin might have 'slightly' radicalised the SDLP. This was not the first time Hume had said something of the sort, however – it was only the most open, unambiguous statement he had made in recent times. In May 1972, he told RTE that the possibility of a restructured North was as impractical as Stormont itself: the only viable option was Irish unity: 'Let's cut the nonsense now and get down to answering the question once and for all.' But in 1972 the SDLP also produced its first document on joint British-Irish authority over Northern Ireland – Ben Caraher helped to write it.

During the 1992 general election campaign Hume said that 'the real union on the table' was European, the union of 'a Europe of the regions'. He was pressed to say whether he meant Northern Ireland would be a region of Ireland or of the UK. 'Quite obviously it would be a region of Europe,' he said, 'quite clearly – both Northern identities transcend the boundaries of Ireland.' An SDLP document produced for the confidential inter-party talks in 1992 proposed a six-person executive commission for Northern Ireland with representatives from the two governments, plus three from Northern Ireland, plus one from the European Commission.

Unionists were outraged at the prospect of an Irish minister having executive power in Northern Ireland, and at the thought of European involvement. Judging by subsequent interviews, the European element of the structure seems to have been dropped – though presumably the context is still important. Sinn Féin, which has only just begun to make unconvincing noises about the importance of 'the European project', as Mitchel McLaughlin calls it, after almost two decades of opposition to the idea of a European community, was plainly baffled all along by the entire plan.

Someone who has known Hume for more than thirty years once said, 'His tactic from the start was to ask for civil rights, which the Unionists couldn't give – in a slightly cynical way it was a safe demand from a nationalist point of view. There was no danger of the book being closed.' But that interprets Hume's original motivation as dogmatically nationalist and anti-partitionist. The increasing emphasis on Europe as a stage or setting that will simultaneously accommodate two Northern identities suggests instead a pragmatism that has been shaped by Hume's lengthy European experience – he first began to liaise with European, and US, politicians, in the mid-seventies – as well as by a growing awareness of the limited Irish government interest in the North.

Hume says now, 'I've never called myself a nationalist. I've always been a social democrat.' For several years he has used the platform of the SDLP annual conference to decry the nation-state as obsolete and nationalism as sterile, a dated, nineteenth-century phenomenon which ignores the divisions between the people on the island of Ireland. In 1984, however, he described the SDLP's achievement through the New Ireland Forum, the meeting of all the nationalist parties except Sinn Féin, as having 'established our position as part of the body politic of the Irish nationalist tradition'.

In 1991, during the SDLP's annual conference, Hume told a
BBC Radio Ulster programme that his position on the unification of Ireland was that he was 'translating its meaning into the
reality of today's life'. What this meant was that 'it's essential the
two governments cooperate as closely as possible in providing
peace and stability for the people of this island'. There is not
necessarily any contradiction here, as the more overtly traditionalist and plain-spoken Seamus Mallon insists. He traces the
new realism in nationalism back to the New Ireland Forum.

'Redefining nationalism is not revisionism, it was absolutely
essential. We came out of a time, remember, when the term "a
united Ireland" had never been defined. In the early seventies,
late sixties, the catch-all was a "thirty-two-county socialist
republic". Nobody bothered to think much about what that
meant...

'The forum gave options in terms of nationalist aspirations. In
many ways it relieved nationalist opinion of the historical
imperative that had built up: that if you weren't simply pursuing
a thirty-two-county republic you were less of a nationalist. It
accepted there could be a staged position and if a united Ireland
was your ultimate aim, you had to decide how to pursue it.
That *is* my ultimate position.'

John Hume is more enigmatic. He guards himself and his
party against the charge of undermining identity and abandon-
ing tradition by lashing out at the 'grievance mentality, which
I think still exists in fairly major areas of the Catholic community. They're happy to keep complaining. It's all they know.
They're whingers. They don't want you to remove the reason
for the complaint in this funny sort of way. They're comfortable
in it.'

Where leading republicans tended to be circumspect in their
public denunciations of the SDLP, mindful that the party is a
reflection of a major strand in the Northern nationalist identity,

Hume has no such inhibitions. The 'whingers', he makes plain, are Sinn Féin and the IRA. By using 'nationalist' as a term of abuse and appropriating 'republican' for his own party, he pre-empts the accusation of 'selling-out' or apologetic nationalism. 'In the real meaning of the word, the SDLP is a republican party, in the original meaning of uniting Protestant, Catholic and Dissenter. The Provos are the nationalists, more in the tradition of the Peep O' Day Boys and the Defenders [nineteenth-century Catholic faction-fighters who committed atrocities against Protestants] – we're more in the tradition of the genuine republican philosophy. I remember as a boy, my father taking me to a nationalist meeting at the top of the street, and they were waving the flag and I was getting emotional. And my father put his hand on my shoulder and he says, "Just you remember one thing – you can never eat a flag."'

As for his own ultimate position, he leaves options open. It is the kind of answer that unnerves unionists and leaves republicans unsure whether to condemn or to borrow some at least of his terminology. 'Unity I've always defined as agreement, not as a takeover bid. And the form of unity? I don't mind what it is. Because the moment the two sections of the Irish people actually agree on how to live together and start working that, it will evolve itself... Once people start working together you grow into a completely new Ireland – and two or three generations down the road, you create new structures that give expression to what has happened.'

The language about new structures and a time scale of several generations has now begun to seep into republican statements, as has the insistence that unity can only happen by agreement. Suspicion about 'internal settlements' remains. In successive elections the SDLP vote has steadily increased, except in Belfast – proof enough for party members that they have given their supporters what they want. It is difficult, none the less, to avoid the conclusion that the SDLP's success has been at the cost of deepening a new and bitter division: among Northern Catholics. The growth of a Catholic middle class is an important factor. But discontented, cynical people in Belfast, Derry, Newry and mid-Ulster are not simply or even primarily bitter at the new economic advantages open only to some. For these people, there is a clear awareness that their aspirations have been pushed into the background by other Catholics as much as by the rest of the political world. They are not all poor; their republicanism is by no means a uniform set of beliefs. Many feel silenced, 'marginalised', in the same way as their parents and grandparents did in the fifties and sixties. What was once a fairly straightforward disaffection from the Unionist state of Northern Ireland is now a more complex feeling. There is no longer a Catholic community of interests within which anger at the state can be expressed.

Máiréad, who dislikes many things about the SDLP but votes for them and has considerable respect for their leader, seemed to me to be expressing something like this.

'What *is* attractive is the idea of Europe, the way John Hume pushes that, the whole notion of a more multi-ethnic situation. At an emotional level that really appeals to me. But I think it's still predicated on an internal settlement of some kind. No matter how you dress that up, it's going to be a settlement where the Unionists are the government of Northern Ireland. Given that we've got Unionists saying "no power-sharing", how does that undermine support for the Provos? As they stand at the moment, their only reason for being is to keep going. They've got to be given some very good reason to stop.

'Their support is ambiguous and very deep, remember. A lot of political argument here is useless for that reason – because it's conducted in terms of: "There's these two hundred bad boys, so why can't we get rid of them?" But the problem isn't that there's open support for an armed campaign. A lot of it is more on the level of: "Well if they keep going, at least it means they'll not be able to impose something on us – we don't want to see these bombs, but on the other hand if the Provos gave up altogether what would that mean? Free rein to internal solutions?"'

Hume's meetings with Gerry Adams during the past year are tersely described by both as intended to discuss the development of a 'strategy' to end the conflict. But they seem an acknowledgement by the SDLP leader of this kind of fear. For republicans, they offer a lessening of their isolation and at least the illusion of participation in mainstream political life. For others, they seem a better, if still remote, chance of progress than further negotiation with Unionists within the unchanged constitutional context of the United Kingdom.

4

'I don't want them to be bad guys'

THE IRA

Among Northern Ireland's Catholics there are, of course, those who only think of the IRA, as one inside observer puts it drily, 'when they blow up MFI', the home furnishings superstore outside Belfast. There is a world of difference in the complex and often intense relationship between the IRA and those who live in strongly republican areas, and the way the organisation is regarded by the affluent Catholic inhabitants of somewhere like Bangor, County Down.

Looking back on his own community's relationship down the years with the force he had served, a retired Catholic RUC man decided Catholics were no more varied now than they had ever been: 'They've always run the gamut from IRA to Castle Catholic.' No matter how distant many are from the IRA, in sympathy and knowledge alike, no matter how assiduously clerics assure the rest of the world on their behalf that members of the IRA should not be thought of as true Catholics, the armed, secret organisation exists now in a form more deeply rooted and more widely established than ever before. In such a small society and after so lengthy a period of unrest, few families have absolutely no personal links to republicanism either by blood or by marriage, no matter how opposed most of the family might be. The IRA has become a considerable element of the Catholic community, like it or not.

Many dislike it, but they are unable to disown it. TONY, the academic from Derry, the first in his family to have a salary, raised to 'be respectable and be grateful for a job, any job, and to keep my head down', was fifteen when Bloody Sunday happened. All round him friends joined the IRA, but Tony stayed clear. It was as much luck as anything else, he says. 'Falling in love at fifteen had a lot to do with it. But it wasn't distaste for them. In those days there was an absolute communal bond – the IRA could operate without masks, nobody would contemplate approaching the RUC. It wasn't fear, it was solidarity. They had an accountability and a support they've long since lost.'

He now thinks the IRA are misguided, counterproductive and sectarian (though not in Derry), and that they exist by rules of their own . . . But that's not the whole story.

'You're sitting talking to republicans for hours, arguing. You just have a feeling there are no goalposts here, there's no framework you'd agree on. A smile comes over their faces at the end of the night: because you have a threshold, they don't.

'But I don't know how the Church or anyone else takes them on – it's not an even playing field. Edward Daly felt stronger to do it than anybody else, when he said there's only one oppressor in Derry now, that's the IRA . . . but there's so many like me. I'm a classic example, that can't 100 per cent come out and just say in black and white they're wrong, they have no justification.'

SUPPORTING THE IRA

Republican paramilitary organisations are responsible for approximately 1,800 of the Troubles' violent deaths inside

Northern Ireland: the IRA are guilty of most of those. They have seriously injured many thousands more people, damaged buildings and installations costing billions of pounds, destroyed lives, homes, jobs and helped further entrench the bitter divisions of centuries. The havoc the IRA causes to those they consider enemies and the accidental victims who get in their way is immense: they have killed more people than loyalist paramilitaries, the British army, the RUC and the UDR combined. Yet on any occasion when republicans are gathered in public, when for example the members of the IRA's political wing, Sinn Féin, hold their annual conference, or ard-fheis, there is an overwhelming sense that this toll of death and misery has no reality for them.

Speakers insist, to applause, that the British government is responsible for the entire conflict. Deaths are commemorated, meticulously – but only from one side of the battlefield. The conference hall is always hung with the names and often with the photographs of those who have 'given their lives' during the previous year: IRA volunteers 'killed in action by British forces', Sinn Féin members killed by loyalist paramilitaries. Dying 'in action' has a unique status, but the deaths of Catholics, and in particular republicans, at the hands of loyalist – 'British, or pro-British, murder gangs' – are even more forcefully rehearsed. The 'suffering of the nationalist people' is a powerful refrain, taken up by speaker after speaker: republican losses blend into a wider picture of a community victimised through the ages. Victimhood is an important part of republicans' sense of legitimacy, effectively screening out guilt for their own violence. 'It is not they who can inflict most but they who suffer most will conquer' is a favourite quotation.

Over the years of the Troubles more than 5,000 people, the overwhelming majority of them from the North, have passed through the IRA's ranks. Several thousand have served sentences as tightly disciplined and motivated prisoners. Over 300 have died as foot soldiers, blown up by their own bombs, shot by soldiers or police, or as 'touts' and 'informers' by the IRA itself. There are less bloody but traumatic hazards: broken marriages, relationships with children shrunk to irregular contact. Women struggle to bring up children on their own and to maintain some kind of bond with imprisoned or fugitive men. At each stage of an IRA member's 'career', whole families are worked into the fabric of a secret army's essential business, stitched firmly in the margins where they can have only the slightest of influence but where activities like demonstrations provide a visible fringe for public consumption.

But for the relatives of people who shoot and bomb for the IRA over any considerable time, the effect is anything but 'fringe'. Their lives for intense periods are dominated by visiting prisons and hospitals, the pattern of their days derailed in many cases by police and army searches and harassment, or the demands of a husband, son or brother – less often a wife, sister or daughter – 'on the run' for weeks and months at a time. For those of them who live outside the biggest and most secure ghettos, there is also the ever-present fear of being identified – by appearance in court, or prison visiting – as a loyalist target.

The majority live on the economic margins: on the dole, dependent on other relatives for money and help with children. It only takes a visit to the Maze prison – Long Kesh, 'the Kesh' to republicans – to be reminded that the prisoner class in general is not wealthy. Swamped by worry and its own grief, a whole section of the Catholic community is not so much blind to the victims of IRA violence as numb to it. The 'blanket' and 'no-wash' prison protests of the late seventies – begun when the Northern Ireland Office withdrew the privileges that paramilitary prisoners considered accorded them 'political status' – kept relatives of prisoners in a fever for several years. Outrage, fervour and despair at the thought of men living in their own excrement or starving themselves to death in turn possessed parents, wives, sisters and brothers, often to the exclusion of normal life. Derrywoman MARY NELIS, tracing her own development from tenants' rights organiser to fully committed republican and Sinn Féin election candidate (she was elected to Derry council in May 1993), maintains that the blanket protest was decisive. Two of her sons took part in the protest; in the early Troubles another son had been killed in a road accident. 'Donncha was one of the first arrested as political status was withdrawn. He was eighteen, and I knew nothing about his involvement until he was arrested. He felt really bad for me – we were just over Peter's death. But I don't believe I will ever go through as much suffering as during that H Block protest. Even my son's death paled into insignificance.'

Such intensity may sound implausible to those who did not witness the period. At the time there was no denying the sense of spreading crisis and bitterness among many Northern Catholics – and a corresponding distaste and hostility among Protestants. In 1981 eight IRA and two INLA men starved themselves to death in jail in the attempt to force the British government to recognise them once more as political prisoners. Communal emotions pulled hundreds of thousands who had never offered active support before onto the streets for the hunger strikers' funerals, 'by their umbilical cords', as one dismayed observer described it. The upheaval of the hunger strike renewed the IRA's roots in the Northern Catholic soul with fresh grievance and sense of isolation. The then head of the Catholic Church in Ireland, Cardinal Tomás Ó Fiaich, and the Bishop of Derry, Edward Daly, were seen to plead with British ministers, and were as visibly rejected. Northern nationalist politicians, watching their supporters turn out for hunger strikers' funerals, had no British government concessions to show for their moderation: their Southern counterparts, as opposed to the popular feeling at the time in the South, were either openly unsympathetic or lacked conviction. Republicans had fasted to death in the past in Southern jails too.

GERRY ADAMS, then Sinn Féin vice-president, became the chief link between the strikers and the campaign supporting them. He was accused at the time by unionists, and by some anti-republican nationalists, of discouraging the end of the strike because Sinn Féin was profiting from it. Asked if he has regrets, he says, 'I don't refléct like that and I haven't had the time – perhaps some day I will. Those of us tied in would feel rightly or wrongly that we stuck by them. They had worked out certain conditions and despite the pressures on us – which in a funny way may have been as severe on us as their experience was on them – we stuck by them. The hunger strikers were absolutely geared to the political consequences, the mass mobilisation.

'A person said to me during the hunger strikes that it was almost back to the civil war time. What she meant was the country had never been so divided since the civil war days.'

For the IRA, meanwhile, it was business as usual, with an occasional set piece in tribute to a dead or dying hunger striker – like the landmine ambush that killed five soldiers within miles of the south Armagh homeplace of Raymond McCreesh, days before his clearly imminent death. That south Armagh ambush is logged by the prisoners' leader in David Beresford's vivid insider book on the hunger strike, Ten Men Dead (London, 1987), built around 'comms' – smuggled letters – from the H Blocks. A comm from 'Bik' McFarlane (serving life for the murder in 1975 of five Protestants in the Shankill Road Bayardo Bar bombing) to a Sinn Féin official charged with coordinating statements and protests about the strike describes McFarlane's mood at the prospect of another death in the jail. Written for private, not public, consumption, it conveys strongly how seamlessly in the eyes of republicans the prison protest, Sinn Féin activity on the outside and the IRA all fitted together. It also catches something of the contrast between the grief with which republicans regard the deaths of comrades, and the relish with which they chart their own ability to kill the enemy.

> Personally I'd whack the Concorde with a Sam 7. Then where would we be, sez you? Oh, I don't know!! Did you ever feel totally frustrated? No, don't answer that. I've a blinding headache just now – a rarity for me which makes it all the more annoying. . . You know something – I feel really terrible just sitting here, waiting for Ray to die. I haven't prayed too much since Bob died – I don't know what it is. Perhaps I should try harder. Love to all. Take care and God Bless.
>
> P.S. Have just heard about that cunning little operation in S. Armagh. Oh, you wonderful people!! Far from home they perish, yet they know not the reason why! Tis truly a great shame. They kill and die and never think to question. Such is the penalty for blind folly. God Bless, Bik.

With hindsight the hunger strike marked a uniquely close identification between the nationalist population – North and South – and what used to be called 'physical force' republicanism. The nature of the protest, the fact that the British prime minister of the day, Margaret Thatcher, had already acquired an image as singularly unbending, and above all the widespread sense of a contest over a bureaucratic formula to save official face: the hunger strike had all the qualities necessary to extract the last drop of sympathy from Catholic ambivalence about the campaign for British withdrawal, and about the IRA itself. In the process, republicanism in truth for the first time emerged as the 'movement' it had long proclaimed itself, complete with political representation; and the IRA broadened and deepened an outer ring of support for a refined killing machine, after the reverses of the mid- and late seventies and the long ebb of sympathy from the previous high point of internment (introduced on 9 August 1971). Eleven years into an armed campaign, the IRA at last developed a political wing – and as many years later may very well be wondering what to do with it, now that the potential of the twin-track 'Armalite and ballot box' phase seems exhausted.

The Belfast IRA man, thirty-six years old, gave me the official line on the present state of development of the IRA – and then expressed some of the realism about its limitations that is increasingly voiced by leading republicans.

'*This* IRA has gone beyond the point where others collapsed. In the mid-seventies, the 1974–75 ceasefire and the period immediately after it under Mason [Roy Mason, secretary of state 1976–79], that should have seen its demise. But it survived. It became a popular army, so entrenched in the community that it was seen as the only hope in the face of onslaught. In fact it emerged stronger from that period, with a leadership politicised in the jails. Previously freed prisoners formed a political party or split or went purely military, went for a strong army with no politics.

'We're very forceful with recruits. We tell them we offer prisons or graveyards – and still the organisation has the luxury of more people than it needs. It takes you to keep recommitting yourself, recharging. But there's young blood coming up all the time ...

'The only power we have is in the struggle. We can't of ourselves move this situation along. But we can condemn future generations by making the mistake of ending the conflict. We're not going to do that.'

The fatalistic tone is increasingly familiar, though the bleak estimate of the IRA's limitations was less hedged about than that of most Sinn Féin spokespersons. What seems to be a growing republican awareness that their campaign must look to factors other than the deployment of ever greater violence if it is to make progress, coupled with the long-established realisation that only their violence gives them any relevance, has produced what has begun to sound like an almost robotic fatalism. It is an analysis that has begun to make some observers doubt whether '*this* IRA' has in fact got an off button.

Before the Troubles and for the four decades back to the twenties, the IRA barely existed. Veteran Belfast lawyer PADDY MCGRORY's description of the 'half a dozen guys sitting down there in the lower Falls' who were sceptical about the South's verbal republicanism in the forties and fifties fits with other estimates. The 'border' campaign had no reality for most Catholics, even in border areas. Former SDLP vice-chairman BEN CARAHER grew up during the fifties in Crossmaglen – a place that gained the name in the early Troubles, though to some locals' dislike, as the 'capital of the republic of South Armagh'. Republicanism did not revive locally until 1971. Ben Caraher's father was a Sinn Féiner in 1917, his uncle was in the old IRA. To him, that was history.

When the fifties campaign began, what struck Ben as an eighteen-year-old was 'the absolute irrelevance of it, what on earth was it all about? I had a first cousin involved, he was caught, occasionally I visited him in Crumlin Road. I liked the man – but as far as I was concerned the thing was insane. To me what they were trying was impossible by the method they were using and it was questionable whether it was desirable anyway. I think now, though I wouldn't have put it like that then, that it was an example of the dominance of ideology on people's minds, the world through the spectacles of the twenties. It had extraordinarily little impact on people's daily physical lives. It went on, it was on the border, it made headlines, but it was outside people's experience. You weren't running across patrols on the streets. Who cared?

'There *was* a bit of guff in the background – talk about "the boys" and "sure they're doing no harm blowing up the odd pylon". There was also the terrible semi-religious thing, that they were daft and impractical and wouldn't get anywhere – but they were purer in heart than the politicians. And the songs came in there . . . about Fergal O'Hanlon and Seán South from Garryowen. Patrick Pearse-type figures: South used to go round cinemas in Limerick putting out courting couples in the back row. But they were tremendous songs, like "The Patriot Game" and the one about South. They perfectly encapsulated the ambiguity. On the one hand, if put to the wall you would disapprove of what they were doing – but the songs allowed you to participate emotionally in some part of their activities. I suppose that's the purpose of rebel songs: part of your inheritance, the emotional ambiguity that allows you to take part whereas your strict political expression would say, Well no actually, I don't think it was a good thing for Fergal O'Hanlon to go and try and shoot policemen with Seán South in Lisnaskea and Roslea. Meanwhile, while you had the IRA sanctified in song, nationalist politicians were a curious mixture of pathetic ineffectuality cum petty corruption . . . there was a contrast there.'

BRIAN MCCAFFREY, former Sinn Féin councillor for Roslea, on the Fermanagh–Monaghan border, the countryside where many of the fifties attacks took place and where South and O'Hanlon died, was only a child in the fifties. All he knows from his own memory is that the songs about the campaign were not sung in his own non-republican family. From listening to family talk and from local conversations since, he is sure there was little local support. 'It probably existed in spite of a lot of people rather than because of them. There was a great apathy: that's what people remember. Talking about it one night in the pub, somebody made the point about the road closures [the blocking of cross-border roads by the British army – to hinder the IRA] that are such a big thing now. For five or six years the roads were spiked during the border campaign, they said, there were four steel girders across one of them – and they stayed there, and nobody even thought of trying to remove them. Now they're putting in hundreds of tons of concrete and it's getting shifted [by local people] the very next day.' By way of measuring the growth in modern republicanism in Derry, MITCHEL MCLAUGHLIN, Sinn Féin's Northern chairman, told me, 'Twenty-odd years ago there was this tiny, totally mar-ginalised and inconsequential republican tradition centred on no more than five or six families. Now there's a network right across the Derry area.'

From its shrunken state in the late sixties to an organisation large enough to maintain violence on the present scale, over such a period, is an amazing leap. Northern Catholics from all parts of the political spectrum agree that the IRA we know to-day was effectively born in the ghettos as a defence force during the loyalist attacks of 1969. John Hume has said that 'the IRA emerged after the pogroms of Bombay Street'.

Former Sinn Féin director of information DANNY MORRISON is now in jail sentenced for the unlawful imprisonment of a man the prosecution depicted as a double agent, IRA man and police informer, held in a west Belfast house and allegedly about to be shot dead after an IRA trial. Morrison grew up on the Falls. In letters from Long Kesh in answer to questions about how he sees his identity now, he described the growth of his own involvement, catching in the process something of community tensions and of the development of a new, spontaneous and programmeless IRA. In August 1969, he was sixteen, due to start studying for A levels. On Broadway, where the road from the Falls ran straight down into Protestant territory, he helped build and maintain barricades.

'Overnight [15 August] the shooting had been very heavy and hundreds of homes had been burned. The barricades were being built from early that morning and there was major panic, unbelievable fear. I don't think I can convey the sense of defencelessness.

'But at first people were still very law-abiding. For example, Broadway was left open and barricades were built across the two side streets which ran off it, Irwell Street and Iveagh Street... Bombay Street was burned down on Friday morning and that afternoon the soldiers began pouring in. They billeted in the Protestant school at the corner of Iveagh Street. We held meetings in one of the classrooms to elect a defence committee. Even though the SDLP hadn't been founded yet, our community even then was polarised. SDLP/Churchy types had great faith in the Brits, as had our parish priest.'

Those who warned about 'getting too close to the Brits, or trusting them' tended to be people interned in IRA campaigns of the past. From what he learned about the state of the IRA, Danny Morrison recalls that then, and even a year later, 'republicanism hadn't articulated any coherent political line, simply represented the aspiration for Irish reunification, and was preoccupied with defence – though quite a few, no doubt, had the continuation of the War of Independence optionally or opportunistically in mind'.

Circumstances since – the Falls curfew, internment, Bloody Sunday – have repeatedly renewed the first rush of recruits, while an underlay of inherited memories and legends from earlier IRA generations makes up the mix of sentiment and historical justification that keeps an outer circle of second-rank supporters and sympathisers in place. The basis of support is what it always was, but constantly renewed.

MYTHS AND MEMORIES

In his *The Politics of Irish Freedom* (Dingle, 1986) Gerry Adams says that in 1961 when the last of the republicans interned during the IRA's fifties campaign were released, 'they found that in Belfast they had 24 people and two short-arms'. But internment itself constituted an IRA resource and was part of the folklore that rippled out into the wider Catholic community – beyond the families of those commonly referred to as 'mad republicans'. The term did not suggest condemnation – instead it conveyed semi-derision, mixed with sceptical admiration. Republicans willing to conspire against the state might always have been a tiny minority of the minority, open to ridicule as fanatics; they gained stature because the authority that interned them in each decade of Stormont rule was Protestant, Unionist and discriminatory... and because there was a strong, if flattering and inaccurate, image of the IRA as a bulwark against loyalist attack.

In the childhood memories of many, no reference to internment was complete without the reminder that even in the twenties, in the years of the most blatant and prolonged violence against Catholics (described as 'pogroms' in contemporary English newspapers), no more than a 'handful' of Protestants were interned in all compared to hundreds of Catholics (about 480 Catholics to a 'dozen' Protestants, according to Michael Farrell's *Arming the Protestants,* Dingle, 1983). Folk memory may not have been exact about the number, but it got the proportions right.

The twenties cast a long shadow: assassinations carried out by uniformed men, by members of the police and by 'special' constables of the new, Protestant state of Northern Ireland. Accounts passed down through families often came complete with gruesome detail. History bears out an interpretation that emphasises a considerably greater Catholic share of suffering, and the involvement in sectarian murder of members of the state's forces. (The dispassionate Jonathan Bardon [*A History of Ulster,* Belfast, 1992] describes the perpetrators of two of the most vividly remembered multiple killings as, variously, 'uniformed men, thought to have been RIC' [Royal Irish Constabulary, the predecessors of the RUC], and 'uniformed police'.) But in the memories of many as formed by childhood tales, it is as though only Catholics died.

For all the traces of it in Catholic folk memory, IRA action at the time against the newly formed RUC and the Specials might as well not have happened. The word 'reprisal', for example, to many growing up in the twenties and thirties meant unlawful revenge killing by members of the state's forces. But often, in the stories parents or grandparents told, the IRA shootings or burnings that triggered the reprisals melted away, leaving only traces. When the IRA got a direct mention, it was instead as the defenders of Belfast's embattled Catholic districts, though the words of some of the songs of the period are far from defensive, as in 'The Battle of Raglan Street', which related how a bomb ensured that 'the Specials went up, and they never came down'.

The McMahons and the Duffins and others in Belfast taken away in the night by DI (District Inspector John W.) Nixon's soft-soled murder gang to die horribly on the side of the mountain: all this came early to many. But not the shooting of B Specials or police in Belfast, Fermanagh, south Derry; not the Protestant Donnelly children killed by a bomb thrown through their window after the McMahon killings, and not the story of the seven Protestants, one a woman, only one a Special, taken from their homes and shot dead on the roadside at Altnaveigh in County Armagh (near the spot at Kingsmills where in 1976 ten Protestant workmen were taken from their minibus and killed by the IRA).

Memories come filtered down the generations to leave only pure, distilled Catholic victimhood. They are still powerful, to judge by frequent republican references today: an evocation of a time when the IRA was massively outgunned but valiant in defence of vulnerable people, a tug of terror at the heartstrings when present-day police or soldiers can even half-credibly be accused of collusion with loyalist paramilitaries. The twenties are not so very long ago, after all. One politician told me that his canvassers in a recent election refused to go anywhere near the house off the Antrim Road where the men of the McMahon family, in 1922, were lined up against their sitting-room wall and shot by 'the Murder Gang'.

JOSEPH, fifty-three, came to Belfast to work from a small farm near Trillick, County Tyrone. He says he has 'no time for the IRA, they make nothing but trouble for Catholics now. I worked for a while in Stewartstown, with Protestants all around me. When an IRA thing happened, you hated to hear it, because of all the comments you'd get, and what could you say? But I wouldn't always have felt like this. When I was only a lad, the most exciting thing I ever heard was Liam Kelly at the sports in Tempo, I think it was. He was the Saor Uladh man [Saor Uladh was a republican splinter group that helped to push the IRA into beginning the fifties campaign] – he managed the co-op in Tempo and he was very well liked. They had the Tricolour up in a bush for the day, and the police told him to take it down. And he said, straight out: "We owe no allegiance to the foreign intruders of a bastard nation." Like that. I can remember it yet. There was a shiver down my back. The police were there in hundreds and they moved in and arrested him and a scuffle broke out. I remember the inspector's cap rolling down the street.'

Joseph's romantic memory, complete with detail, catches

much of the flavour of the fifties IRA that Catholics retained. It merged with memories of internment: in the thirties, forties and fifties hundreds of men and women, almost all of them Catholics, were held without trial under the Special Powers Act in prison ships or Crumlin Road jail, and even among anti-republicans, there was a certain respect in references later to X or Y who had spent 'years of his life in Crumlin Road'. Jimmy Drumm, the veteran republican whose wife Máire was shot dead in the Mater Hospital by loyalists, famously spent fifteen Christmases in jail without trial.

'You might deduce from the tone of voice that X or Y was wrong-headed, maybe even a bit mad,' says a fiftyish civil servant of the tales his avowedly anti-IRA parents related, 'but you came away with an impression of a principled maverick on the one hand and vindictive discriminatory authority on the other, equipped with a battery of special powers. Remember, a lot of those men lifted in the fifties could have got out years earlier if they'd signed to be of good behaviour. They wouldn't do it, because they didn't recognise the British right to ask them.'

The small scale of the IRA campaigns of the thirties, forties and fifties – bloody though the bombings in England were – made scarcely a dent in the mythology. No wonder that the introduction of internment on a large scale in 1971 set off emotional depth charges. Several of those taken from their homes in the early hours of 9 August had been interned before, some as young men in the forties, some in the fifties campaign. Suddenly in a clatter of bin lids and helicopters, myths and memories came crashing into the seventies, to be added to this time – months after a raft of eyewitness description of early-morning arrests, beatings, men pushed out of helicopters – by a detailed and factual account of white noise and high-tech interrogation in a military barracks at Ballykelly, County Derry.

Middle-class Catholics in public positions protested by resigning. In Ardoyne and the Bogside young men – and some women – queued to join the IRA.

THE TROUBLES

Across the range of political opinion from instinctively or rapidly republican to the unaware and indifferent, events shaped people: the riots and burnings of 1969, police and Specials seen once again as nakedly partisan and threatening, the mass intimidation and movement of families, most of them Catholic, from their homes; awareness that Unionist prime minister Brian Faulkner had called for internment as much for his own political survival as for military considerations; Bloody Sunday. The Falls curfew and the sight of British soldiers with their rifles pointing towards Catholics and their backs to Protestant rioters had within a year transformed initial reactions to British army intervention. There were crucial moments: as when General Officer Commanding Sir Ian Freeland allowed a junior Stormont minister, the son of former Unionist prime minister Sir Basil Brooke, to tour the defeated and battered Falls in an army jeep after the 1970 curfew. Half a century of resentment fused with ancient anti-Britishness.

The arrival of soldiers on the streets of Belfast and Derry, and in the square of Crossmaglen, among other places, in time sucked in people who had watched the civil rights movement from a distance, seeing it as a mixture of students and the middle class – not for them. The retired RUC man who always thought his own community varied from 'IRA to Castle Catholic' says he believes that placing soldiers in two places only in August 1969 might have prevented the emergence of a new IRA.

'That was a mistake – they took over everywhere. They were only required in two places: Belfast and Derry. But they were even up in Coleraine, they took over the whole province. They were never needed in Crossmaglen or Newry.'

Inheritance of memories and folklore with their message of implicit semi-approval did not necessarily mean inheriting IRA membership, or sympathy. I was struck by the sizeable number of those who talked to me who had fathers, grandfathers, grand-mothers or uncles in the 'old IRA' (a historic term that stretches from the War of Independence, the Tan War, to the fifties). They included stalwarts of the Church and of the SDLP such as Bishop Eddie Daly, Paddy Duffy and Ben Caraher as well as present-day republican leaders like Gerry Adams, Mitchel McLaughlin and Danny Morrison. What determined their adult beliefs seemed to have less to do with personalities and character than with where they were in 1969 and what they were doing then with their lives.

For some, circumstances did indeed fuse with legend, or so they convince themselves. The senior Belfast IRA man describ-ed his 'awakening' in 1966, at the time of the fiftieth anniversary of the 1916 Rising, to the idea of 'republicans embattled, Irish people in battle with British people for centuries in the struggle to remain Irish'. Within a few years, he was helping to build barricades against loyalist attacks. But in 1966, when he main-tained that this concept of the historically embattled Irish occurred to him, he was nine.

He joined the Fianna, the IRA's youth wing. When I asked what joining the Fianna meant then, he pointed to a child's picture book, in Irish. 'We used to read this kind of thing, Diarmuid and Gráinne, Finn, the legends: from romantic nationalism to republican beliefs, you could say. I was aware of who the Fianna were, historically. I had the sense of the ancient Fianna, then the Fianna founded by Constance Markievicz and Bulmer Hobson. In 1966 all that awakened in the celebrations of the Easter Rising – we talked about it in school – there was the major parade along the Falls Road to Andytown. Those years at the start, it's difficult to remember what your impressions were at the time but there was that uneasy sense that things were going to get a lot sharper – people were generally terrified of what was coming. And at the same time you had the sense of being Irish, trapped within an area which the British controlled, and in danger.

'My mother and father were the generation that fell between two camps: probably the memories of the twenties and the thirties were sharp. They were very nationalist but we weren't a traditional republican family: I had uncles who'd been in the Army [the IRA], yes, but we weren't like the families who go back generations and they're all members, it's handed down. Still, we were bloody antagonistic towards the state and Britain – we were well aware we were kept in our place. We understood that for staying outside there was a price to pay. You were always aware that there were people in our area who'd been imprisoned by the Orangemen and the British – they'd only been out of jail a few years then, after the end of the fifties.

'I remember the first UVF bombing just vaguely: an old woman from Ballymacarrett, standing at the corner talking to my ma, the men were up at the bookies and we were arsing around listening. This wee woman said, "It's coming again." Her husband was shot dead by the Specials in Ballymacarrett, I think in the thirties.

'By 1968 I was involved, there'd already been incursions by that time. There was the beginning of organising defence groups within the area – solely to protect against attack. To me the IRA were still old men in trench coats and slouch hats. Yes, the Fianna was seen as a junior, training wing, and I saw it like that. But the IRA was in no sense active, like starting anything on their own. And there was such a gap between the Fianna cubs and any idea of an active IRA. We didn't see ourselves as the same thing. Certainly though, by the time people had

started defending the areas and when Gerard McAuley was shot
dead helping people to get out of their houses in Bombay
Street, we heard very fast he was a member of the Fianna – that
had an effect.'

The evocation of a community under attack from 'Orangemen' and 'loyalists' – delivered here in classic propaganda style
but with touches of clearly personal reminiscence – underlines
a powerful factor in the growth of the Provisional IRA through
the early 1970s. As always before in Northern Catholic history,
the IRA in this generation has brought as much death to the
community it comes from as it has warded off. But the wave
of loyalist house burnings and intimidation of thousands of
families between 1969 and 1973, and the initial stages of loyalist
paramilitarism – when random murder of Catholics was often
accompanied by sadistic mutilations – propelled many into the
IRA to 'defend the areas', and to take revenge. Loyalists said
they were retaliating for IRA attacks. 'The consciousness of the
people who are fighting in the streets is bigoted and sectarian,'
left-winger Eamonn McCann said at the time, regretting his
own movement's inadequacy and unpreparedness for the chaos
of the early Troubles. The British army and the RUC behaved
as though the only threat to order came from the IRA: the
police in official comments habitually kept 'an open mind' or
believed murders of Catholics were 'motiveless'. A leading
loyalist paramilitary once explained that the multiple knife
wounds and time taken over murders in the early seventies was
'just because we could – there was no hurry'. Security force
sources have since admitted that in the struggle to counter a
full-blown IRA campaign, they could not cope with the notion
of a second front against loyalism.

Bishop EDDIE DALY is fifty-nine, fated, somewhat to his embarrassment, to be forever the priest in the 1972 photograph

waving a bloodstained white handkerchief while men beside him try in clumsy panic to carry a boy with a huge stomach wound. Alone among Catholic clergy, he is willing to admit on the record that once he had romantic ideas about violence. Describing how his attitudes have changed, he suggests something of how his community also shifted, and was forced to shift. Like his close friend the SDLP leader John Hume, he now blames the IRA as chief agent of destruction, and says their campaign has no justification.

He lived as a child a hundred yards from the border, in Belleek, County Fermanagh. 'My father was a member of the old IRA in the War of Independence. He never spoke about it to me. But I grew up avidly reading the stories of Tom Barry and Benson's Flying Column and all that. I was full of that stuff and loved it and when the IRA campaign in the 1940s began and Hugh McAteer and the others escaped from prison, I was full of excitement and admiration – I remember as a child the wanted notices outside the RUC barracks and hoping we might see one of these guys to tell them the police were still looking for them, to warn them. I was only about eight or nine then but I remember it vividly. I can still picture the mug shot of Hugh McAteer on those wanted notices.

'And my childhood also existed through World War Two. I was fascinated by the war – reading everything I could get my hands on about it – collecting maps of Europe, those maps with the great arrows pointing in all directions . . . a lot of local people tried to get Lord Haw Haw on the radio but we were not really pro-German – it would have been hard to be so – the people who were really kind to us as children were the American GIs who were based in camps near home and they gave us candy and chewing gum. We were pro them. They were great characters locally – but generally speaking the real fighting war was something enormously thrilling and glamorous. And above all, it was distant. We saw the war planes flying over, the beautiful white Sunderland flying boats going out from Lough Erne . . . and then all those Flying Fortresses and Liberators and the American planes which came across the Atlantic, the bare bones of them with as little fuel as possible for fitting out in Britain . . . we were all the time fantasising about what happened to those planes in far-off parts – the drama of war and conflict.

'But then, thirty years later, confronted with real-life conflict for the first time on the streets of Derry and seeing the results – the blood and bits and pieces of guts and brains on the street – war and conflict took on a different hue. The glamour went out the window very quickly. Then I started to see the whole thing, including the childhood stuff, in a completely different light. I saw the obscenity of war and conflict, the cruelty of violence, at first hand, and it was so different.'

In the civil rights movement a very powerful point was made, he says. 'But then the guns came out. It went sour. It was like a huge orchestra playing in tune with great flair and enthusiasm and suddenly the whole thing goes flat – we came face to face with reality. It was an enormous sea-change in my whole perception of the glories of Irish and even, I suppose with hindsight, the glories of British and American soldiery – a radical change in my perception of war and struggle. And it fundamentally challenged my understanding of patriotism and conflict. . . I underwent a major change in attitude in the early seventies after first seeing for myself what a high-velocity bullet or a bomb could do to the human body: and not just what they did to people's bodies but what they did to people's minds. The brutalisation that takes place, the way people begin to justify things which are totally unjustifiable, the way that laws are corrupted, truth made irrelevant, the way that everything is manipulated. Morality is really a very thin film over society and once you puncture one part of it, it tears in all directions.'

ANN, from north Belfast but living now in Craigavon, has raised twin girls and two boys on her own. Her husband served fourteen years of a life sentence as an IRA prisoner for the murder of a soldier. She discussed her own sense of identity with me in the months when he was in the prison's pre-release programme, getting home at weekends; we talked on the understanding that for her husband's sake, she would not be asked about his IRA involvement.

Ann grew up in Ardoyne through the sixties, occasionally hearing the older people talking about past republican campaigns. She did not find it in the least attractive. 'You thought it was crap, you didn't want to listen – it was all old guff.' She says, nervously, that yes, she does support the IRA, but immediately adds that killings are hard to stomach. 'A lot of people would deny it – but most people that I know would support the aims and objectives of the IRA. What they don't support, what people can't stomach, is the killings. That's just a human reaction. It's difficult too because it's a guerrilla war – when people are away at war and everybody recognises it, you accept it – deaths etcetera. But a guerrilla war is harder to come to terms with. You're supporting something that's not quite legitimate. And people are naturally very opposed to doing something like that. Plus, to support the IRA, you're putting your own life at risk first, aren't you really?'

In 1969, when the Troubles started in major fashion in Ardoyne, she was thirteen. 'What I remember of the burnings was the tracer bullets first, over the roofs so they were all lit up, and my father made us all lie on the floor on mattresses. The bath was filled with water, every night. You'd hear people shouting: "They've got control of the area" – meaning the loyalists – "they're going to turn the lights off, they're going to come in."

'I remember running down our path and looking down the

street and seeing women and children running along – the streets in Ardoyne are very long and, you know, there's gaps then – seeing women and children running along in their pyjamas and nightdresses with the light behind them, the flames, wee black running figures. They had to jump from the backs of their houses on the Crumlin Road, the front of the road – because their houses were being shot at first and then they were being burnt out, in the early hours of the morning. I can remember my mother crying at the bottom of our path. I was just looking. You know how when you're young there's no emotion, you don't understand, I was just looking and going Wow! But my mother was crying and my father was biting back the tears and I could see him getting angrier by the minute. People were taking them into their houses and stories were spreading, how a pregnant woman had lost her baby because she jumped from the window . . . they felt they were going to be killed in their beds. They were in mortal terror.

'But internment, that really united all the people of Ardoyne. I remember the bin lids and the whistles, the automatic thing to do was pull your jeans on and run out. You felt you had to go and look – and there was strength in numbers, you felt you were doing something to protest. All the women rushed to beat the police and the army away to get young fellas – and so many escaped like that. As it went on the women got hit back by the Brits. You weren't having any effect – and people were dragged out of their houses with nothing on them but a pair of trousers and beaten over the head on the way out. Then getting internment explained to you, that there was no trial, the news coming back into the district of the beatings in the holding centres, being hooded, helicopters dropping men. It was so frightening, as though your whole world was totally changed. Ardoyne – it was like a big cloud over it.

'But the togetherness of fighting it and the pride in who you were – that you were standing up to all this oppression by some means – and sticking together as a community very tightly: there was a real sense of excitement. You felt that you were part of a struggle or a revolution or change, part of history, of the civil rights thing continued, that you as the young generation were going to make changes, that your idealism was going to be fulfilled. Now what truth there was in that's another thing. There wasn't helplessness, absolutely not – which there had been initially, before the Troubles, and cynicism. Instead there was a great surge of going for it – the feeling, we're so united and so strong now that nothing can break this wall that we've built round ourselves.'

It is hard to avoid the conclusion that a factor shaping attitudes before the Troubles was the IRA's lack of ability to take on the state. Massively outnumbered and outgunned by B Specials and police, the 'old IRA' was unable to protect Catholics in the twenties, and in the next three decades special powers and internment effectively saw the movement off. Then in August 1969 people pleaded with ageing IRA men to dig out their guns, and priests welcomed their protection for their churches. A defensive role became offensive over a period when British soldiers also changed roles: the concept of heroic, outgunned IRA defenders was slow to fade. There was also the powerful sense of solidarity Ann describes, which for a time gave a new, directionless IRA and whole communities a sense of common purpose. But the reality of a late-twentieth-century guerrilla force armed with ammunition that pierces armour, rifles that see in the dark, plastic explosive, rockets and mortars and surface-to-air missiles is very different from the mythologised and largely ineffectual past, hard to square with the picture Northern Catholics have had of themselves as underdogs, and difficult for many to rationalise away.

Prolonged exposure to IRA methods has removed much of

the romanticism – and some at least of the ambiguity. It is difficult to retell exploits of local heroes in the early days without
also recalling the unheroic and the callous. The Troubles began
on television, and the cameras have caught Enniskillen as well
as Duke Street (the civil rights march on 5 October 1968 that
was batoned by police) and Bloody Sunday: there are new songs
now, an altogether more raucous bunch than 'The Patriot
Game'. In the memories of everyone who has lived through the
Troubles, even for those who immediately balance every IRA
atrocity mentally with a loyalist equivalent, the Abercorn,
Donegall Street and Bloody Friday linger. They were all
examples of city-centre bombings that caused deaths and
horrible injuries. On Bloody Friday, twenty-two bombs went
off in Belfast inside seventy-five minutes.

But there are new myths, constructed upon elaborate tales of
warnings withheld by conspiracies of RUC and media, deliberately premature detonation of IRA bombs by army devices, and
by the even simpler method of judicious omission. MARIA,
thirty-six, is a former SDLP supporter who teaches in north
Belfast. She may no longer have faith in the SDLP, but she
dislikes the tactics of republicanism even more.

'In Modern World Studies, we do Northern Ireland. Some
do the Arab–Israeli conflict because they can't face Northern
Ireland. It always strikes me that when we talk about it, the kids
just aren't aware of the early no-warning IRA bombs in Belfast,
like the Abercorn. "Was that the UVF?" they'll say. A lot would
be IRA supporters. They don't know about the IRA bombing
atrocities of the seventies, even Bloody Friday here in Belfast.
It has not been passed down in the mythology.'

She does however have sympathy for people in the district,
and says she can understand how they support the IRA: her explanation sounds like the SDLP theory of 'urban deprivation' to
account for Sinn Féin's hold on west Belfast. 'All I know is that

people in Ardoyne, New Lodge, west Belfast, are a very small minority. I know they have no hope, and they have no money, and they have no anything. For them to blow up the centre of Belfast, for them to keep everybody back from their work – they're not going to work anyway. It's a culture – in a way it ceases to be an Irish issue. But because of the political situation people are able to use poverty and deprivation and sublimate it to this political cause.'

Some emigrants I spoke to were more sure of how their own feelings had changed over the years than people who have never left, perhaps because those who go away have been forced repeatedly to explain themselves and the Troubles to an often unsympathetic and rarely knowledgeable audience.

DEIRDRE went to England as a twenty-year-old in 1972, as the death toll climbed sharply. She comes from east Tyrone, from a strongly republican family in a Catholic village surrounded by countryside equally loyalist. Her mother 'just thought England should get out of Ireland', her father was an 'old IRA man' who fled north from Limerick one step ahead of internment there, went to live with cousins in the Sperrin mountains and married a local girl. They 'always had to scratch for a living', she says, and her father started going to England to work for most of each year when she was a baby. Most of the neighbours were no better off. Two-thirds of her class in primary school emigrated.

'At the beginning in England I was more intense, forever into rows where I was nearly in tears. I couldn't argue rationally and gradually made up my mind I wasn't going to get involved. I was very patriotic to begin with, up against very British attitudes. I began by defending the IRA because I knew people in it from home and I thought that's who the IRA is, not cartoon monsters like the English papers were drawing – though I didn't know myself that these people were in it until they were caught, I was a right eejit not to realise about a couple of them in particular. But it just never occurred to me. The IRA was in the past, it was my da, old men. To me the new IRA grew in response to the house searches, the way the soldiers behaved, internment. When that happened I was more pro-IRA, that was when I had most sympathy for them.

'Then I began hearing stories from friends in Belfast and Derry, of them being tyrannical. I began to make room for that possibility – that they were so ruthless, using people who weren't all right in the head, on top of innocent people getting it... When the bombing really started here, Birmingham, Guildford, warnings that weren't warnings at all, that was hard to take. I've never reconciled it. I still don't think I've got what the IRA is. For years I had a very idealistic thing about nationalism and the rebellion against British domination. Emotionally, I don't want them to be bad guys.'

Much of what Deirdre said has echoes of other people: watching the IRA grow on the anger at British army behaviour, internment, the growing disillusionment about IRA behaviour, 'warnings that weren't warnings at all'. Few volunteer a similarly open and childlike conclusion, though many clearly think it.

'THE ARMY'

The IRA man who described his romantic youthful attachment to the Fianna in a Belfast ghetto makes an effort to paint an equally idealised picture of the identification of 'the community' with 'the Army' – that is, the IRA. But it is clear that he recognises the limits of communal support. 'It started very early for me and for everyone when the soldiers came in first, you became aware very quickly of people who talked to them and people who didn't. You became aware of the term "Castle Catholic", that they weren't dead sound, that they were half-

friendly with the Brits and the peelers, would have dealt with
the Brits and the peelers. You began in your head to see who
was to be trusted and who was not. That would have grown
with involvement in the republican movement.'

IRA membership plainly induces a grim realism and a
heightened sense of mortality, while simultaneously making it
possible to contemplate methods of killing continually without
dwelling on the consequences to those bereaved.

'There'll be a new generation in charge within the next four
to five years. They're coming up now. The difference between
us and previous generations is we know we have to stand aside,
people now are more in touch with the realities. The longer
you move in the IRA the more you know you're moving in a
very incestuous community . . .

'It's easiest to explain geographically – I can't go into the
town for a drink for example, or some RUC man would be on
to — [reputed to be the UVF leader] and the boys in the
Shankill, and I'd be blown away in two seconds.

'The odds we're up against are just phenomenal. Look at west
Belfast. What is it? A hundred and twenty-five streets? And
every conceivable ambush point, every safe house has been
videoed and photographed and heli-tele-d and driven past
countless thousands of times. The idea that we can still move
from here – that twenty Brits and three sets of jeeps'll be passing
and I'll know the way they're passing because I'm told, if they
change the way they move I'm told, if there's something out of
the ordinary, I'm told. In every street I'm told "Watch it – do
you want to come in for ten minutes?" . . . I can move from here
along with two or three and ambush the end of that patrol –
that's surely remarkable, after nearly twenty-five years of this.
And some time I'm going to get killed, but there's more where
I came from.'

Through the window and off to the side, a patrol was just

visible in the distance. I had not noticed it, nor noticed that he
had looked. He talked about the 'sense in republicanism of
where we're going as a people, it's egalitarian'. The volunteer
out 'engaging the Brits', the woman of sixty sitting all day in
a polling booth, the supposedly 'minor figures', were as
important as Gerry Adams. When I questioned this, he was
indignant. 'Those are the people who sustain and carry us. I
have immense respect for them: I'll go into their houses, bring
in weapons, prepare to go out on operations. They'll give you
grub and you know they're going with less themselves. After
almost twenty-five years, to sustain this – I don't think I rate
anyone more than the "minor figures" (he puts up fingers to
make quote marks).

'The sustaining factor is the unshakable dignity of the
ordinary working-class people who say no one should have
to live the way we were forced to live and we're prepared
to do what is necessary to ensure nobody else has to live this
way. I don't know that Adams is in any sense more important,
for all the momentous decisions he's made and for all that he's
moved in certain directions. There are no "minor figures" in
this struggle.'

As in the accounts of many others through the years who
describe becoming involved with the IRA – because their areas
were under attack by loyalists, or having seen the British army
behaving badly – there was no attempt here to interpret the
support of 'ordinary working-class people' as a commitment to
republican ideas. This man instead suggested, like many others,
that the history and experience of Catholics in the state of Northern Ireland, particularly poor Catholics, to a large degree
explains attitudes towards the IRA and support for them. The
only person he described as impelled towards the IRA by
republicanism was himself – through the Fianna, at the age
of nine.

When he spoke about 'the community' and the remarkable support they gave, it was clear that for this man the community meant Catholic west Belfast. Some young west Belfast people told me what they thought about the IRA's relationship with the community they live in. They did not refer with respect to 'the Army' or 'the struggle'. All but the most middle-class of them talked about 'the Rah', 'the Provies', or 'the fucking Provies'. The only one who was 'middle-class' – a self-description – called them 'the IRA', and was by far the most supportive.

None of them is old enough to have had any opinion about republicanism when the Troubles started: two were not born then. They have had to make it up as they go along, and they are still changing.

Nineteen-year-old GEMMA has a child aged eighteen months. 'See before I had the baby, I was in the YTP [Youth Training Programme] and school and that, and you used to go home and you'd see people getting kneecapped when you were walking up the street – it was nothing. You'd see it happening and you'd say, "Well, they must have deserved it", because that's what you were brought up to believe. You'd see people getting shot.

'I've seen three people shot dead. It wasn't until after I had the child I realised, I thought about it – you do get more emotional. There was this fella about a year ago, me and friends were walking past when he was found. It's called Dead Man's Alley because a lot of men are shot dead in it. They thought he was a tout, apparently. I was pushing the baby and everybody was standing going, "Well, he must have been a tout", because of the way he was shot through the head.

'But he was young, and he was small. He was very tiny. And I thought to myself, Jesus, imagine if I was sitting in the house waiting on someone coming up and saying, "Your son's only after being shot." I was nearly crying. I was standing there, a couple of us, and I was shaking. And even one of the police –

he came over. You know how you don't talk to them. He came over and he just said, "You're young, you should get out of here. I can't even go over and look at that. I've seen too many of them", and he just walked away again. He knew we were young too and he just said, "You should wise up and get out of here. Look at that on your doorstep – it's ridiculous." And it made me think.

'I have seen it all and I don't want my baby to be brought up to see it. I have seen too much and we just took it under our skin and thought nothing of it. It's just here, bombs going off and people getting shot. It didn't register. It was just normal. You'd be standing in the shop buying sweets after school or you'd be in at night for fags and people were brought out from beside you and kneecapped outside the door. And you'd say, "He must have done something, he deserved it." I wouldn't think that now. Everybody has their rights. Who has the right to go and shoot somebody dead? I just hate this place, it's ridiculous. I really hate it.

'It's so close-knit round the Falls – everybody goes to their own wee club, not many go to different ones every week. When you go in you either support this – the Rah, the whole bit – and you're in a crowd, or you don't get on with them. It's always the one thing. If you walk in and you're a stranger, you're not a regular, you're not welcome and that's it. They're very aware of different people coming in.

'You feel deep down the Brits shouldn't be here, it's not their country. That's what you're brought up to think. Nobody'd say anything else. And the way the soldiers come into the area. . . But I still don't feel that much about the army or the police. I don't feel strongly about getting the British out. I wouldn't say that, of course I wouldn't. Can you imagine living in St James's, say, or Iveagh, and turning round and saying, "The police are all right, I like them"? Well, I don't like them either.

'I've seen people getting tarred and feathered for offering drink to them...if they were drunk, in a group, you know: "Here's a wee tin of beer" to a Brit. Girls. I've never personally been there but you say to yourself maybe they were doing no harm, being friendly and the Brits being friendly back. But somebody went and told...'

TERESA sits beside Gemma, too shy to meet me on her own, and content to let Gemma do most of the talking. She is eighteen. They were at school together but see little of each other now. Gemma stays at home with her baby and her boyfriend in the evening, Teresa likes to go to clubs in the city centre. She suddenly bursts into speech when Gemma mentions the IRA's treatment of joyriders.

'I don't know much about anything that's going on or any of the organisations – because I don't want to. But the hoods – you were brought up to believe hoods is all, not human beings, they're animals. And if they get shot it's all right. My daddy, he's worked with them, and he doesn't like them, he's going, "They deserve all they get." But when you actually know the hood himself, he's just normal.'

'And it's a web it's easy to get tangled into down here,' Gemma adds. 'It's just as easy to get into a [paramilitary] organisation up or down the Road as to get into joyriding but nobody seems to think of that. They just say, the hoods are animals.

'We're the unusual ones – because we don't like the Rah. And I would think the majority here support it.'

'Between Divis and Andytown, most people would support them, yeah', says Teresa.

'It's a big thing,' Gemma adds, 'the main thing in their lives – they're fighting for the cause, or involved or working for Sinn Féin. There's not a lot of people in west Belfast who don't support them, I think – even at our age. In the YTP I was in, everybody was into IRA/Sinn Féin – and you say to yourself what's the point, what's it doing for them, they're young. It's because they all live on the Road, they just go along with what's happening.

'Most of the parents have grown up with that, remember, and they're putting it into their kids. Many have lost their lives believing in what their parents believed in. You go into the clubs round this area and it's all the Rah – I don't go to clubs here and that's the main reason why I don't. When you're going in, it's not for a drink just. You're going in to what they're all thinking and it's either who's lifted, or *Republican News*, or who the Rah's got – who they killed. Cheering, stuff like that.'

JIMMY and SEÁN are 'hoods', Jimmy apparently more reformed than Seán. They sound much younger than their ages. Seán has been glue-sniffing for ten years (and stealing cars for eight) and is twenty-three. He behaves like a childish thirteen-year-old and says the glue has 'done him in'. Jimmy is all of twenty-five and sounds like a reasonably mature seventeen-year-old. He says he stopped joyriding some time ago and is working with an educational scheme to help others to stop. They talk with intensity about the evil of the IRA, their violence against 'innocent people', without the slightest suggestion of awareness that they themselves might have injured or even killed people while driving stolen cars. Neither has any reason to like the IRA. Jimmy has been badly beaten, Seán threatened. But they maintain they originally fancied joining up.

Seán and his family were 'put out' of their home in Lisburn by Protestants when he was fifteen. 'You know the Anglo-Irish Agreement? Well it was because of that. I was really Provie-minded after that – then I got into this stolen car one night, it was left up the back of the house, jumped into it and then drove it. Thought, it's better flying about in cars than getting in with the Rah and all, and I started stealing them and all, started hating the Provies. They gave me a bad time.'

Jimmy's family was burned out of Ardoyne when he was two – in the year Seán was born. 'There was always a lot of rioting and shooting when we were younger. Everybody thought, aye, I want to join the Rah, when you were running about as kids. Then when you see what damage it does to people – they're only hurting their own people.'

Seán adds, 'I think it's fifty–fifty hate the Rah. People just want to live a life, have a happy life, no hassle with shooting.'

'About half see them as protectors, the other half see them as destroyers,' says Jimmy. 'I had loads of beatings.'

'This fella I know might have to get his leg off, when they kneecapped him they shot him through an artery and gangrene set in. They think it's starting to work its way up. He's just seventeen. He's not a joyrider. See when you're standing on the street corner and they come up to move you on and smash your face in and all? This fella, he just doesn't care, he said, "Ah fuck off."' Seán sighs, then laughs. 'He's mental. People call him Simple. That's his nickname. They shot him just to make a – what do you call it? – an exhibition of him.'

SINÉAD, the 26-year-old nurse tutor, votes Sinn Féin and 'can't stand all the Peace People types who keep condemning the IRA'. The hunger strike horrified her: she went on 'all the marches, and every single funeral' until she was seventeen. 'I wanted to belong to this west Belfast world. I thought west Belfast had a sense of belonging, that everybody felt the one way and there was a togetherness – but it's not like that.'

The IRA and Sinn Féin chiefly attracted her because she sees them as 'standing up for second-class Catholics'. 'Maybe this is typical of a republican – but I feel that the killing the Provos do is different from the Protestant paramilitaries. I can't help that. I try not to be like that.

'But there are some things that I wouldn't support. Once, I

believed I would never think twice about anybody the IRA
killed and then, when I was at the funeral where the two cor-
porals were killed [plain-clothes soldiers attacked by the crowd
and shot at Casement Park, Andersonstown, after driving into
an IRA funeral for one of those killed by Michael Stone, see
below], that was the first time – maybe because I was a bit older
– that I felt, this is really wrong. These were people that I knew,
round me, that did that, and I didn't think they were like that.
That sort of – not destroyed what I felt completely, because
people get excited and it was the atmosphere. But that really
shocked me. More than anything else that ever happened.

'I've seen things from the other side: Catholics being shot, I
was there when Sean Downes was shot dead by the police,
people beside me injured, I was in Milltown when Stone started
[Stone, a loyalist paramilitary, staged a lone gun and grenade
attack on an IRA funeral on 16 March 1988, killing three men].
Casement's the first time I ever saw my own side doing
something. Maybe it's something to do with that, with seeing
it and being there. It scared me. Just before, at the graveyard
with Michael Stone firing all round him, I didn't feel afraid. But
at the other I did. Because my own people were out of control?

'I don't think the IRA have created confidence for Catholics,
that's not right. Most people look at them and see them as
humans – not the way they see Protestant paramilitaries. But
they shock too many people. Catholic sympathy with the
underdog, that's traditional in us, isn't it? The IRA have stepped
on that. Maybe the younger generation than me are growing up
to believe the IRA won't let anybody step on us. But mostly as
you get older, you say, what's the point?

'As many in west Belfast would say they've given the place
a bad name as would say they give us dignity, or pride. There's
a lot in the protection thing, that they give the area a certain
amount of security, that any Protestant will not come very deep

into west Belfast without being afraid at least. That gives Catholics confidence. But step outside and you've lost it.

'It annoys me about other areas, people there are for the IRA and they think they're great, they're doing something, and they don't understand that most of the time the people who suffer a lot from the IRA are the people in west Belfast. And they suffer an awful lot. There's a girl I know, married to this boy, they took his car and said drive into town, and I won't say what they used it for. They told him they had his wife and kids. He had been for them – and he's going, how can they do this to me? Others would say they have a war, they can't go into Protestant areas and take cars, can they? And that's true – who did he think they took the cars off when he was *for* them?

'Another girl, her brother owns a wee firm, the IRA asked for the van. He wouldn't give it. They threatened the whole family. Three masked men came to shoot him, this girl she got between them, she went to Sinn Féin, she had some pull or other, they got someone to come and she talked to the IRA. She screamed and shouted, and they dropped the whole thing. And they were republican supporters. But that's very unusual, what she did, and what they let her do.

'A lot of people outside west Belfast who support them, they don't know things like that go on: they glorify them, but the IRA can be very hard. Catholics who support the IRA – they don't always know that. But they *do* know they won't win. It's just a matter of showing your face, saying "We're not lying down, we're going to do something."'

The IRA of today is a very different organisation from the shell of 1969, and political ideas among Northern Catholics are a good deal more complex: Catholic attitudes towards violent republicanism accordingly vary more widely and are more bitterly argued over within the Catholic community, though it would probably be wrong to say that there has never been such

a range of difference before. Enough personal reminiscences
survive from the years between 1913 and 1922, and indeed for
some years thereafter, to suggest a similar confusion then
throughout Ireland.

Many become impatient, and potentially hostile, at being
asked how they feel about the IRA. If there has been no prior
discussion about the Troubles in general, they think the
question comes pre-packed with suppositions about the way
they ought to answer, or are likely to answer. Since the British
government introduced broadcasting restrictions to keep spokespersons or supporters of banned groups off the air, broadcast
journalists have made a practice of asking people in areas where
republican support is high – before they interview them –
whether they support Sinn Féin. Sinn Féin is of course legal, but
asking people whether they support it is easier than asking about
support for the IRA. Those who say they do support Sinn Féin
are not interviewed. This does not encourage frankness, but
then it is a subject about which people are rarely entirely open
in any case.

There is also the hard truth that attitudes in Northern Ireland,
Catholic and Protestant, nationalist and unionist, do not come
neatly sliced and separate, capable of being defined in clear and
distinguishable form. 'People don't necessarily have a line on
the IRA that they can trot out,' said MÁIRÉAD in north Belfast.
'Many don't consciously work something out, they don't separate the IRA off as a phenomenon – it's part of their circumstances.' Her visible irritation was a useful reminder of how
journalists and political scientists filter reality, where they don't
fictionalise it, by formalising and verbalising human reactions
from the perspective of their own prejudices and often very different backgrounds.

On the other hand, Belfast SDLP member BRIAN FEENEY says
it is 'mandatory for the Catholic community to have a position

on the IRA'. To him there is no great confusion about the broad
divisions among Catholics on the IRA: 'You're for, you're
against, and then there are the sneaking regarders, the third
position, who haven't come to terms with their own attitudes.'
The 'sneaking regarders' are the group most derided and dis-
dained by both other categories of Catholics – and certainly by
Unionist politicians, who do not use the term but who would
define far more Catholics as falling into that category than is
accurate. The accusation of ambivalence is of course made as
readily about Protestants by Catholics, and with as little hard
evidence.

On all sides, there are those who are more sensitive to the
accusation than others – some because they loathe the
paramilitaries, some simply because they are afraid to be thought
supporters. And as Máiréad pointed out, many have no clear
line. Sinn Féin supporters like Sinéad vote for a party which
'supports the right to armed struggle' – the one irreducible 'line'
to have emerged from several years during which republican
spokespersons have deliberately obscured the relationship
between their political party and the IRA. So Sinn Féin votes
are understood by many, especially unionists, to demonstrate
support for everything the IRA does. But Sinéad's account of
her own feelings, franker than most, suggests the confusion, and
the change, in one person's attitudes. It is an account mirrored
by many others.

'Whataboutery' saves some from self-doubt: the selective
memory that is at least an option for almost everyone in the
North, preserving Bloody Sunday and numerous examples of
loyalist murder in Catholic minds, and wiping out the Abercorn, attacks on Protestant pubs, Bloody Friday. But even the
most effective selection mechanism cannot erase personal
witness, as Sinéad found when she saw a crowd destroy two
soldiers. Some can live with that: Sinéad knew very well why

it so distressed her. It was part of the IRA 'stepping on' the idea that Northern Catholics have always been victims, the under-dogs. Like many others, she still supports the IRA, but with something that sounds close to despair.

In the end, even among friends or associates, people may never declare themselves either for or against. Within many families, disagreements are well-established and dangerous ground is well-signposted. In the pockets of middle-class, religiously mixed society, unspoken rules keep discussion to a minimum. In strongly republican areas people tend to keep their reservations to themselves. When they voice them, the contradictions come tumbling out.

In south Armagh, where smuggling pitted the community against two states for decades even before the present Troubles, keeping your own counsel is an iron rule, with the neighbour as much as the outsider. MARY-ROSE goes back regularly from Newry to her family home in the border district of Glass-drumman and has watched local attitudes to the IRA change and change again. Only the silence stays the same.

'There's almost a Mafia *Omerta* business. I've discussed it with a few: If you knew, would you tell? and they've said: I would, but I can't. Why can't you? Ah now . . .

'You realise the place hasn't changed that much – they're a bit sick of what's happened, very sick sometimes. Partly it's a fear, a real fear. But there's still the old hankering too, that this state is not honest, there's no chance of getting it honest: that you can talk till you're blue in the face, but the only thing "they'll" react to is . . . and that's it.'

BRENDAN teaches a class of mixed adolescents and mature pupils in west Belfast. They are, he says, almost completely republican. Because they know he is sympathetic to them, and they know he is nationalist, if not republican, they will allow him to put hard questions. In his account, one central dilemma emerges: how to square the fact that the IRA kills Protestants with their understanding of their own republican identity.

'They've got these pigeonholes they put things into: acts of war, mistakes. Interesting how widely those distinctions are accepted: it's not confined to a few militants. They get very uneasy if closely questioned – they can get hostile. You often get a split between people who say "we are responsible for that, it's terrible", and want to disown it or make some individual moral gesture to make up for it – and other people who will say, "I'm not cruel, I see how bad these things are, I'm not hard, but it's not as easy as that. You can't just say we all apologise." The common thing is someone will get angry with the person who wants to apologise and they say, "You sound like the bloody Peace People" – a terrible insult. There's a great depth of feeling about things like that.

'There's another attitude comes out if you condemn, or you want them to condemn: "You haven't suffered yourself, how dare you talk to us?" I think that's understandable. People have a perception of those who advocate "peace in the morning" – as people who live somewhere nice, who don't know what it is to have their front door kicked down, who haven't had members of their family shot dead. If all argument fails, they ask what you've suffered.

'Then there are the people who say, "I wouldn't do that myself – but I have none the less a deep sympathy with those who do it, and with what they suffer as a result." I often think some of the feeling for prisoners comes out of a sense of guilt – I wouldn't do those things, but you can't abandon those who do, they're part of us.

'One of the things I find very discouraging over the last number of years is when you're talking to people who would never be down the town blowing up High Street, the extent to which they have come to accommodate violence. They say,

"I'm sorry about that, I wouldn't want to see anybody's legs blown off, but, you know, the guy's in the UDR." And they don't apologise when they're ex-UDR. You can get people to agree much more readily that it's not really fair. But there's always a rationalisation: like, how many of these guys are under-cover, what's really going on? People have such a level of distrust about the state and how it operates. It's not hard for them, maybe they don't absolutely believe it, but it's not hard to excuse things in a very rational way by saying, "Well, you never know what's going on now, you never know."

'Statements of excuse like that made by the Provos . . . the inclination among those people, even if they don't 100 per cent believe it, is to want to believe it because it's deeply distasteful to them to believe that they are sectarian. It's repugnant to them – because that's what Protestants are, and by definition, we are not. The Provos are tapping into something very potent when they issue statements saying we will not be drawn into sectarian killings. An outsider would say, "God, that's pathetic, imagine them saying something like that." I mean Gerry Adams is say-ing we call for no retaliation against Protestants – against a background of Teebane. But to a lot of insiders, that means something.'

In its twists and turns and description of half-internalised pleading, the account captured much of the self-deception that supporting the IRA involves for many Northern Catholics. Brendan caught exactly the reaction of 'outsiders' who are ut-terly scornful at the idea of the IRA denying sectarianism – and the eagerness of republican supporters to believe the IRA's denials. There was also an echo of Sinéad's regret for lost vic-timhood.

The IRA strongly denies that its campaign has any sectarian motivation: the most it concedes is that, indeed, Protestants may mistakenly 'perceive' particular killings as sectarian. Off the

record, unattributably, prominent republicans in recent years
have confessed that they have constantly to 'keep the lid' on
demands from their grassroots for more explicitly anti-
Protestant actions in retaliation for loyalist attacks. Republican
awareness of the conflict between their public statements and
the reality of many IRA actions makes many tetchy and incoherent. Teebane, which Brendan mentioned, was one example:
eight Protestant men in a minibus, killed in a landmine ambush
on a lonely Tyrone road as they came home at the weekend
from work on repairing a bombed police barracks. When the
Enniskillen Remembrance Day bombing killed eleven Protestant civilians, prison officers in the Maze reported a crisis among
republican inmates about IRA strategy – 'it came nearer to
breaking them than anything else'.

'We may have sectarian individuals,' said the IRA man I
spoke to, 'and of course there is such a thing as Catholic bigotry,
of course there is. But there is a difference in kind between the
motivations of the loyalists and republicans – the idea that a
loyalist organisation would shoot dead a Catholic married to a
Protestant wife, that anybody who stays outside is a threat! Our
community wouldn't tolerate that kind of thing.'

The assertion of a pure, immutable motivation convinces
only the most doctrinaire. Inconvenient truths keep showing
through. The way republicans airbrush violence that does not
fit their own definitions of legitimacy is just one facet of an
unwillingness to deal logically with the reality of the Troubles.
As they have on many other occasions since, the IRA in the
early and mid-seventies in Belfast and in south Armagh in particular committed a series of murders which could only be
defined as sectarian: random attacks on Protestants found
wandering home from the pub, attacks on bars in Protestant
areas, the Kingsmills and Tullyvallen shootings. Some in the
community tolerated all of them, as some in the Protestant

community have tolerated similar attacks by loyalists. One of those now most involved in what seems to be a republican leadership rethink of the official line on the need for Protestant 'consent' to any plan for unification was a member of a gang that in the mid-seventies murdered several Protestant men at random.

Tony, the academic from Derry, says with typical Derry chauvinism that he first saw sectarianism in the IRA when he came to Belfast, and was horrified. 'I never experienced republicans in Derry having this hatred. I remember talking to this quite senior guy in north Belfast, we were standing looking over to the Shankill and we were talking about our dreams for Ireland. And he said – there wasn't drink or anything involved, he was quite rational – he said: "Tony, what I'd really love is to be able to stand here and just see green fields." And I says: "Come on", and he says: "No, that's my dream for Ireland. I would like to see those Orange bastards just wiped out."'

Teaching in west Belfast, Brendan hears instead of any such crude sectarianism the justification and self-exculpation about IRA violence that republicans engage in. The young people in his classes are entirely unaware that the lack of bigotry they pride themselves on in effect dehumanises an enemy they know in any case only at a distance. They simply do not attribute to Protestants the sort of feelings they have themselves about violent death in their own community. There is no doubt, however, that the enemy in the war they speak of is not only British, but also Protestant.

'They say, "Nobody approves of those things the IPLO [Irish People's Liberation Organisation, a republican splinter group] do, shooting Protestants in bars, that's wrong." People defend themselves mentally against the full horribleness of things, and the political consequences. Many who are not rabid republicans will say about the killing of off-duty UDR men, say, and

accusations of IRA genocide along the border, killing only sons
on farms, that kind of thing, they'll say: "There's a war on, people on the Protestant side must see . . ." They mean Protestants
don't really believe it's sectarian, they just say that to make the
IRA sound bad. They're saying "If they spent ten minutes thinking about it, surely they could see . . ."'

5

'Benign apartheid'

PROTESTANTS

Talking to Catholics about Protestants is in one outstanding respect similar to the exercise in reverse. From the least to the most political, these are two communities convinced that one can only gain at the other's expense. Some think it should not be so, some are saddened by the awareness – but they cannot deny it. The perpetual tension between advance for one and reaction from the other, an inevitable consequence of constructing a state on a head count, is a measure of the damage done to both by the experience of living together in Northern Ireland. It can seem as though communal self-respect is never innate, always conferred: the 'we are the people' assurance that depends on marching past silenced, hemmed-in Catholics, the confidence that was boosted by the Anglo-Irish Agreement's role for the Republic, but even more by the sight of the RUC batoning Protestants.

And it all comes back to numbers: crude consideration of how narrow the majority's margin is, how soon it will be necessary to stop describing Catholics as a minority. The calculation has always been contentious. But analysis of the 1991 census produced a figure, agreed by most experts, of an overall Catholic percentage of 42 per cent; it found that Catholics were in the majority west of the Bann, and among students throughout Northern Ireland. Having always been a unionist preoccupation and the subject of nationalist wishful thinking, the population balance has now become a sharp political question. After the 1992 breakdown in inter-party talks, Unionists and Northern Ireland Office sources alike blamed the SDLP leader JOHN HUME, denouncing as 'ludicrous' and 'offensive' his proposal for Irish and European as well as British elements in a future Northern Ireland government arrangement. His comment on this kind of reaction is also a terse, but pointed, reference to the population balance as revealed by analysis of the census: 'What the census figures do perhaps is they bring a little more reality home to the Unionists and might underline to them the generosity that we're offering, given our past history and given the nature of their role – the fact that their basic approach is to exclude everybody but themselves. They ought to understand that in spite of all that, our approach, which is the accommodation of both identities, is not only very fair, but in the circumstances is generous.

'If they don't accept that offer, what's going to emerge in the end could only be worse for them and their people, and therefore for all of us.'

Hume's increasingly explicit declaration of the elements necessary to give his community adequate political expression once again catches a mood. Statistical confirmation of an increased proportion of Catholics has crystallised rather than shifted attitudes: as ever, the reaction of one community infuriates the other. Hume's critics, among unionists but also in the Republic and in Britain, insist that by so stating nationalist demands, and by his talks with Sinn Féin president Gerry Adams on agreed nationalist objectives, he has turned his back on any

accommodation of unionism. But the alienation voiced by a
wide variety of Protestants over the past year – dread of British
disengagement mixed with protest at political and economic
advances for more numerous Catholics – merely confirms
Catholic conviction that the essence of unionism is a desire for
supremacy, not accommodation.

'I think the perception is still that at the drop of a hat Protestants and unionists would go back to square one and Stormont,
if they could,' says a middle-aged County Armagh woman.
'People think they just want to be the boss and have us back
down there.' It is a widely held belief. Many see few shades of
difference between demands as stated by Unionist politicians
and the mood among the Protestant community in general. The
developing lobby of those who argue that nationalists should
back down on their demand that Northern Ireland must be Irish
as well as British – since Unionists will not accept this – is likely
to be disappointed. What many Northern Catholics hear from
the representatives of Northern Protestants at various levels, and
from the grassroots, with very few exceptions, is a continued
denial of their political legitimacy, to be maintained by loyalist
paramilitary terror, if necessary – exactly as many Protestants see
the aim of nationalists backed up by the IRA. One former SDLP
politician describes the argument for nationalist 'magnanimity'
as essentially dishonest, in that it appears to ask nationalists to accept a British context for Northern Ireland in perpetuity: sur-
render portrayed as compromise. But he thinks there is a danger
of nationalists reacting so scornfully to unionists' inability to
adjust that they fail to appreciate the dominant emotion in the
other community. 'It seems to me the major motivating force
in unionism is fear: fear that their position in Ireland will be
either undermined subtly or overthrown violently. They're
simply afraid: afraid of the native population and afraid of
betrayal by the motherland. In any situation, in a contest

between constructive engagement and fear, fear always wins.'

But few Catholics are disposed to empathise with Protestant fear. They hear complaints about alienation, and react precisely as Protestants did when the Anglo-Irish Agreement was described as a treatment for the alienation of Catholic nationalists. To many, the true nature and cause of Protestant alienation is demonstrated by the explanation in the loyalist paramilitary magazine *Combat* (June 1993) that UDA and UVF murders had been stepped up in response to the growing Catholic share of the population to 'stop further encroachment into Protestant areas'. Several mentioned Unionist politicians complaining about the alleged unfairness of the Arts Council and the Industrial Development Board, as happened inside a few minutes in Westminster in spring 1993 – allegations made largely on the basis that both were now headed by Catholics, as far as anyone could tell from the information they provided.

Decades of Unionist assertions on behalf of 'the people of Ulster' – as though Catholic nationalists did not exist – make it difficult for Catholics to take seriously the now frequent complaints by Unionists about nationalist insensitivity. One focus of irritation is the campaign to have the Republic's constitution changed, habitually conducted by Unionists at all levels as though the entire population of Northern Ireland found the Irish territorial claim as offensive as they do.

In June 1993 Sir Kenneth Bloomfield, head of the Northern Ireland civil service until 1991, told an interviewer for the *Ulster News Letter*: 'Articles Two and Three are objectionable. They ought to go. No justice or rightness in them.' The interview sounded several key notes. Speaking throughout of the deep concern, isolation, alienation of 'people' – 'people' here used apparently in traditional style as a synonym for 'unionists', Sir Kenneth at one point explained that it was 'understandable' that British secretaries of state had been denounced. There was a 'feeling that the SDLP has won concession after concession on the back of the IRA [and] the conviction that NIO policy has been to propitiate Nationalists with discrimination against Unionists on, for example, all sorts of public bodies'.

Sir Kenneth is a BBC governor. Asked if 'the BBC here is becoming greener, an extension of RTE', he answered: 'I've heard that said', and went on to comment that it was 'surprising people regard Gaelic as an important badge as to who they are'.

A *Belfast Telegraph* column in May 1993 by the commentator Barry White picked up on other unionist expressions of communal alarm: that Northern Ireland was being 'destabilised' by nationalists' insistence on their Irishness, which White found incomprehensible. 'Most Welsh nationalists are perfectly happy being British,' he wrote. 'Their nationalism is a cultural thing. Why cannot Irish nationalists learn from them?'

Unionist bewilderment at the persistence of nationalist difference, alternating with a policy of ignoring it, produces an exasperation among Catholics that extends from the most political to the least. One of the SDLP negotiators in the inter-party talks – not Hume – said, 'Unionists tell us now as though it was their idea, not John Hume's, that there can't be victors – but there must be a withdrawal of Articles Two and Three and a crystal-clear declaration of the Union. In terms of power-sharing, they wanted nearly total victory there: the SDLP could have some chairs of committees but the final say must be the majority's. They seem to think it's OK to expect us to accept that unionist rights are superior to nationalist rights. Some genuinely can't understand. They think they're being extraordinarily generous and they're making "concessions". Who the hell do they think they are? They're no longer in a position to make concessions. It's a question of coming to terms with new reality.'

Clearly, some at least of this irritation had been voiced at the time. Behaviour across the table from political opponents is conducted within certain rules, however, and allows in a way for an openness impossible in general in segregated Northern society. A shy elderly woman living in a mainly Protestant village in County Armagh described a conversational ritual familiar to Catholics throughout Northern Ireland.

'There's something I notice. You'll be in mixed company – it could be in a local shop, say – when some IRA thing's happened. And a Protestant will say, looking round to make sure you hear them, "Isn't that terrible? Isn't that just awful?" Something goes through your head before you say anything back. You find yourself thinking, now if I say indeed it was desperate, the next thing your woman'll say is they should bring back internment and we'll be off. Someone else'll say it's all because nationalists have got one thing after another and it all started with civil rights. Then what am I supposed to say? What they want is for you to agree that the Troubles are all the Catholics' fault for kicking up in the first place. But if you say nothing, they'll have you down as a Provo, no matter that you hate the Provos' guts.'

Catholics express dismay and disgust at the lack of Protestant reaction to loyalist killings, the years of silence or equivocation from Unionist politicians: but they discuss it among themselves. They tend not to solicit Protestant reaction either because they assume those Protestants they know are as disgusted as they are – or because they are afraid to discover that is not so. In any case, many are convinced that Protestants who think all Catholics should feel remorse about the IRA are not inclined to feel self-conscious, much less guilty themselves, about loyalist killers.

'I came from strong republican roots,' a 44-year-old Fermanagh woman says. 'At the beginning I felt responsible for every single thing that was done, the IRA car bombs in the early seventies, all that awful stuff. It didn't seem to me that this was at all the same thing as the rebels I'd grown up singing about. I could see where it started, in Ardoyne and Conway Street, in the burnings and the intimidations and then the army on the streets – but all the same, these were my people blowing the legs off human beings, and I felt bad. It was guilt by association, I suppose. Other people wanted to talk about it too. You would spend hours and hours discussing who was responsible for the climate that made those things possible and about what could be done. But Protestants don't feel the same guilt on their side. They never said – they never offered anything. They'd let you do it instead. I don't know what that means, and I don't know now whether it's still true. I haven't been in those arguments for years because people don't want to talk like that any more – no one bothers now.'

This woman lives and works in comfortable, mixed districts and has kept some Protestant friends from student days in the late sixties. Then, she thought her generation of resolutely non-sectarian civil rights campaigners could break the old barriers and overcome what they called 'local, sectarian politics'. When she said that Protestants in discussions about the origins of the Troubles 'never offered anything', it was clear that she meant they never said they believed unionism or unionists bore any responsibility. In admitting that she did not know whether Protestants still reacted like that, and in her assessment that people did not want to have such discussions any more, she spoke for a large number. The unusual feature was that she had been accustomed to genuine political argument, however unsatisfactory from her point of view, in what Northern Ireland calls 'mixed company'. Many both older and younger than her have no such experience.

Numerous Catholics deny that they feel anything about Protestants as a group, deliver sermons on sectarian stereotyping and insist they judge people only as individuals. Others volunteer from the outset that their lives are largely bounded by their own communities – through circumstance, or by choice. Many skate between their reactions to the few Protestants they know and their feelings about Unionist politicians, loyalist paramilitaries, and the Northern Ireland state. But there is a widespread and exasperated feeling that the dominant Protestant voices – leading Unionist politicians in particular – still spend more time implicitly denying the past than attempting to deal with the present. And to a very large degree, that exasperation blunts or entirely negates Catholic sympathy for Protestant fears about domination in a Catholic Ireland. To the same degree, opinions are formed without anything resembling open and honest discussion with Protestant friends. Fear, like hostility, is viewed at a distance: the one minimised and the other exaggerated accordingly.

Others refuse to equate unionism and Protestantism, some because they think the unionism of someone like Ian Paisley is clearly more concerned with the dominance of his own brand of Protestantism than with any union with Britain. There are those who still argue, as some Catholics always have, that Protestants must surely be more politically diverse than they seem. A few cling to the idea that working-class unity must still be possible some day: 'The Workers' Party dream,' a Belfastman said. 'Wouldn't I just love to vote the non-sectarian ticket they always talked about? If only it wasn't a state built on sectarianism – but that's a big "if only".'

Past loyalist paramilitary flirtations with vaguely left-wing politics have left some impression. In several interviews, people launched into wishful thinking about the loyalist world. They hoped some kind of political thinking was developing that they did not know of, they said. But it tended to sound more like a search for reassurance. One woman said she was 'curious about the type of Protestants I don't know, who are really ruthless and would kill anybody'. An older Belfastwoman thought there 'had to be more to loyalists than just killing Catholics because they're Catholics. I'd hate to think that's all there was.'

The impression in most such conversations, even where people have contacts in the other community, is overwhelmingly of distance, lack of understanding, and a nervous, repelled fascination with what is universally taken to be widespead anti-Catholicism among Protestants. Many Catholics unhesitatingly blame the IRA for 'deepening division' and adding to hatred. But the explanation that loyalists attack random Catholics because they have no more obvious and accessible target like the security forces, is not one that convinces many. Experience and memory predispose most to see sectarian hatred as the prime motivation. Republicans habitually reject the suggestion that the IRA provokes loyalists: others disagree, but are still convinced that only anti-Catholicism can explain the savagery of loyalist paramilitary history. Few believe the republican conspiracy theory that makes British secret service agents the origin and chief inspiration of loyalist paramilitarism. It may suit republicans to believe that loyalist murderousness towards Catholics is really British in origin; others do not, though it is clear that often they would prefer to.

Catholic attitudes towards Protestants, once shaped by the inferiority born of economic disadvantage and political repression, have become less focused, more confused – where once they tended to be an uncomfortable mixture of inferiority and superiority, the superiority built largely on a conviction that the nationalist identity was much more secure than the precarious Britishness of Protestant unionists. The gradual lessening of discrimination under direct rule, and an increasing perception that the fickle British have shown more liking for nationalists than for unionists, have increased Protestant insecurity and a

corresponding Catholic confidence. Republicans still use the
language of subjection and victimhood to justify the IRA, but
have to strain to align it with their theme of a risen people, freed
by their own struggle. But complaints about 'oppression' now
seem hopelessly old-fashioned to many, who none the less still
see disadvantage and above all institutions of the state to which
they cannot feel loyalty. In the third successive decade of
unbroken violence, the bulk maintained from within the
Catholic community by the IRA – although loyalists have killed
more than the IRA has in the past two years – the traditional
Catholic communal self-image as victim is under stress. It is sustained only by the immediate memories of thousands, and by a
lingering, untreated mistrust: a Catholic fear that mirrors that of
Protestants.

THE PROTESTANT STATE

Discrimination, fear of physical attack and conviction that the
state was 'alien, not ours' are the themes that surface repeatedly
when people talk about how they first became aware of being
'Northern Catholics'. The focus changes according to where in
the North they come from. In majority-Catholic areas, it tends
to be a memory of the 'Protestant' state beyond an immediate
Catholic world: not a threat, more an annoying and occasionally
insulting irrelevance. In small Catholic enclaves surrounded by
larger Protestant districts, as in the towns and villages of mid-
Ulster or in Belfast streets, it is the perpetual awareness of
greater, unfriendly numbers. For many older people, awareness
of gerrymandering and discrimination in housing and employment coincided with the realisation that employment in the
public service would be on terms designed to remind them that
they were powerless.

There is a considerable reluctance now to 'rehash it all', a
consciousness that the grievances charted by the civil rights

movement sound ancient and much-catalogued. But people cannot deny what shaped them. The memories are of the noise and bluster of the Twelfth, police guarding Orangemen who drummed their way past Catholic homes and churches, of the Union Jack flying on public buildings and country crossroads, of Tricolours taken down by police, of a mandatory oath of allegiance to the British monarch to be taken by teachers and civil servants, of Unionist politicians who had made anti-Catholic remarks being installed as judges, of Protestant civilians in uniform as B Specials stopping their Catholic neighbours and asking their names; and, in small but unforgotten riots in Kilkeel, Newry, Derry, of the police batoning Catholics while Protestants looked on.

Many are aware that in the past both communities behaved as though their sense of identity depended on the distance between them – as perhaps indeed it did. 'And we were inclined to look at Protestants and lump them all together,' a fifty-year-old from County Fermanagh said. 'I think our generation had a warped concept of Protestants because they felt downtrodden themselves. All our fathers were on the dole or off in England, and it never occurred to us that there were poor Protestants in Belfast and Derry and all over the place.'

But although they can see now – and some felt then – that there was a narrowness in their own community, an authoritarianism and rigidity fostered by the Catholic Church and prevailing nationalism alike, the overriding consciousness is of having little choice but to be 'agin the state' and anti-Unionist. Younger people, however, repeatedly told a somewhat different story: growing up in the sixties, they disliked 'old-fashioned talk' of sectarianism, of anti-Catholic 'pogroms', of the IRA. MÁIRÉAD was born in one of the poorest parts of north Belfast, in a street demolished for redevelopment in the early sixties. She was fifteen in 1968.

'My father would have been very nationalist-minded, and him and I used to fight – I'd say, "You're absurd, you're stuck in the past", and he'd say, "Oh you think you're very smart, you think it's all about American imperialism. Well, let me tell you, it's actually about things like housing, and sectarianism, and partition."'

Máiréad says now that she is a reluctant nationalist, that the Troubles forced her to conclude that the Northern state 'in effect institutionalised sectarianism' and had to be replaced. In the years leading up to the Troubles and in 1969 to 1970, many similarly found themselves discovering common ground with their parents. 'A bit of that attitude about the police being the Unionists' private army had died away,' said a 45-year-old from Newry, 'and then, there they were side by side with the Specials and the Protestant mobs in 1969, doing nothing to stop them burning Catholic houses.'

Older people watched the arrival of Terence O'Neill, a few with an initial optimism they now find hard to credit, then witnessed with rapidly growing disillusionment the location of new investment and allocation of resources to economic re-organisation. New-style Unionism, under a veneer of modern-isation, in some ways seemed to pose even more threat to Catholics. 'Christ, they're really going to wipe us out,' one Derry-man remembers thinking, as Stormont built a new city called Craigavon, east of the Bann and named after the first Unionist premier, and placed a new university in the Protestant town of Coleraine instead of on the existing foundation of Derry's Magee College. Unionist resistance to civil rights demands left many people cynical, but disappointed others. Some still think O'Neill had good intentions but no control over his party, others that he was a phoney liberal throughout. Most find it difficult to think back beyond their disillusionment. 'What did he do, after all?' one man summed up the views of many others.

'Shook a few nuns' hands, and caved in to Ian Paisley away back in 1964 about taking the flag down on the Falls, when Paisley was only a crazy preacher on the edge of everything.'

The received wisdom now is that of its nature the Unionist state could not initiate reforms, and that the momentum created by agitation for civil rights could not have been halted by earlier and more substantial concessions. It does not seem like that to a few people still willing to look back. For all the weakness of 'ifs' and 'might have beens', their reflection lends perspective: if nothing else, they point up the distance Catholics have come. PADDY DUFFY is fifty-nine, a solicitor and businessman, an early member of the SDLP and, prior to that, part of the attempt to energise and redirect the old Nationalist Party.

'It was all too late, always too late. Very little would have settled the problem in O'Neill's time – Faulkner setting up the committee system, if that had happened six months earlier – and if Sunningdale was offered today, wouldn't Unionists grab it? Sunningdale wouldn't settle the situation now. The problem from the Protestant point of view is they've never been able to take the thing that's there, and the stakes have increased, all the time: to the degree now that Catholics won't settle for anything that hasn't an all-Ireland dimension.'

A former RUC member, a Catholic who insists the force today is devoid of the bigotry he grew accustomed to in his early service, is more dramatic about the effect of heightened nationalist consciousness. He is loyal to the force he served, insists it has a record of decency and impartiality, and remembers a period when it 'sat easily in the community' – but he also has no hesitation in linking the record of the Protestant state to the rise of the IRA.

'To have Stormont back would be totally unacceptable, even to the mildest of Catholics. If there is an internal settlement, it would finish the SDLP, and the IRA would just go on. Things like loyalist killings help them: the "they're all we have" syndrome. But the seeds were well sowed – discrimination and housing.

'Initially people would have accepted crumbs, if anyone had been willing to give them crumbs. Now they wouldn't accept the cake and all. The whole cake wouldn't please them now, and they've got so they wouldn't let the others have the crumbs.'

As the former RUC man, and many others, see it, fresh anger animated and directed an old and innate awareness that had been fading but had never died. Regional differences that produce a shading of attitudes – to the point where some observers have been tempted to detect different concepts of identity according to place of origin in Northern Ireland – do not affect fundamental conclusions among Catholics about the nature of the Northern state.

From a childhood in the fifties in Crossmaglen, County Armagh, BEN CARAHER remembers how the state looked from its southern rim, and recognises the same features of alienation as many others, but from a vantage point that makes Protestant Northern Ireland appear stagy, almost exotic. 'Being brought up in south Armagh, in Cross, the dilemma of being a nationalist in Northern Ireland was only on the edges of my consciousness. We were very marginal to Northern Ireland. Culturally and every other way we were part of south Monaghan and north Louth. My first consciousness of the Northern state being alien would have been during the general election of 1949 as a kid, playing around enjoying the crack of meetings in the square. This was the election after the South declared a republic and left the Commonwealth. Basil Brooke took the opportunity – as ever – to call an election, and the Anti-Partition League cooperated by putting up as many candidates as it could. The Unionist for Armagh was Isaac Hawthorne. I remember standing outside the polling station and Hawthorne came along doing the candidate's tour, and I was struck by how different he was. He wore spats: he was wearing what I'd now recognise as country gentleman disguise. But the spats conveyed what they were intended to: "I am different from you – there's us and there's them" – my first insight into a dress code. The Nationalist candidate, Malachy Conlon, won by 10,000 to 3,000. We were told we were for him and a united Ireland, whatever that meant.'

In Ben Caraher's description, there is no awareness of Protestants as a threat – because there were few Protestants. Those he knew were unexceptionable human beings: unionism was the alien force, and the state was Unionist, controlled by others, who turned out to be Protestant.

'There were no sectarian tensions – a very small Protestant population, perfectly acceptable to the locals – so that people's political ideas and attitudes didn't have the edginess you got further into the North. There was no concept of not getting a fair crack of the whip: local government was nationalist-controlled, there was no discrimination in housing, local authority jobs, no industry to exercise discrimination in. If people didn't have jobs, it was in the nature of things, rather than because there wasn't fairness. Poverty was the nature of things.

'But we were well aware of allegations of discrimination elsewhere. And very well aware that the machinery of government was not ours. It belonged to somebody else. There was an alien force in the country, right in the heart of the town: a police station that flew the Union Jack on state occasions, and on the Twelfth of July.

'There wasn't the same distance from the police that there is now, but nevertheless the police were the Other – and they were the most visible sign of the Other, of state power. There was no identification with it: it was not ours, it was not us. You either came in conflict with it, if you were unlucky, or you ignored it for most of the time, or you took advantage of it: education, health services etcetera. So the state was something that belonged to somebody else, could occasionally be exploited, was usually to be let, severely, alone, and sometimes you came into conflict with it.

'The visibly alien Northern Ireland, apart from the barracks, started around Newtownhamilton – you thought of it as not friendly. Or rather, you didn't think about it.'

Since the term 'alienation' began to be used, largely by the then taoiseach, Garret FitzGerald, and his foreign minister, Peter Barry, in the 1984–85 run-up to the Anglo-Irish Agreement, endless debate has revolved around the degree to which nationalists have become reconciled to the state by direct rule, by the agreement and by the growth of a Catholic middle class that has been able and willing increasingly to participate in civil administration and the economy. But regular surveys of opinion on police and army responses to terrorism still show the most glaring contrast between the views of Catholics and Protestants. Protestants regularly express near-total confidence in the 'security forces' – Catholics tend to have reservations even about the degree of acceptance implied by the very term 'security forces'. There is little doubt that the Protestant community still thinks of the security forces as 'theirs' – as do Catholics.

One recent finding, typical of previous years, showed 84 per cent Protestant approval for the use of plastic bullets to 85 per cent Catholic disapproval. A 1991 survey found widespread Catholic conviction that the legal system had a strong element of bias and that the RUC and UDR, like the British army, lacked public accountability. Some 70 per cent of Catholics surveyed believed that 'when the police or army commit an offence, they usually get away with it'. Given the tendency of poll respondents in Northern Ireland to moderate their views, this suggests little change down the years in basic Catholic responses.

A 75-year-old man remembers as a child of about four in the Bone (then one of the smallest and most vulnerable Catholic districts in north Belfast) coming in to tell his father importantly that on the street people were saying 'the police are black bastards. My father said then, and he repeated it often as we grew up: if there wasn't a policeman on the corner, son, there's people around here wouldn't let you sleep in your bed. And he was right. The trouble is, we still can't trust them.'

The anxious desire to accept authority, undermined by endemic suspicion, is typical of many older and conservative Catholics. This man was retailing street talk from the Troubles of 1922, when members of the B Specials and the Royal Irish Constabulary were involved in reprisals for IRA killings and attacks, with minimal response from the state. It was a period that helped form two communities and their thinking. Protestants remembered and still remember being targeted for murder North and South, the groups taken from their homes in Bandon and Altnaveigh to be shot, the burnings of mills and businesses, and the establishment of a Unionist state in the teeth of an IRA onslaught. Catholics recalled, and relayed to their children, how gangs forced thousands out of work and hundreds from their homes, and how men in uniform came for Catholics during the curfew, 'arrested' them, and shot them. In general, and as is true today, neither remembers the dead from the other side.

The clash between inherited views of the state's forces and of the climate in which the state was established still resounds, straining relationships between the two communities and dividing the least political. In May 1993, loyalist paramilitaries shot and killed a man working at the west Belfast home of a Sinn Féin councillor, Alex Maskey, during an attempt to kill Maskey. Republicans led a chorus of local suspicion in which the SDLP MP Joe Hendron quickly joined: there had been a heavy army presence around the street for days, it was said, then the soldiers withdrew and within an hour the loyalist killers arrived. In north Belfast, an ecumenical peace and reconciliation group devoted to encouraging trust and friendship between Protestants and Catholics had been holding a seminar. They broke for a meal. One participant, a nun, returned angrily after the break from her west Belfast convent to tell the meeting what had happened, in exactly the language of those who were alleging collusion. Cross-community harmony dissolved. Very quickly the organisers decided that the subject would have to be shelved to restore tempers. But there was another exchange before people settled down.

'Grievance' and 'alienation' have become the language of politicians and journalists, words that have lost impact through over-use. Few Northern Catholics use them in describing their own lives: instead they talk about how it felt to be burned out of their home, intimidated out of a job. But many Northern Catholics are also reluctant now to talk about experiences in this generation that for them revived all the folk memory of the twenties – and they are also resentful of the pressures that have made them reticent. Many Protestants find such accounts intolerable, as does a section of Southern opinion: the standard reaction is to ask whether the narrator is trying to justify IRA violence. For the same reason mainstream Northern media coverage, more responsive to unionist than to nationalist opinion, has throughout the Troubles tended to downplay the continuity and scale of loyalist paramilitary attacks on Catholics.

Among the people I interviewed, several mentioned in the course of describing something else that they had been forced to move house: by 'loyalists', some said, 'Protestants', said others. The stories spanned the decades: Belfast lawyer Paddy McGrory described how his parents pushed a handcart piled with their belongings over the hills from Lisburn to the Falls Road in 1920. Two of the youngest people I talked to had moved into squats and other temporary accommodation in Belfast in the early seventies: one had moved four times before he started school. Another's family had been forced out of Lisburn in 1986 by loyalists protesting about the Anglo-Irish Agreement: his father sat up 'night after night waiting for them to come back after the first petrol bomb. He got this heart condition out of it.' The father was thirty-four at the time.

Those I interviewed were not deliberately chosen to represent Catholic suffering in the Troubles. The fact that they included a number with experience of the mass movement of the early Troubles, and later repetitions, was a reminder that a considerable part of the Catholic population in what are now totally segregated areas in north and west Belfast, and where the IRA have strong support, have similar family memories: of petrol bombs, beatings, having to leave a mixed area because of threats and violence from Protestants, of the RUC either unable or unwilling to help. Many, like the family of Bobby Sands (the first IRA hunger striker to die) forced out of Rathcoole when he was nine, had deliberately settled where they could bring their children up with both Protestants and Catholics. Rathcoole was attractive, a spruce new estate on the outskirts of the city. One woman remembered, 'The rest in Andytown all said you're mad, they'll burn you out – but I went, I wanted to live in a mixed area. Two years later they did burn us out. We went back to Andytown and they said, "Told you so."'

Official reports found that between August 1969 and February 1973 a total of between 30,000 and 60,000 people, between 6.6 per cent and 11.8 per cent of the Belfast population, were forced to leave their homes. A 1974 report from the Northern Ireland Community Relations Commission estimated that 80 per cent of those forced to leave were Catholic: between

24,000 and 40,000 people. Most poured into the big Catholic ghettos, and many had to make further moves.

In standard accounts of the Troubles, the mass migration of 1969 to 1973 tends to disappear in the sequence of rioting, the arrival of the British army and the rise of the Provisional IRA. In the process, the fact that most of the victims of 1969 were Catholic also disappears – as does the number of Catholics killed in the early seventies by loyalist paramilitaries while coming home from bars, or on their way to or from work in mixed areas. Many of these deaths were described at the time by the RUC as 'motiveless murders'. Perhaps the basic reference book most popular with journalists is *Northern Ireland: A Political Directory 1968–88,* by former BBC political correspondent the late W.D. Flackes and Queen's University of Belfast political scientist Sydney Elliott (Belfast, 1989). The book begins with a chronology of major events that makes no mention of the forced migrations of the early seventies and includes no loyalist murders of Catholics in the events of 1972.

By 1973 twenty-three out of the thirty Catholic-owned and Catholic-frequented bars in north Belfast had been bombed by loyalists. But what preoccupied the media was IRA car bombs and killings of soldiers and civilians. Except for the *Irish News,* the Catholic-owned Belfast paper, the local press and broadcasters took their line from the police. The *Belfast Telegraph,* intent on supporting Terence O'Neill and later Brian Faulkner as reforming Unionists in their struggle with their own hard-liners, steadily played down loyalist violence and focused on the IRA. *Belfast Telegraph* reports talked of 'random' shootings, and frequently omitted the religion of the victim, as the BBC did for some time. The explanation was that giving the religion of the victim 'fed sectarianism'. There is, in other words, a period of recent history that is unrecorded and all but hidden – except in the memories of whole districts.

'It was all you ever heard: the IRA gunmen and bombers,' says an elderly County Down woman, 'as if the others didn't exist. The one I still remember is McGurk's bar [bombed in December 1971]. Fifteen dead, the publican's wife and child among them, and most of them over fifty. The army put it out it was a bomb they were making on the premises. Some outfit like "the Empire Loyalists" claimed it inside hours – but they still kept saying it was the IRA, and there was no outcry about loyalist violence.' Many years later, a UVF man was convicted for the bombing.

British, Unionist and indeed Southern depiction of the violence as largely or wholly caused by the IRA is resented by many Northern Catholics, both supporters and opponents of the IRA. An outside observer, having studied the death tolls, bears out the Catholic perception that loyalist attacks on Catholics have always been downplayed: 'You get reports and analysis and the continuity of loyalist violence in the *Irish News*, for all the paper's faults. But it isn't anywhere else. It's minimised, physically and psychologically – and all you get is, why don't the IRA stop? North Belfast, for example, is the story of a community under attack: the Catholic community. But it's presented in exactly the opposite fashion by unionist voices, and their view is increasingly reported as the truth.'

The Northern Ireland Office's refusal until 1992 to ban the UDA caused considerable nationalist anger. There is a widely shared conviction that loyalist paramilitary violence has never been condemned or confronted by the British government or by the security forces as readily as that of republicans. In conjunction with revelations about double agents such as Brian Nelson, who passed army intelligence on suspected republicans to the UDA killers of Catholics, this resentment feeds endless conspiracy theories about collusion – cherished by republicans, but shared also by others. The tacit admission by security force sources and officials that they have always been reluctant to wage war on two fronts does nothing to soothe nationalist offence.

SEPARATION

Suspicion of the state may have lessened for some Catholics as they find doors open to participation. But as the pattern of segregation hardens, there is little mutual trust about the future of that state. And where people do still mix, they behave with only slightly less frozen etiquette than their parents taught them: don't talk about religion, politics, Britishness, Irishness. Seamus Heaney has immortalised the poisonous maxim every Northerner learns: 'Whatever you say, say nothing.' People lived by it, and still do.

BRÍD RODGERS, for twenty years the SDLP's most prominent woman representative, came from Donegal to live in Lurgan with her dentist husband nearly thirty years ago. She was struck by the way everyone else obeyed unspoken conversational rules.

'I remember in one of the few mixed situations you'd have had, a social function in 1967, some discussion about the British abortion legislation and I said: "Well, I suppose I look at it from a Catholic point of view because I'm a Catholic." And I got a thump under the table! Everybody *knew* I was a Catholic. But the thing was, you didn't say that. You weren't allowed use that as part of an argument. You were supposed to keep all that quiet, the division, and the rules of Catholicism – it was thought to cause offence.'

The rules of conversation in 'mixed' company excluded politics, identity, religion, all the vital subjects of mutual exploration that friendship thrives on. Such exclusions make for straitened relationships, though there are many, both Catholics and Protestants, who deny it. It is, after all, shaming

for everyone. Bríd Rodgers described the habits of the late
sixties. Jumping backwards and forwards through the decades
suggests little variation.

MARGARET, now eighty, thinks she understands her Protestant neighbours better now than before the Troubles. The one
good thing in the last two decades is that there is 'more openness', she says. Most people in her small, mainly Protestant town
in County Tyrone have made bigger efforts to build up social
contacts. 'The Protestants here did try after O'Neill's time,
they realised there was no contact before, so they invited you
to functions and associations. The Business and Professional
Women's Association – I joined that. And they were lovely
people, really good friends.'

Contact went only so far, however. 'You didn't talk about
the IRA when it started up, that sort of thing.' You certainly
didn't talk about loyalist paramilitaries either. She said she felt
sorry for 'the unionists, Protestants, because they've been let
down by the British, haven't they? They know the British don't
like them and they'd love to get out. That must be hard to take.'
Again, it was something she had never raised, like the many
others who said they thought it must be true.

The 74-year-old Cardinal CAHAL DALY recalls friendships,
some of which became lifelong, from his student days in the forties in the then overwhelmingly Protestant Queen's University.
He remembers thinking of the state of Northern Ireland as
'something other, separate, not *our* state' – but insists that this
did not mean he lived in a Catholic world. From an early age
in north Antrim, his family had Protestant neighbours and
friends. Some neighbours were among his friends at Queen's.

'People of a Protestant tradition, of a British background –
that was a very positive thing. It is true the divisive issues were
carefully avoided. It might be said that this meant personal relations were at a superficial level, and that we didn't really face

up to it and get to understand how other people felt, out of politeness and courtesy – one wasn't exactly aware of the implications of that at the time . . . yet it seemed to me valuable, meeting others, seeing and admiring their human and Christian qualities.'

Many others recalled Protestant friends of pre-Troubles days in similar fashion, making the point in some cases forcefully that 'at least we did mix a bit' and that no matter how constrained the friendships, they had known more 'of the other side' than the next generation did. Many had met their 'first Protestants' only when adult – but it had at least been possible.

In Derry, TONY (disgusted later by the anti-Protestant bigotry he met among Belfast republicans) grew up with a number of Protestant friends in a district mixed until Bloody Sunday.

'I remember fancying a young girl, about ten or eleven, and I had the notion that she fancied this other guy, whose name was Mowbray – and I said to him one time, "I think X fancies you, would you be interested in her?" He said: "A Fenian? I wouldn't touch a Fenian with a bargepole!" And I remember thinking, wonderful – I don't know what he's on about here but if it means I've a chance with her . . .

'On Bloody Sunday, I remember coming home that night and the parents, they were just so frightened, there was nothing they could say to me, I was sixteen, a very angry young man, and as you know people were just queuing up to get a crack at the army. So we were standing at the street corner debating that night what had happened and what we were and weren't going to do – and we had a Protestant friend called Hammy, and we didn't realise, he slipped off and he never came back. Somebody said: "Where's Hammy?" But he was away, and we never felt the need to call for him.

'The same way, we never realised, but the whole Protestant

community there just overnight disappeared – when I say overnight it took eighteen months I suppose – the Mowbrays and
Hammy, all those people. But I never even noticed them leaving, so much was happening. They were just not on my agenda
at all. They were just forgotten, pathetic people – where we had
this moral argument that was so overpowering we would inevitably win out and get equal status. In that eighteen months the
old "whatever you say, say nothing", my parents' "for heaven's
sake, son, don't rock the boat" – that all changed. We weren't
going to apologise any more for being what we were.'

Over much of Northern Ireland, massive segregation has
now succeeded the phenomenon of two distinct communities
in some places living side by side but maintaining separate social
lives and customs to a high degree – which, in spite of warm-
toned reminiscence about friendship and neighbourliness, is the
essence of what existed before the Troubles. The mental walls
and barriers of the past are now translated in the cities into the
brick and concrete of 'peacelines', and a flurry of estate agents'
signs as one group flees another's arrival. Analysis of the most
recent census data showed that by 1992 only about 7 per cent
of the population of Northern Ireland lived in areas with
roughly equal numbers of Protestants and Catholics (*Independent
on Sunday*, 22 March 1993). And even within those areas the
communities tended to divide into segregated clusters.

About half the people of Northern Ireland live in areas that
are more than 90 per cent Catholic or 90 per cent Protestant,
and the number of segregated areas has more than doubled in
the last twenty years, the degree of separation increasing year by
year. Belfast and Derry show the sharpest divide. In the May
1993 local government election, the last Unionist representative
on the west bank of Derry, the old city side of the River Foyle,
lost his seat. Belfast has only pockets of integration in two areas,
both in the process of becoming more Catholic than Protestant.

Fair Employment Commission research shows that workplaces are as divided: more than 250 sizeable firms draw their workforces virtually or completely from one or other community.

The youngest people I talked to had much less friendly contact with Protestants than their seniors, and only the most superficial knowledge – sometimes hostile – of the other community. In several cases their families had been intimidated out of mixed areas in the early seventies. One remembered nights in a school in Ardoyne, bullets coming through the windows. Living in Catholic west Belfast, they had come through school without ever meeting any Protestants in a setting that encouraged familiarity and friendship. They had only ever known the Troubles, and had learned simultaneously that they were Catholics, and at war with Protestants. Those in their mid- and late teens seemed more bewildered than convinced they should hate these unknown people. Listening to them was a bit like hearing a children's story about trolls or other odd, potentially frightening creatures: adult consideration of political conflict, party allegiance and paramilitary support was suddenly reduced to crude stick drawing of enemies on the streets, with words to match. Protestants are 'Orangies' and 'Jaffas'. A teacher in a Catholic school remarks, 'The kids talk routinely about Jaffas and call themselves Taigs: it's as though they don't know these are insults.'

Nineteen-year-old GEMMA remembered that at 'thirteen to fourteen I learned from the others at school about the UVF and the UDA, and that we were Catholics – they would say, did you hear about that bomb? Did you hear about him getting shot? And you'd say to yourself: We're Catholics, we're targets for the UVF and they're targets for us. And you started to put two and two together and say, Oh Jesus, we're a Catholic area.'

Living on the borderline upper Springfield Road, Gemma's introduction to Protestants involved stones and petrol bombs.

'You used to hear everyone saying they're fighting with the Orangies tonight – and when you saw your whole district fighting the Protestants, you just thought well that's it, you don't associate with them. You just thought they're people we hate, we have to hate them because everyone else hates them. So you went up and you stood while the men were fighting with them.'

Somehow, in spite of the friction across 'peacelines' and the depths of mutual suspicion, people in districts pitted against each other for years still manage to meet and marry. The most recent survey of social attitudes puts the proportion at 9 per cent of all marriages.

When we had been talking for half an hour, and when her shy eighteen-year-old friend Teresa had suddenly become vocal to tell us that her aunt married a Protestant – 'the first one I met, and you wouldn't notice any difference, he's real nice' – Gemma said her mother was Protestant – or had been Protestant. Twenty-five years after marrying Gemma's father, she is now a 'very holy' Catholic, her daughter says. 'Very Catholic-Catholic.' She never talks about her background, and nor does Gemma.

'You can't run about the area saying my aunt lives such and such a place, she's a Protestant. It's hard on my ma, because she's got to hide what her family was.' Neighbours, even some family friends, do not know the secret. She doesn't tell them her maiden name. She always thought the community she grew up in, one of Belfast's most hardline loyalist districts, was 'very bitter,' Gemma says, and she met her husband in a 'mixed' disco. Her mother and father died without forgiving her and without ever seeing their grandchildren.

'They only met my daddy once, in the town, they ran into them – they just asked her what was she doing with herself. That was the last time she saw them.'

She keeps in contact with her sisters and brothers, and Gemma has seen her 'a bit on edge' when republicans have shot someone in the streets she came from. 'She sees things on both sides, she thinks one side is as bad as the other . . . but my daddy's very into Sinn Féin, so they don't talk about it. They get on great.'

Gemma relayed the story as though it was perfectly understandable that in her own city a woman should live a life of disguise and concealment – which, of course, it is. Helplessness dominated her description: of her mother's life, of her own first realisation that she had to hate 'the Orangies'. It was one of several occasions when a woman was described as swallowing her own beliefs or politics to line up with her husband. For many, talking about their attitudes towards Protestants is just one measure of how little control they have over their lives. The facts of who they are and where they live are great blind forces: only luck, intelligence and willpower can push these forces back. Even then, friendships are strained by memories, experience, mutual fear, and bigotry.

'PROTESTANTS ARE THE BIGOTS . . .'

Marriage across the divide strips away pretence. The Northern Ireland Mixed Marriage Association, which exists to help people deal with difficult parents, friends and clergy, say that they have always had as many distraught Catholics on their books as Protestants. Every Catholic knows someone in their circle who has either reacted with horror when told their child intended to marry a Protestant, tried to prevent such a marriage, or been wounded by such a reaction from a relative. The objectors may say their concern is based on religious conviction, that they fear for their child's religion, their future grandchildren's religion, even their child's safety. But the sheer distaste many show when confronted with the imminent arrival in their family circle of a Protestant cannot be explained as anything other than prejudice.

'On my side it was my mother, on his it was his father,' said JEAN. 'Religion didn't matter to us, but it mattered to his da and my ma. Of course people all over Northern Ireland say it doesn't matter but when it comes to families, nine out of ten of them it bugs.' Another woman described the care she and her husband had taken not to talk about the news in the first years of their marriage, in the mid-seventies when 'tit-for-tat' retaliatory murders spiralled. 'You just didn't want to risk saying the wrong thing.' In Lisburn, a woman said she knew they both had to 'watch out for strangers – you can feel that wee bit of a threat sometimes, you have to watch what you say'.

A large number of parents who choose integrated schools for their children are in mixed marriages – one statistician wonders whether these children will in time develop the elusive 'third identity' so sought after by some in the community relations field. Occasionally a person in a mixed marriage proclaims that she or he has become 'more what I started as' in the course of the marriage. More often, people estimate that they have learned about facets of the other community for the first time. It is not a universally recognised benefit. 'He knew nothing about the plantation, Catholics being pushed into the hills, and it was a shock to me that his mother had spent a lot of her early life in and out of the pawnshop' was how one woman sketched the lessons both learned. But many Catholics in mixed marriages list relatives who have broken off contact, ignored the birth of children, or asked directly if they will now be 'betraying your politics like you've betrayed your religion'.

These are not the kind of tales people repeat for tape recorders, however. Gemma's innocent account of her mother's hidden Protestantism was unusual: others in an area so accustomed to hostile publicity would have added that, of course, she did not need to hide her Protestantism, no one would think anything of it. Most Catholics are well aware that bigotry does not reflect well on the speaker. They realise that Northern Catholics have benefited precisely because Northern Protestants have forfeited sympathy in the outside world by repeatedly venting unadulterated anti-Catholicism to visiting journalists. It is also true that while Protestant anti-Catholicism is thought by some to be a theological virtue, there is no equivalent contemporary Catholic respect for anti-Protestantism. Constitutional nationalism has for years glossed over its former narrow equation of Catholicism and Irishness: republicanism prides itself on its non-sectarianism. As a west Belfast teacher said, describing how his republican teenage pupils wanted badly to believe IRA 'explanations' that Protestants are never targeted because of their religion, it was 'deeply distasteful for them to believe they are sectarian – because that's what Protestants are – and, by definition, we are not'.

He went on, 'When I ask is there anything inherently sectarian in Catholic nationalism, can we look at the history – they are appalled. They'll say, "Oh, certainly, the likes of the SDLP, they trace themselves back to Daniel O'Connell and his type – but us, no, we come from a very pure ideological position, ultimately derived from Wolfe Tone and the United Irishmen." They'll be able to quote you a few lines: "The unity of Protestant, Catholic and Dissenter, that's what we're all about."'

A number of Catholics and probably most Protestants deride this kind of argument. But the conviction that 'Protestants are the bigots', founded on Northern Ireland's history of anti-Catholicism, sustains many. It underpinned the sense of superiority that, even in the days when they recognised their second-class citizenship, made it possible for Catholics to regard as in some way inferior those who controlled the state and dominated employment. But the conviction of a superior culture, a coherent identity, in some also relies on adherence to a religion that has always proclaimed itself the one true Church, from which all Protestants are schismatics. Many have clear memories of being taught that all those 'outside the faith' were lesser Christians, lacking the fullness of truth. Catholics who complain of a Protestant master race attitude see no contradiction in their own sense of superiority: because, they say, they have no desire to treat Protestants as lesser beings. Many refuse to see Protestant distaste for the Catholic Republic as anything but anti-Catholicism and political obduracy – a view shared even by people who themselves see the South as dominated by a reactionary Church.

This kind of thinking is in some a worldview shaped by an environment entirely coloured by Irish Catholicism, and all but devoid of Protestantism. Tomás Ó Fiaich succeeded the cautious and correct William Conway in October 1977 as Catholic Primate of all Ireland. Nationalists loved him: unionists called him 'the Sinn Féin Cardinal', initially largely because of his Irish name and his origins near Crossmaglen, County Armagh, which had by then become tabloidised as the capital of IRA 'bandit country'. An Irish Church historian and language scholar and a warm, gregarious man, the cardinal regularly invited large groups of people from many backgrounds to his official home in Armagh, clearly in an effort to reach beyond his own Church. Comments and statements he made, however, offended many Protestants, and alarmed some Catholics.

He once said he thought 90 per cent of bigotry was Protestant; he made no secret of his desire to see a united Ireland, called for British withdrawal, visited republican prisoners on the dirty protest and made an emotional statement comparing the Maze prison to the slums of Calcutta, and was photographed laughing heartily – a characteristic image – with Gerry Adams at an Irish-language function. He also frequently condemned

IRA violence – and on the occasion of the Enniskillen bombing
which killed eleven Protestants he emotionally apologised on
behalf of the Catholic community, which infuriated numerous
anti-republican Catholics who believed this equated them with
IRA supporters. But he was primarily seen as a republican, by
Protestants and Catholics alike. The Catholic RUC officer, now
retired, says that was a total misunderstanding.

'I liked the man – never saw him as antagonistic. But what
struck me most about him was that he couldn't understand the
opposition to the Orange parades through the Tunnel [a small,
poor Catholic district in the Protestant town of Portadown,
through which Orangemen and bands were in the custom of
marching twice each Twelfth]. He didn't understand what Protestants could do and what they could be like. He lived in an
all-Catholic Irish world. But that didn't mean he was a bigot or
the Sinn Féin Cardinal. He never saw Protestants as a threat:
they were alien to him, they didn't belong. He was a fella raised
in a single community. Now Cahal Daly [Ó Fiaich's successor]
on the other hand . . . he realised the fears Catholics had, he's
better balanced, thinks things out. He's very careful.'

The choice of comparison was revealing. Cardinal Cahal
Daly is much admired by many who regarded his predecessor
as a political disaster for the Catholic Church – and much
disliked by those who loved Cardinal Ó Fiaich. Ó Fiaich's
appeal for Catholics of republican views is easy to understand,
but he had wider support. A considerable number of Northern
Catholics liked him precisely because he caused controversy,
because he spoke without considering whether Protestants,
Unionists, British or Southern opinion would regard what he
had to say as lending support to the IRA. They might have
flinched at the laughing photo with Gerry Adams. But when
the cardinal said he would like to see a united Ireland, spoke
emotionally about young republican prisoners, and perhaps

most of all when he attributed most bigotry to Protestants, he said what many Northern Catholics thought but dared not say.

The single-community worldview the retired Catholic policeman recognised in Ó Fiaich conveyed a simplicity and an unselfconsciousness impossible for those brought up 'further into the North', as another south Armagh man puts it, accustomed to worrying whether the majority will think them subversive. In at least some minds, minority self-respect requires an amount of macho grandstanding by figureheads. The same people think of Cahal Daly as 'too apologetic', because his style is to balance every assertion of nationalists' rights with a statement on the respect due to unionists – and because his condemnation of IRA violence has been more absolute and unremitting than his criticism of the government and security forces.

It is possible to defend the robust statement of your own community's beliefs as dignified, even praiseworthy, in a minority. But there were many Catholics who felt that for the titular head of intolerant and authoritarian Irish Catholicism to ascribe 90 per cent of bigotry to Protestants not only ignored the normal bonds of diplomacy but also defied fairness, sense and Irish history. Though the humane and decent Ó Fiaich would have intended nothing of the sort, there were also many who thought his words reinforced the covert thinking of those who view contemporary Northern Protestants as essentially alien and deserving of punishment for the sins of twentieth-century unionism and seventeenth-century plantations. In both communities, teachings that depict the 'others' as essentially different also make it easier to kill them without conscience.

MUTUAL IGNORANCE

Older Catholics who have had more contact with Protestants than the almost completely segregated young, who grew up in the same small townlands, in the same Derry and Belfast streets, are at least able to think beyond images on TV screens and remember real people with names and personalities. That does not always mean they are more free of prejudice; and because relationships were always confined, they may have little more insight into the other community. 'What we have here,' said one politician sadly, 'is two communities who don't talk to each other.'

And who don't know each other, he might have added. The most striking quality in most Catholic conversation about Protestants is the high proportion of speculation and plain ignorance to sure-footed knowledge, and the same is certainly true in reverse. Most Catholics have met Protestants who say things like 'What sort of ridiculous name is Fionnuala/Sinéad/Tarlach? Which bit of the South are you from?' Both sides treasure little nuggets of what they take to be inside information about the other, polish them, hold them up for admiration against a great blank backcloth. So some Catholics, for example, lovingly dwell on those Protestants who tell them that they covet the wealth of Irish traditional music and that they feel deprived of their heritage.

A more intriguing nugget is the legend of Protestant guilt about the plantation, 'stealing the land'. This almost has the status of urban myth. Though a considerable number of people insist it happened to them, the tale scarcely varies: in a setting of unusual intimacy and confidence, a remarkably frank and open Protestant has at some stage told them that 'at the heart of the Protestant psyche' there lies a guilt about the plantations, and a fear that 'in a united Ireland, we'll lose the land'. The odd thing is the power of this notion of concealed Protestant guilt, given how many Catholics are galled that Unionist politicians deny it so comprehensively. SDLP leader John Hume diagnoses Unionist political paralysis as caused by 'the siege mentality – inbuilt in that is a guilt complex and an inferiority complex'.

Protestants who hear this kind of thing have been known to point out that this misapprehension must be because Catholics are themselves famously beset by guilt. The notion that any but an untypical few might in 1993 agonise over the dispossessions of the seventeenth century is laughed off, especially by those from the kind of working-class background Catholics have always professed to respect, but in the past found difficult to envisage.

It is equally difficult now for younger Catholics to credit how demoralised an older generation once was, and how humiliated they felt by Protestants in spite of their conviction of their own spiritual superiority.

'You went around with your head down,' marvels eighty-year-old Margaret, listing the many ways in which society has changed. 'If you were in a bus conversation you spoke very soft. I suppose a lot of young Catholics now wouldn't believe that. The others talked out loud. We were afraid to. Well, that has gone.

'There has been a movement towards fair play, there's no doubt about it. There was so much discrimination, I don't think there was a Catholic who didn't know it. Once there were no Catholic inspectors in the schools, the matrons in the hospitals and all the top jobs that I can remember – there was never a Catholic. Now you keep hearing about people who've done well. We do feel now we have a part to play, which is good. We were so subdued. We just felt Protestants were better off than we were: they seemed to have the better houses and the better land and they had a feeling of superiority. And we . . . just felt inferior to them.' The admission came in a rush, after a pause, as if even now she found it difficult to say. 'But that has all changed. We've got up off our knees. And they have changed too, very much. I think they're more understanding of us.'

Though such Catholic perception of greater Protestant understanding is rare, the determination to be positive is typical of a considerable number – as is the representation of Protestants as decent people, bent out of shape by self-interested politicians. 'Unionists' are guilty of discrimination, 'Protestants' are upright, honest, hardworking, straight, deluded into anti-Catholicism to deliver a sectarian vote, divide the working class, and maintain upper-class Unionists in power. There is considerably less of this now in Catholic folklore than prior to the Troubles. Upper-class Unionists on the old model no longer exist, and Ian Paisley, the UVF and UDA are difficult to explain away as puppets.

For both communities, a range of personalities from the other side attracts special blame for 'stirring up' the Troubles. Protestants revile Bernadette McAliskey and John Hume, a most unlikely pairing; Catholics particularly abominate Ian Paisley. The Paisley repertoire of lurid anti-Catholicism and bombast about the justice and righteousness of Protestants fighting to defend their faith long ago disintegrated into self-parody. But there is still Catholic incredulity and considerable, if tired, disgust that for twenty years a man with such a reputation has been an acknowledged Unionist leader, topping the poll in each European election where he can reach beyond his own Democratic Unionist Party support. In 1989 he got 160,000 votes, 41,000 more than the Ulster Unionist candidate – 29.9 per cent of the total vote, and 57.4 per cent of the Unionist total. In the early seventies his *Protestant Telegraph* described Catholics as 'two-legged rats'; in 1992 he told his supporters that in talks with the SDLP and the Irish government his party's delegation had taken care never to 'sit with these people or sup with them and nor did we enter their habitation'. As one SDLP man said, 'He still takes as his text "Come you out from among them and touch not the unclean thing" – it's a seriously malevolent text.'

Anti-Catholicism among Protestants is still painful for many Catholics to contemplate: awareness of it makes strange alliances. The only report for which I have ever received approving letters from Catholic clergy, including a bishop, was an account of the Ulster Unionists' annual conference in 1984, which laughed and clapped a delegate who recited a list of the 'names that have crept into the BBC'. There followed a list of Róisíns, Éamonns, Séamuses and Seáns, several names of people who worked for other broadcasting stations and some who were not broadcasters, read with much grimacing and the maximum stumbling over Irish pronunciations. The delegate kicked off with a plaintive 'How often we've been irritated by that dreadful pronunciation of H.' Much laughter. 'I hate the H.' More laughter. The most heartfelt note in my unusual fan mail came from an old Belfast priest, retired now and living in the South. 'We always faced this hate,' he wrote. 'If it wasn't shootings and bombings it was insults and blasphemous attacks on Our Lady and the Mass, or just plain ignorance and hostility about the Irishness of our names. From your account, it sounds as though nothing has changed.'

In fact, something had changed. The Ulster Unionists were supposedly debating 'Ulster's Cultural Heritage', not a subject for party conferences in the fifties, sixties or even seventies – for all that it turned out to be simply an excuse to exercise old reflexes. The list of those who had 'crept in', the arrival of obvious, audible Catholics on the airwaves, was in itself meant to be a demonstration of how Ulster's heritage was under attack. The delegate chided his audience that their passivity had allowed this to happen: he urged them to complain every time they heard something, or someone, they objected to. The reactions were interesting. A newly promoted BBC political reporter, a Catholic but with a name that did not identify him as such, lost his temper and threw down his pen as the list progressed through friends and colleagues. This was noticed. When the speaker sat down, a small group rushed over to surround the BBC man, aware now that he was Catholic, demanding to know why he was angry. No other reporters were present. He floundered; I tried to make it obvious I was taking notes. Party managers became uneasy, several moving in to detach the noisiest protesters: this was the kind of behaviour the Reverend Ian Paisley's Democratic Unionists might revel in, but not the senior Unionist party. The BBC man, embarrassed, asked me not to report his part in the incident.

A few days later, a television presenter phoned to confirm that his was one of the names on the list. He thought this constituted intimidation and was considering legal action. Out of habit, I made a note of the call: 'Every night I'm subject to phone calls of this calibre,' he said, 'the situation has become almost impossible. I can't interview certain people because it would be assumed there'd be a slant. When we did the thing about Sean Downes [the man killed by an RUC plastic bullet in Andersonstown, during an arrest operation at a demonstration], the abuse that came through was amazing.' He did amaze me. The report he mentioned had been minimal: not an investigation, not a commentary. He was not a political reporter. If he took legal action, it never became public. He left Northern Ireland to work in London.

In a small way, the incident pointed up one considerable source of pressure on local broadcasting, known but tacitly ignored by the rest of the media. Working for a Dublin paper as I then was, other pressures were more immediate: Dublin's lack of interest in Northern Ireland, the constant demand for 'good news' to balance the diet of violence, considerable wishful thinking about the allegedly hidden Irishness of Northern Protestants, which manifested itself for example in an annual jamboree of folksy Twelfth coverage – and a steadily growing distaste for the complaints of Northern Catholics, who were more and more equated with the murderousness of the IRA. Struggling to balance my own innate sympathies with an attempt to imagine the thinking of Northern Protestants, I never in those years thought of suggesting that as part of our annual Twelfth double-page spread, we ought to have someone in Portadown in the narrow streets of the Tunnel, through which Orangemen and bands marched twice to their gathering place and back again – which meant the RUC kept the residents behind barriers for several hours in the day.

The Twelfth parade no longer marches through the Tunnel. Although local Catholics had been complaining for decades that the parade humiliated them, it took steady pressure from the Irish government over several years, and the then RUC chief constable Sir John Hermon's particular determination to demonstrate impartiality, to produce an alternative route for the march. Unionists expressed anger at this disruption of 'tradition'. When the routes of other parades were similarly altered, Unionist politicians said – and still say – that the police have become the tools of the Anglo-Irish Agreement and the Dublin government. The SDLP welcomed the changes, and some Catholic opinion decided the RUC was beginning to display even-handedness. Others gave them no such credit. In places like the Tunnel, people had spent too long corralled in their own homes, watching police laugh and chat to Orangemen who deliberately chose routes to give maximum offence. The exhortation to drummers to 'beat it up as we pass the chapel' is part of Orange tradition.

As an offensive manifestation of public Protestantism, the Twelfth's only rival in Catholic perception was the B Specials, dissolved in 1970 to be replaced by the UDR, which in turn has now merged into the RIR. Changed names did not change or improve the original image with many Catholics: 'Uniformed neighbours stopping you on the way to Mass and asking your name, holding your Rosary beads up for their friends to laugh at,' as one fiftyish man from Aughnacloy, County Tyrone, recalls. There were 'a few good Specials, decent fellas who were in it for the few bob and the crack, but there were fellas who just liked putting you in your place with a gun in their hands'.

In exactly the same fashion, of course, rural Protestants have always distinguished between their 'decent' Catholic neighbours and those whom they suspect are IRA supporters. One of the best evocations of the deep and mutual suspicion between the two communities is the study of a border area in the fifties by Rosemary Harris (*Prejudice and Tolerance in Ulster*, Manchester, 1972), in which she maps long-lived local memories on both sides of the 'others' who give allegiance to shadowy, violent groups. The groups are no longer shadowy. A Presbyterian moderator has spoken sadly of noting in almost all his churches across rural Northern Ireland a plaque listing parishioners killed by the IRA. In Fermanagh and Tyrone, Protestants are convinced the IRA has deliberately targeted border farms and 'only sons' while professing to be targeting members of the police reserve or UDR, and now the RIR. The IRA denies this, but its murders, often of people who have never been security force members or who have resigned, in a number of cases of the one male in a family due to inherit a farm, have forced Protestant families to give up land and move away from the border. In parts of Tyrone, Derry, Antrim and north Armagh, loyalists murder Catholics, occasionally with Sinn Féin or IRA connections but more often not. In many cases, local people suspect the killers are themselves soldiers or police, or have UDR/RIR or RUC help. There are frequent protestations of good neighbourly relations, and a simmering, mutual bitterness and dread.

In the same way as Protestants deride the notion that they feel guilt about the plantations, Catholics scoff at the idea that anyone imagines a political settlement that would take farms from Protestants and hand them to Catholics. But in every country district where the two communities are present in strength, people on both sides can reel off farms by the religion of the owners. Catholics habitually break the list down into good land and bad and note that almost always 'the good land is Protestant'. It is clearly a live issue – on which no one will be quoted by name. Several SDLP representatives and a number of priests, however, insist that there is an unspoken republican vote-catcher. 'The voting patterns reflect decades, centuries of bitterness,' says an SDLP veteran, 'you can't miss it. Our vote is in the old, settled parts of towns – the Provo vote is concentrated in the wilder countryside, and in the new housing estates where people are just in from the country. There's an ancient, tribal conviction about dispossession.'

He might have added the somewhat more recent grievance about lack of housing under Stormont. 'My father was in the council,' says Paddy Duffy, 'and year after year he got nowhere. He couldn't get houses built in Ardboe, but they were being built in Tullyhogue.' In Derry, 57-year-old MARY NELIS remembers the consequences.

'We're talking about epidemics of TB when it was practically eradicated everywhere else, in the fifties, late on. It was a big scourge here, and it was clear the overcrowding in the houses had a lot to do with it: that and the poverty. Until they built Creggan, there were thirteen of us in a two-bedroom house – my sisters had got married and they were there too.'

Of the complaints about Unionist rule addressed by the civil rights movement, discrimination in housing 'was the sorest because it was always with you,' says a Tyrone woman. But it is now recalled with little heat as one of the first and most comprehensively tackled of grievances. The problem of discrimination and inequality of opportunity in employment, on the other hand, still rankles. Campaigning on these issues has been marked by fundamental disagreement among Northern Catholics from the start: broadly speaking between those who believe the British government should be pushed hard to take all measures necessary, and those who have always feared Protestant resentment would prove counterproductive. John Hume, for example, has constantly argued that more jobs are the first prerequisite for producing fair employment.

A government approach that for years was half-hearted and ineffectual has achieved only patchy progress for Catholics. But in a narrowly based economy, heavily dependent on the public sector and with a much higher rate of joblessness than before the Troubles, some Protestants still claim fair employment legislation victimises them. Their complaints leave most Catholics cold, especially those either specifically discriminated against in particular cases or convinced that the structure and spread of industry in Northern Ireland has left them at a disadvantage. Present-day Protestant attitudes towards efforts to eliminate discrimination have added to the lingering bitterness about Stormont: many Catholics see only that the statistics demonstrate a continued Protestant advantage. In July 1993 a league table of UK regional male unemployment showed Northern Ireland Protestants next to the bottom, at 10.1 per cent, just above East Anglia. Catholics in Northern Ireland topped the list at 24.2 per cent, double the rate for any other region.

Though the collapse of many traditional Northern Ireland industries has increased the proportion of Protestants on the dole, the gap in rates of male joblessness between the two communities remains wide: more than twice as many Catholics as Protestants are unemployed. A considerable number of Protestants made redundant by the textile and engineering industries have found work in the security forces. Recent research shows that the 80 local government areas where unemployment is lowest are exclusively or predominantly Protestant. Of the 50 wards where unemployment is highest, 45 are Catholic, including the top 8. Male unemployment in the Catholic districts of Brandywell and Creggan in Derry and in the Falls, Whiterock, New Lodge and Ardoyne is between 52 and 60 per cent: overall figures hide pockets where the rate of joblessness is even higher.

In *Interpreting Northern Ireland* (Oxford, 1990), which surveyed the major literature on the Northern conflict, the respected John Whyte concluded that the argument was not whether discrimination still existed but to what extent; he selected as a moderate judgement on the Stormont years the verdict of John Darby that 'there was a consistent and irrefutable pattern of deliberate discrimination against Catholics' (John Darby, *Conflict in Northern Ireland*, Dublin, 1976). In 1987, eleven years after the implementation of fair employment legislation and fifteen years after the dissolution of Stormont, a government-appointed commission reported that 'serious and substantial' inequalities of opportunity for Catholics persisted in both public and private sectors (Standing Advisory Commission on Human Rights, *Religious and Political Discrimination and Equality of Opportunity in Northern Ireland*, Belfast, 1987). Only a small minority of employers had sought to achieve a balanced workforce, the report said: very few had done more than sign a declaration of principle. The commission called on the government to set a target for bringing down Catholic male unemployment that would reduce it inside five years to 1.5 times the Protestant rate. The government rejected the idea, and the differential remains substantially unchanged.

Striking advances for Catholics in the public service and in some occupations previously dominated by Protestants, particularly the law, have not been matched by increased opportunity for the unskilled and semi-skilled – in large part because of continued recession and high unemployment. Meanwhile a steady stream of successful cases through the fair employment machinery, almost all taken by Catholics, demonstrates a continued, if diminished, will to discriminate. The cases continue to emerge right across the board: from public employment in health and education boards through the older and more prestigious of Northern Ireland's two universities, Queen's, to private industry. Until recently, it was fashionable for government officials to talk of a 'legacy of structural discrimination', the product of actions in the past and beyond the reach of short-term solution. Official complacency has been dented.

In September 1992 the leak of an internal Northern Ireland Office briefing paper made public a civil service assessment of the task facing a 'central secretariat on targeting social need', already the subject of a significant speech by the then secretary of state, Peter Brooke. Brooke referred to, and the leaked memo listed, the 'serious differences [that] exist in the social and economic conditions experienced by Catholics and Protestants in Northern Ireland'. The persistence of the 'differences was central to the continuing divisions in Northern Ireland', but existing policies seemed unlikely to reduce the gap significantly or quickly. So 'Targeting Social Need', the 'TSN initiative' in civil service jargon, must 'skew' the allocation of public spending, of support for new jobs and temporary employment towards 'those in greatest need' – namely, Catholics.

The TSN assessment pulled together a range of official statistics, with dramatic cumulative effect:

> On all the major social and economic indicators, Catholics are worse off than Protestants. Catholics are more likely to be unemployed (23% of Catholic males are unemployed as against 9% of Protestant males). Catholics are more likely to experience long-term unemployment (67% of the long term male unemployed are Catholics). Catholics are

significantly less likely than Protestants to hold professional, managerial or other non-manual positions. More
Catholics than Protestants leave school lacking any formal
educational qualifications. Significantly fewer Catholic
pupils follow science subjects to A level. There is a greater
provision of grammar school places for Protestant than
Catholic children. Significantly more Catholics than
Protestants live in public sector housing and experience
overcrowding. Catholic households have a lower gross
household income than Protestant households and almost
double the proportion of Catholic households are dependent on social security. Catholics suffer from higher levels
of disability and ill-health.

An official 'review' of the efficacy of fair employment measures
is to be completed in 1995 – the TSN initiative is supposedly
working towards the same date. Unionists greeted the leak with
shouts of 'discrimination': politicians and some other Protestants
continue to insist that claims of widespread and systematic
discrimination during the Stormont years, in housing and
employment, are wild exaggeration or simply untruthful. In one
case, amelioration of Catholic grievance bolsters that of Protestants: about 50 per cent of housing in Protestant west Belfast
now dates from before 1919, compared to less than 11 per cent
for Catholic west Belfast. Adducing the new prominence of
individual Catholics, some Protestant representatives deride the
idea that any Catholics might still be disadvantaged or discriminated against. The DUP's spokesman on employment, Gregory
Campbell, told his party conference in 1990: 'I'm going to deal
with fair employment legislation in the only way the representatives of the Protestant people know how to deal with it –
because RCs are at a disadvantage, everything we do has to be
aimed at helping them. The poor RCs.' Laughter and applause.
    Although most Catholics would say that the British government

should take the blame for lack of commitment and urgency, and some concede that even if the will had been demonstrated the problem could still not have been solved speedily, sour Unionist attitudes and awareness of the continued advantage of Protestants keep alive bad old memories. All the research suggests that a range of factors is relevant to continuing inequality. Some Catholic opinion highlights present-day discrimination and the skewed location of manufacturing employment: some Protestant opinion dismisses discrimination – past or present – as a cause of disadvantage, and instead emphasises the size of Catholic families and traditional weaknesses in the Catholic education system. Meanwhile, long-term unemployment, two-thirds of it Catholic, sometimes second- or third-generation in a family, and a pattern in many places of female part-time, low-paid employment supporting a family, have eaten into the Catholic community. But despite several studies, among them a 1992 survey conducted for the SDLP on voter behaviour in west Belfast, showing a marked preference for Sinn Féin among the low-paid and unemployed, the most vivid denunciation often comes – off the record – from the more successful and those who have been most involved with the state at various points in the past thirty years. Others tend to be quietly cynical. It is as though those who rejected the scepticism of their own community and tried to participate in the Unionist state – or who have been determined to see those Protestants still in place near the top of the system as all equally reformed – are all the more galled to discover that their Catholic identity is not in fact irrelevant.

A retired senior public official still bristles when he recalls how he learned in the mid-sixties that his religion debarred him from a job he was otherwise well qualified for. 'I was taken aside and told very quietly by a very senior guy, a Scotsman and a nice man who liked me: "You haven't an earthly there." I was stunned. "Why's that?" I said. "Well," said he, "put it this way – you're not well enough versed in the Scriptures."'

A passing reference at a social function to discrimination provoked a fiftyish woman to recount her father's career as a Catholic in the RUC, stationed for years in central Belfast. He was head constable for forty years, she said, a perfectionist, 'and they wouldn't promote him'. When he complained they told him he was so good at organising big events, they wanted to keep him in the centre for royal visits. 'When Paisley had to be arrested for some demonstration in the fifties, guess who they sent to arrest him?' The family lived in the station until she was fourteen. They had no friends: Protestants did not like them because they were Catholic, Catholics did not like them because they were police. Then a couple of years before her father was due to retire, soon after the IRA fifties campaign began, there was a big meeting of officers 'and he heard about it by accident only when it was over. He asked why he hadn't been informed. "We don't trust Fenians because they're rebels," he was told. It pierced him. More and more things fell into place, and he went away, and retired, and he died.'

Of those I met for the first time while interviewing, the most apprehensive about being identified was a well-known lawyer who had nothing but contempt for 'Catholics with a chip on their shoulders'. He was particularly scornful of those who used discrimination as an excuse to malinger on the dole queue. He had only met prejudice once in his working life, he said – apart from a recent occasion when he had walked out of a dinner late at night when the guest of honour and several associates, all major figures in the legal world and all Protestant, had become drunk and 'reactionary'.

'What annoyed me was that they obviously thought I would sit and take it. And when I left I found myself thinking for the first time, so what do they say about me when I'm not there?'

He would not repeat what they had said.

All over Northern Ireland, there are pockets where individuals from the two communities live peacefully side by side and maintain friendships. But the pattern of growing segregation mirrors mutual mistrust and mental distance. Peacelines in poorer districts are matched by the signs of fear and flight in areas of former Protestant privilege: a brain drain to English universities of the brightest Protestant school leavers, a steady and increasing drift of established, almost always Protestant, residents away from Belfast's oldest area of wealth as upwardly mobile Catholics move in, and a less-noticed but no less definite version of the same trend in towns like Newry and Dungannon. 'The rise of the Catholic middle class has begun to promote a bit of Protestant paranoia,' said an expert on the statistics whose roots are outside Northern Ireland. 'There's fear, they're seen as a threat, taking over south Belfast for example, and yes, there's a degree of Catholic triumphalism.'

In a sense, this is a second wave of upward mobility and consequent flight, the second built on the momentum of the first. The new, larger Catholic middle class owes much to direct rule, but it has developed primarily because the number of Catholic graduates has grown. Education reforms, which made third-level education possible for working-class Catholics, were not the sole factor: the beginning of the Troubles left more room for Catholics in university and eventually more room in the job market because Protestant students in greater numbers chose English universities and foreign students stopped coming to Belfast. And as Queen's University's student body steadily changed from being more than 70 per cent Protestant to more than 50 per cent Catholic, the trend became self-perpetuating. Protestant students began to feel uncomfortable in what many now see as a Catholic-dominated university student body.

Education officials shy away from spelling out the implications – but in the past four or five years the numbers of the most
highly qualified Protestant school leavers opting for university
elsewhere has in fact increased. It is a permanent loss: studies
show that two-thirds of Protestant undergraduates stay away
compared to half the Catholics who go at the same age. And as
the sharpest of political observers have noted, it is also a reversal
of previous patterns – in which traditionally more Catholics
than Protestants emigrated from Northern Ireland. As in all such
developments, this drift of eighteen-year-olds feeds into another
movement and speeds it up. That Protestants leave traditional
middle-class districts as Catholics arrive is in part direct reaction:
but there is also an element of parents at retirement age leaving
to follow the children. The overall picture is of a confident
Catholic group, young and growing very rapidly, faced with
nervous and retreating Protestants: a middle class in the making
watching another in flight.

Nowhere is this more obvious, and more noted, than on
Belfast's Malone Road. A flock of bright blue Rathmore convent uniforms at school coming-home time where once the
colours of Methodist and Victoria colleges reigned: the Sunday
morning fleet of Volvos and BMWs outside the church of
St Brigid's, Derryvolgie, built in a side street at the turn of the
century by benevolent Protestant employers for their Catholic
servants: these are by now hackneyed examples of new money
inside the fortress of old Protestant privilege. There is nothing
subtle about the shift. When falling rolls pushed a Protestant
girls' school next to the overcrowded Catholic primary into a
merger on another site, St Brigid's parish quickly bought up the
empty premises. The church is now in the middle of major and
much-needed expansion, to a plan some parishioners think is
unnecessarily elaborate. Land has been cleared, a hoarding
surrounds the building site. Sour Protestant jokes at mixed

dinner parties are already anticipating the moment when the
frontage of a new and immodest 'chapel' bursts through onto
the Malone Road itself – only a few hundred yards from a well-
camouflaged and long-established RIR barracks.

While many seem content to simply enjoy their new surroundings, some Catholic arrivals are alarmed by what they see.
A man in a high-profile job, originally from a part of Northern
Ireland with a traditional and relaxed Catholic majority,
expressed with the fluency of considerable reflection an anxiety
others have just begun to struggle with.

'The Protestant middle class feels threatened – not by the IRA
but by the sight of Catholics arriving – so what do they do?
They send their children to England and they follow them, or
they head for north Down. What do we get? A middle-class
Catholic ghetto in south Belfast, demanding bigger schools,
bigger churches, next a Gaelic football field I expect. I want the
kids to play Gaelic, but that's not the first thing we moved
here for.

'The Protestant middle class is abdicating. Why aren't their
Church leaders, the archbishop, the moderator, why aren't they
saying to them "Don't jump the ship – stay and work it out with
Catholics?" In our immediate area, it's increasingly difficult for
the children to find Protestant friends – I resent that very
strongly. I want Protestant kids in my home, so my kids can
practise what we're saying about treating each other as equals,
recognising each other's way of life. I don't want my kids to
leave the place after school – and I don't want to see Protestants
going either. I want the best talent and brains to stay, I don't
want them to run away. There's no advantage in that for any
of us.'

As he described how he saw the drift in his area repeated in
other parts of the North, this man became increasingly depressed. He seemed equally downcast by attitudes he saw on

both sides: the Protestant rush to leave, and among Catholics a lack of enthusiasm for mixing. He suspected he knew what lay behind Protestant flight at a personal level: 'They're exporting their kids because the political environment is changing so dramatically. The parents find the changes in the Anglo-Irish Agreement so hard to come to terms with. But as well as that, I'm nearly afraid to say it – I think they just don't want to live side by side.'

On the other hand, he knew that his own yearning for a mixed society was unusual. It was clearly not among the social ambitions of many others: Catholic friends, he said, found it odd that he felt so comfortable with Protestants. He thought it came from the confidence of his original homeplace. 'There's still an unease for many. I feel I'm as good as anyone else and I'll take people as they come. Others would say they do that too. But they're on edge, they have preconceptions, they expect slights. And what I dislike most: there's a whisper of triumphalism among some of them, that the system is breaking down for the Protestant community and "they're beginning to get a taste of their own medicine". I don't like that sort of language. I've heard it on a number of occasions.'

This man's clearly genuine distress at the prospect of still greater separation, of Protestant flight and Catholic entrench-ment, is shared by people in different parts of the North – perhaps expressed most strongly by those in their forties and fif-ties, who in bad moments see their own children facing an even more shrunken world. But anxiety is strongly countered by a widespread inclination among Catholics to stand back from events and allow shifts to happen without examining each stage. Neither pessimistic nor triumphalist, they watch developments in the Protestant community with interest, not much sympathy, but a degree of dark humour.

'The divisions are getting clearer, aren't they?' said an Omagh student, twenty-eight, belatedly training to be an accountant. 'Some want to get rid of the agreement. Some want integration, some want devolution, some want to talk to the British and they might even want to talk to the South. But they don't want to talk to the SDLP. And they don't want, ever, to talk to the Provos.'

For him, as for others, it was time to get on with life in a changing Northern Ireland while Unionists evolved a political strategy. Meanwhile he thought the SDLP leader John Hume had done 'the only thing he could really' by reopening talks with Sinn Féin leader Gerry Adams, and producing an agreed statement. He is resolutely optimistic about the future. Criticism of Hume from Unionists, the Alliance Party and some Southern opinion for making common cause with republicans had made little impression on him. He voiced the instinct among many Catholics that no settlement would be achieved unless Sinn Féin was brought into political discussion, and the equally common derision of Protestant outrage at the prospect: 'How dare Unionist politicians lecture Hume about talking to the men of violence, with *their* record!'

Whatever the shape of any future settlement at governmental level, the legacy of grievance and recrimination seems to have set the limits within which most will want to live. 'You feel comfortable in Dungannon now,' said one apparently confident, successful man. 'It's become a Catholic town.'

While there may be traces of triumphalism among the affluent, many Catholics still feel vulnerable. The implications of the 1991 census have only begun to sink in, and fear of a Protestant backlash is deep-rooted – many think it may already have begun. Questions linger: if Hume persuades the IRA to stop, can the British be trusted to give nationalists parity with unionists? Or will some new British 'internal' solution be imposed? ANN in Craigavon looks at unionists from the perspective of a republican brought up in Ardoyne, and sees no reform.

'It's going to take a long time to shift unionist attitudes – and the only way to start to erode them is to take away the power and the privilege they've had for so long. There's decency in every human being – but they've been reared to think that they are the special people, Catholics are lazy, to be treated like the blacks: dirty, lazy, whatever.'

It is a fairly typical republican view: a leading Sinn Féin official insisted that 'unionists still have their hands on the levers of power', although he conceded that none of this power was directly political. A more widely shared conviction is that Protestants have not come to terms with what needs to be done to give Catholics equality inside Northern Ireland: socially, economically, and politically. The continued unionist denial of the equality of nationalist identity translates directly, in many Catholics' minds, into hostility.

The expansion in size and self-importance of the ghettos has not yet soothed old fears. SINÉAD's west Belfast assurance dissolves, as she says, when she leaves the area. She described with embarrassment at her own nervousness a visit to the tiny Catholic Short Strand district, surrounded by the bulk of Protestant east Belfast.

'It was the first time I'd been in Short Strand. I knew there were Catholics all round me, but I felt uncomfortable. I know it was because it's a lot smaller than west Belfast, and the Protestants are an awful lot closer to you. A lot of people say to me, "How can you live in a place like that?" – meaning west Belfast – "Protestants would know immediately who you are." I don't feel like that when I'm there. But I did in Short Strand: I'm here, and I'm vulnerable and they'll know what I am.

'It's a thing that's inside you. When you're in town, you don't want someone identifying you, saying your name, if

you've a name like mine that could only be Catholic. I'm sure
a Protestant doesn't feel like that. Do they? That's a sign that
we're not equal. We'll always feel like that, because we're in a
minority.'

A veteran community worker reckoned most colleagues no
longer even pretended that making 'cross-community links'
should be a major aim. 'Locally people all understand there are
no victories to be won: we're all net losers. Protestants don't
really want to hold hands with Catholics and vice versa – on
both sides they just want to be left alone. I'm working towards
acceptance of two traditions of equal validity, living apart if
necessary. No patsy notions of reconciliation. I'll settle for that
for the time being, because I think people reconcile from
strength. If you're feeling vulnerable about your own identity
and culture and status, you're not going to hold hands. So you
have to build people up first. Even though that's a very narrow
goal, I'm actually working towards benign apartheid.'

It was not a phrase I had heard from any Catholic previously:
when last I'd heard a Northern nationalist reference to apartheid, it was as one of the swearwords used to draw damaging
parallels between the social vision of unionists and the whites of
South Africa.

6

'If we could trust them . . .'

BRITAIN

Britain no longer obsesses Northern Catholics as the author
of all their woes, if in truth it ever did. Even the most
political, convinced that the British government carries the
main responsibility for finding a solution, have little enthusiasm
for diatribes against 'perfidious Albion'. What were once standard denunciations of the treacherous oppressor, the occupying
forces, now have an old-fashioned, almost comic ring in many
ears. Protestant Unionists have always been the immediate focus
of dislike rather than the distant British – and what are now
widely perceived to be altered British attitudes towards
Unionists, the Union, and towards nationalists, have significantly softened and refashioned traditional hostility.

None of which is to suggest that Catholics tend to absolve
Britain of the sins of the present and the past. But for many, particularly those who live in comfortable middle-class surroundings at one remove from the most obvious manifestations of the
Troubles, it is possible to speak of a British 'role' with some
distance. In a way, they separate consideration of British motives
and of the British presence – largely because the presence in

their case consists of a non-discriminatory direct rule rather than helicopters overhead. In the places where most middle-class Catholics live, there are no army vehicles in convoy, no soldiers with rifles aimed on the footpath as they go shopping. On the other hand, army patrols in the most republican parts of the North continue to irk many, whether republican sympathisers or not. They are not impressed by the standard Protestant, unionist response that the security forces are present in force only where there is likelihood of terrorism. There is still an automatic reflex of resentment, shared by a large number, to being stopped and asked in an English or Scottish accent for name, address and destination. In much of Northern Ireland, however, the questions come from the RUC or RIR, setting up different and, for many, more hostile vibrations.

Awareness of British faults may no longer obsess, but it persists none the less across a wide band of Northern Catholic society. The list scarcely varies. Surveys regularly show that Catholics blame British direct rulers in Stormont for refusing to be accountable for the security forces they control; many are critical of extended special powers and repeated tinkering with the legal system. The American academic Richard Rose, who conducted the first major survey of political attitudes in the mid-sixties and analysed the first years of the Troubles, decided in 1972 that 'the alternation of conciliation and coercion since 1968 has once again led to the making of Fenians' (the nineteenth-century secret and violent republican brotherhood), a judgement still widely shared among Northern Catholics.

Perhaps most heat across the widest spectrum is caused by the British pose of disinterested observer at the scene of a sectarian squabble. Northerners in both communities occasionally use the word 'tribal' to describe local attitudes, but almost unanimously, they object to it in British mouths. 'They're just so bloody arrogant, so superior,' said an elderly County Down priest long retired from his urban Derry parish. 'They won't listen. They're two days here and they think they know it all.'

But many also recognise that British ministers preside over a regime that increasingly brings Catholics into positions of influence and which has made equality of opportunity a watchword in public employment, even if patchily achieved. Some are not disposed to regard this as much more than a belated attempt at just administration; others increasingly regard British officials as the neutral administrators successive secretaries of state have begun to describe. Traditional distrust of Britain is fatigued, as weary as British politicians are of Northern Ireland affairs. But it survives. At a point in 1992's talks between the two governments and Northern politicians, when Unionists were expressing angry conviction that Britain had obviously adopted John Hume's agenda and all of seven years after the SDLP leader first began to suggest authoritatively that Britain was no longer opposed to Irish unity, a senior SDLP negotiator agreed that yes, indeed, the language of the talks' communiqués as drafted by senior British civil servants owed much to Hume. Then he added, in the driest of voices: 'And wouldn't it be nice, now, if we could *trust* them.'

The growing recognition that Protestant Unionist opposition to any far-reaching change is at least as much a problem as British inconsistency or lack of interest does, however, lend a new perspective to dislike of British attitudes. Recognition of the growing divide between Unionists and Britain has an even more powerful effect. SEAMUS MALLON, the SDLP's deputy leader, the nationalist politician whom many Protestants dislike even more than John Hume and almost as much as Gerry Adams, mainly for his criticisms of security forces behaviour, puts this in characteristically stark terms, though he also adds the tinge of doubt that many others feel about the benefit of this change to nationalists.

'The Unionists are optional extras at Westminster – as we are – though we command much more respect because we know who we are and say who we are. But I see them grovelling and currying favour, talking about our boys in Bosnia.

'The British, I see no signs they're prepared to grasp the nettle. I think renegotiating an internal settlement is their core position, with little token things stuck on. They've got to the stage where they might rethink their position. But in twenty-five years they haven't rethought anything. One of their characteristics is permanence: they've never been invaded, or had internal subversion. That breeds arrogance and incompetence.'

BRITISH DISINTEREST

Growing Protestant anxiety about British intentions gives pleasure to a considerable number of Catholics, an emotion others deride as in itself a 'colonial' reaction. 'Isn't it what all the best imperialists always did, divided the colonised, pleasing one lot by humiliating the other?' said an Omagh student. At the peak of angry Unionist reaction to the 1985 Anglo-Irish Agreement's recognition of an Irish role in Northern affairs, while nationalist opinion in general watched with some satisfaction as loyalist demonstrators clashed with the RUC, republicans had to struggle to construct a coherent response. They wavered between condemnation of the agreement as a British ploy to further compromise the Southern state and Northern nationalists, and a claim that any benefits it brought to nationalists had in reality been won by the pressure of the IRA.

In effect, the *ad hoc* and occasionally contradictory nature of much British policy has left many puzzled. 'I think there's a decision in the Northern Ireland Office that the SDLP must persuade Unionists to come to some accommodation, that it's not for them to do,' says an SDLP politician, 'and that's just a cop-out. Their greatest exertion is to make common cause with Alliance, as though the Alliance Party is the happy medium here – as though Alliance isn't a unionist party.'

Ministers and civil servants who encourage Unionists by suggesting that nationalists should settle for an 'internal' Northern Ireland settlement with minimal recognition of Irish political identity, often seem at odds with the line Foreign Office mandarins appear to have laid down in the early seventies, of close cooperation and recognition of shared interests with Dublin governments. Some Northern Catholics think the increasing instability in unionism is encouraged by Britain, and will in time lead to a pragmatic settlement. Others see only drift and muddle, inspired by nothing more elevated than a desire to mollify those who insist on their Britishness and a refusal to give Northern Ireland sustained governmental attention.

MARGARET, a warm, lively woman of eighty who went on civil rights marches in 1968, says she blames Britain more now because she blames Protestants less.

'Whitelaw I liked. Some of them have done their best, including the man we had before this one [former secretary of state Peter Brooke]. And there have been changes, great changes: there's Catholics in jobs now they never would have had a look at before. There was no fair play before – but I didn't blame the Presbyterians for that, I didn't blame my Protestant neighbours. I blame England for that. For partition, for letting it happen.

'And on the politics of it now, the British aren't getting anywhere. They're not really tackling it. So there has to be, I think, a colonial solution. There'll have to be compromises all round.

'I'm not an IRA man but I think what Gerry Adams says is right. The British have to go. It won't work until they do. I'm sure the Unionists, the Protestants do feel that England is not behind them, nobody knows what they're at. We could get on perfectly together here if we were allowed to. It will be a long time frame but it's inevitable. They always say you have to talk to your enemy. Well, Britain has to talk to the republicans. What are they waiting for? They should do it now. There'll need to be a settlement over a period of years, with money from Britain. The Free State government will have to help too.'

But Margaret's conviction that a settlement, and peaceful coexistence with her Protestant neighbours would follow swiftly and surely on British withdrawal was not shared by many of those who talked to me. In general those over seventy had considerably more optimism about solutions than younger people, though often they were also the most critical of Britain. There seemed to be no contradiction and no hesitation there: Britain had caused the trouble, Britain should get out, and peace would follow. In this kind of argument, there was no heat. Margaret's appreciation of Peter Brooke and Willie Whitelaw was widely shared, as was her awareness of the improvements direct rule had brought. British withdrawal had become a dry legal formality: necessary, of course, not in the least contentious. The impression from some was of a quarrel long settled, with only paperwork to be completed.

SINÉAD, twenty-six, living in west Belfast and supporting Sinn Féin and the IRA with reservations, believes 'there has to be a united Ireland – if you feel you're Irish and you say anything else you're settling for less, you're treating yourself as a second-class citizen'. Her attitude towards Britain and her views on British responsibility are less definite. She visits England often, to stay with friends in London and Manchester.

'The atmosphere and the variety's great in London, nobody caring what you are, not like here. I think it's the Britain of the past that was responsible. I don't feel that John Major or even Margaret Thatcher really are the enemy – they came to power and that was the situation they inherited. I don't think they have any control over it really. Yes, there are things British governments could have done and don't do. You could criticise them for that. But could you really go the whole hog and say take out the troops? I don't think they could. I don't think there's anything in it for them, being here. Like other countries they gradually let go of, I don't think they want to be here. But it's not that simple to get out.

'I know a lot of people don't like the army – and I can understand why – but I wouldn't dislike the army as much as the RUC. I don't like the RUC at all. But the army, to a lot of them it's a job. They sit in their barracks and say Catholics are this and that, they're led to believe that Catholics are their enemy. But they don't really feel it. They're just an army – whereas the RUC . . .

'I think it's the Protestant thing – I don't think the British bit has all that much to do with it. On the whole it's the Protestants, they feel it's their state. Not even that it's a British state. Sometimes I think I wouldn't mind that half as much. If the Protestants thought, we're part of England, we'll be like England. . . Well, Catholics in Britain don't feel like we do. They aren't treated differently because they're Catholics. I wouldn't feel the same if the Unionists were like that.'

To Sinéad, as to many others, 'the Protestant thing' is clearly much more real than hostility towards Britain. The theme of absolving modern Britons also recurred, although Sinéad's blithe 'they're just an army' was remarkably charitable and benign for a resident of west Belfast. As she said herself, she is fortunate to live in one of the most middle-class streets in the district, where soldiers tend to be less likely to come under attack and where they behave in a less abrasive fashion than the jumpy patrols through Ballymurphy and Beechmount. But like others in similar districts, she said that house searches by the army have steadily become less widespread and less rough in recent years – something few Sinn Féin supporters would volunteer so frankly.

Sinéad also recognised, as do many Northern Catholics, that Britain may want to leave but is in some difficulty. The recognition in itself undercuts old hatred. Even where the history of dispossession is visible to people in their own surroundings, contemporary political awareness forces out temptation to brood on the past.

PADDY DUFFY was an SDLP local councillor until 1993, though he has not been involved in party organisation for the past ten years. Tirelessly political, he invests most energy outside his business into the selection of projects for grants from the International Fund, set up in the wake of the Anglo-Irish Agreement with money from the USA, Canada, Australia and the European Community to pump-prime self-help and industrial development. In the mid-seventies he met loyalist paramilitaries and Unionist politicians to discuss the idea of independence for Northern Ireland.

'I never espoused the cause of independence for its own sake. It attracted me in that it got the British out. I must be on record as saying the British presence is the problem – John Hume objected to that as too simplistic. I think it has been, though. If they had said ten years ago, twenty years ago, that they would go, our problems by now would have been over. We'd have had some kind of a solution: for me it would mean a pluralist society here above all, not any kind of absorption into the South.

'I *would* be anti-British, in the sense that I look back. It's quite wrong, actually, and I know that well, to visit the wrongs of the past on the present population of Britain. But when I look at history and see people starving and these boys sitting with their sacks of corn and I see the amount of money that they've taken out of Ireland, landlordism, the Catholics living up in the bare Sperrins and down around Lough Neagh's shores [he laughs], you begin to think – that's what they've done to us. And of course that's the thing you've got to forget about. You have to say that's away in the past and nothing to do with the present British. And in that sense I can put it to the side.

'In the present, some of them have behaved very well. I think Edward Heath in power a bit longer would have faced up to the whole thing. And while I'd be critical of Thatcher on a lot of things, I think if she'd got a chance she might well have faced it. But the hunger strike – she couldn't be seen to concede. Major might be the type to do business in a positive way, maybe, rather than harping back...'

MYTHS AND EXPERIENCE

Going to live in England produces a variety of attitudes. It is common to hear Northerners – Protestant and Catholic – talking irritably about brothers or sisters developing English accents within months, and starting to lecture them on their 'bitterness'. Others who leave develop a stronger sense of Irishness.

DEIRDRE, forty-one, is a middle-ranking civil servant in London, left home in the Sperrins twenty years ago and talks with less and less conviction about 'coming home'. Her accent is as strongly Tyrone now as ever, and the attitudes towards Ireland of people she meets at work and outside it still perplex her. How she feels about Britain and the British is a subject of considerable heat: more exasperation, though, than dislike.

'It's all mixed up with my own ideas about identity. I know I felt Irish at the beginning of the Troubles, but that was really just anti-Britishness – in a very unreal way, not real British people. It was to do with things like the Black and Tans, what my parents told me. My mother was from Galway, she said they were thugs, they shot people indiscriminately, a child in a woman's arms, they burned whole villages. There was this whole picture: British justice, that was always mentioned, we were poor people, persecuted, the language stamped out. And religion: I remember an actual picture – maybe in a book or it might have been in an aunt's house – of the redcoats closing in round a Mass rock, a priest in the middle, people in ragged clothes and snow on the ground. And stories about priests in hiding with a price on their heads. Stories like that are very strong, what they invoke in you. We used to visit a cousin in the Glens and I remember going in a procession to the Mass rock at Cushendun. We walked... when I was very young, maybe four.

'If I had to choose I would still say I'm Irish, certainly. I just feel the Irish people are my people. But I don't have the same anti-Englishness, though I could still be provoked. Even the Troops Out Movement annoyed me. I wondered if they knew what they were doing. Generally, I'm more tolerant of British people than I used to be. I think they really don't understand us – it's as if there's a big difference in values, social behaviour etcetera.

'I think the British – the Scots and the Welsh as well as the English – they find Irish people very charming individually and I think they're nice for being charmed. But they're not very good at the nitty-gritty stuff, like responsibility for their soldiers and the RUC and the UDR and collusion and stuff like that. And what I think of as the 'big British political attitude' – I mean what governments do, their arrogance about Northern Ireland and generally getting on as though they're a major world power: that's hard to swallow and doesn't seem to square with the man in the street. I don't know where it comes from. Empire seems too long ago. Fear, maybe? Military considerations? It's all way beyond me. I notice British people are pretty anti-Europe too but I don't know where that fits in.

'The PTA [Prevention of Terrorism Act] and the cards you have to fill in at the airport annoy me but I'm almost used to it now. There's still something uncomfortable there. Ken Livingstone I really like because he's prepared to talk to them – Gerry Adams and so on. I really admire that attitude in this country where they're so goddam bigoted, not prepared to speak to them. There's no percentage in not speaking to people. I think Livingstone has integrity.

'Apart from him, and Clare Short, though I think of her as Irish really, British politicians I don't trust at all. But I'm not so keen to say Britain is the cause of all our woes any more. Some fault must lie with Ireland. It's a cop-out blaming Britain.'

Growing out of anti-Britishness for most people requires some thought about how to apportion blame for the present conflict and responsibility for moving on. Deirdre was brought up in a traditionally republican home and has been galled by the British refusal she meets to take any responsibility. She has been forced to the conclusion that blaming Britain is a 'cop-out', in part by a growing distaste for the IRA – but also by meeting Northern Protestants, in England, and becoming curious about Protestant attitudes. She still does not much enjoy admitting that there must be Irish faults in the relationship with Britain.

JIMMY, the 25-year-old former joyrider living in the lower Falls, went to England and worked on building sites when the IRA threatened to shoot him. Now unemployed, he would like to go back to school. He has started reading: books on the Troubles (Bobby Sands's prison diary, Martin Dillon's *The Shankill Butchers*) dealing with the recent past he was too young to understand. He separates in his mind what he feels about English people and Britain's involvement in Ireland.

'In London the people are too ignorant. You're Irish scum and that's it. Manchester and Liverpool they're more down to earth. I stayed in Manchester two years, went to London for eight months and then up to Liverpool. Scousers, they're something between the Irish and English, and most of England hates the Scousers too. I was in the hospital in London one night and someone had written on the toilet wall, "They should get all the Irish, put them in Liverpool and drop a nuclear bomb on it." And the Scousers when they were talking to you, there's like a bond, maybe because it was such a big port between Ireland and England. Some of them said, "What about the Troubles then?" – and you didn't want to talk in case there was any friction. But they said, "I understand, we shouldn't be in your country." They shouldn't. They've no right to be here. It's like when Iraq went into Kuwait and took it over, the whole world went out against them because it was wrong. It's not right, it's just dictatorship more or less. That's the way I look at it.

'But if they left now, I reckon there'd be a civil war.'

Views on Britain tend to heat up when people recall specific events in the course of the Troubles – the Falls curfew of 1970, internment, Bloody Sunday: the progressive transformation of British soldiers, in Catholic eyes, from welcome peace-keepers into the prop of Unionist government. Until his recent retirement from local government politics, 46-year-old college lecturer BRIAN FEENEY was the SDLP's most abrasive and most articulate Belfast representative. Brought up in a middle-class Andersonstown family with no interest in nationalism, on Bloody Sunday he was in England as a postgraduate student.

'It was in England that I became conscious of being Irish. I went there, the south of England, a very conservative bit, the August after the Falls Road curfew and stayed there for three years. And when Bloody Sunday happened I watched it on television, hardly slept that night, and I can remember very well going into the university the next day. In the staff common room, nobody wanted to talk. There was a certain amount of guilt. You're talking now about highly educated people,

English intellectuals, and there was guilt but they wanted to avoid the issue. That sticks in my mind as an example of being made to feel Irish.

'They resented the way it impinged on them. Internment didn't in the same way. Then the number of shootings and bombings in 1972, they were always asking for explanations and I was getting into rows with them – more and more I would know people involved or places where things had happened. By late '72, we decided we were coming back again, because we decided we didn't want to have English children. And we really didn't want to live in England any more.'

But it was the July 1970 army curfew in the lower Falls, an event that famously recruited hundreds to the IRA, that first made Feeney feel anger at British behaviour. Following an arms find in a house, soldiers were stoned: rioting spread, 3,000 troops poured into the area and General Sir Ian Freeland, from the air, ordered all residents to stay indoors while his soldiers began a house-to-house search.

'I just missed being inside the curfew zone – I drove through as soldiers straight up from the boat piled out of lorries putting on steel helmets and gas masks and blocked off the road. The supreme idiocy of Freeland in his helicopter flying over the place, over streets of tiny houses with no hot running water, a toilet at each end of the street as it was then – roaring instructions out of a loudspeaker to the people to put arms and weapons aside. Nobody could hear a word, there was mayhem. There was this real gut feeling of revulsion against the British army, it enraged people who wouldn't have been prepared normally to go and do things, like the women did who broke it in the end by just marching in from the upper Falls with food. And we certainly regarded it as the first fruit of a new Conservative government who weren't going to adopt this softie Labour line of conciliating these troublesome Catholics.'

TANKS AND GUNS

The British army, of course, for all that it became controversial within a few months of arrival on the streets, had never been a uniformly hostile or an unfamiliar organisation in Northern Catholic minds, to be equated in its entirety with government policy and British history in Ireland. Sinéad, the nurse tutor who supports the IRA with reservations, can still think of British soldiers as 'just an army'. Brian Feeney remembers that regularly in the early sixties some of the boys who failed the eleven-plus in his Andersonstown primary school went on to 'join the British army – which is what you did – when they got to be seventeen'. But in a comparatively short time, attitudes that were muddled and flexible set hard.

Even by the late summer of 1970 when the army had undoubtedly made itself unpopular, Catholics were not yet ready to support shooting them. DANNY MORRISON told Patrick Bishop and Eamonn Mallie, the authors of *The Provisional IRA* (London, 1988): 'The reaction would have been, "God Almighty, did we produce people who are capable of doing that?"'

At the time of the Falls curfew, Morrison was still at school doing A levels. Despite his family's close ties to the old IRA (his uncle Harry White was a locally famous 'forties man', one of the group arrested with Tom Williams, the only IRA man ever hanged in Northern Ireland, for killing an RUC man in 1942) – but the family disapproved of Morrison's growing involvement, as he described in a letter to me recalling changing attitudes.

'By June 1970 I was selling the first editions of *Republican News* from underneath my jerkin outside St Paul's chapel and hiding when I saw my da coming. At home meanwhile, I often had to share my bedroom with a British soldier who was courting one of my sisters. [Two sisters married soldiers.] Their Irish history started only a few months before and I'm sure they hadn't got a clue what I was talking about until four in the morning. I was very intense. I was appalled at how shallow their convictions were.' Morrison points out that 'they weren't based immediately locally – but one of my brothers-in-law stayed the occasional weekend until early 1971'.

Internment was introduced on 9 August 1971. On 30 January 1972, Bloody Sunday brought the IRA another surge of recruits and created an updated anti-Britishness in another generation. For SHEILA, then a young mother in Moyard, west Belfast, those years meant gradually developing strong anti-British-government feelings from a family background with no special place for Irishness or nationalism.

'My da would have seen himself as left-wing, a trade unionist, and it was him who talked politics to us. My mother stayed out of it, it was his business. The view in our house would have been that things Southern, whilst attractive in some ways, were a bit backward. English, British politics were important because there was a left-wing angle. There wasn't a sense of national identity or Irish nationalism. It was very much my da, being interested in British politics, talking about workers and bosses. We voted for Harry Diamond – Republican Labour, was it? I remember talk about the Northern Ireland Labour Party, and then voting for Paddy Devlin and Gerry Fitt.

'I was working, married young, had babies. The beginning of the civil rights movement passed me by. Internment though, that was a key moment, people being lifted around you. Suddenly this didn't seem removed at all. It was me and my community, people I knew, the army on the streets, barricades. I'd gone back to study by then, politics. The "break-down of society"!' She laughs. 'That was happening at the bottom of your estate. You started making connections then all right between Catholics, the state, and state oppression, seeing it that

way: the army coming in waves with their shields and their guns
and the kids at the barricades.

'And then Bloody Sunday... It was a lovely sunny day, there
was the elation of thousands of people on the march, I felt very
positive – then being caught in William Street with my sisters
who were forging ahead. I pulled them back, real coward, and
said let's stick with this priest, it'll be safer. Eddie Daly, it happened to be. Then heading back to a lorry and hiding under
it with Lord somebody or other, I've forgotten his name.
Everybody's story's the same of that day, of eventually getting
back to the Bogside and hearing the numbers dead, just the
shock of it.

'There was a fall of snow that night when we walked up the
Whiterock and the next day it was still lying. I remember looking out at the white, soldiers coming up the white street, and
opening the window and shouting at them. Screaming, cursing.
For me to have done that – I suppose that was political initiation
of a kind...'

A NEW DEAL?

Cardinal CAHAL DALY's emphasis has always been on British
responsibility towards Northern Ireland, rather than on their
sins of the past. The week after Bloody Sunday, as Bishop of
Ardagh and Clonmacnois he preached a sermon at a Mass for
the victims in St Mel's Cathedral, Longford (*Violence in Ireland*,
Dublin, 1973), in which he said that the British had been
warned repeatedly of the need for resolute action and radical
structural reforms:

> They did not listen. Will they listen now? Will they ever
> learn to take Irishmen seriously? Must there be tragedy
> piled upon Derry's tragedy before Britain's leaders learn
> that there is not a military solution, that there is now no
> alternative to a radical new deal for all Ireland?

He says now that Bloody Sunday was traumatic for large sections of the Republic, the British media and the British government.

'Since then they have conducted one of the most comprehensive studies and most perceptive analyses, which resulted in Sunningdale, and which recognised the anomalies in the Northern Ireland situation. That has, with some setbacks and some hesitations, formed the basis of British policy since up to and including Hillsborough and the Anglo-Irish Agreement. There has been a consistent thread: perhaps stronger on analysis than on prescription and on action. There is still a very great deal of thinking to be done. It is not easy for the British government – nor for the Irish government – to know where to go from here. But I think great progress has been made and it's going to be further encouraged by political developments in Europe itself, where Ireland and Britain have so much in common.'

Cardinal Daly habitually tries to find an optimistic concluding note – in this case an echo of the John Hume emphasis on Europe as a wider stage 'on which to soften the edges of sovereignty in the region of Northern Ireland', as one of Hume's associates puts it.

MÁIRÉAD is not disposed to be so charitable to Britain. Aged forty, born in north Belfast, it upsets her, she says, to realise that she is now more nationalistic than she was at eighteen. 'I would drive a harder bargain now.' She now sees the Northern Ireland state as beyond reform, a situation for which she thinks Britain should be held responsible. But she can still see the dilemma the British face.

'People don't have to be personally embittered to see that there is a real grievance. One of the things that's wrong and seductive about the new version of Irish history is this line: "If we could just clear our minds of these anti-British feelings then

nationalists could solve a lot of their problems more easily."
Now I doubt that. Sometimes it's been taken to extremes, the
types who blame the British if there's too much rain. But most
people don't feel like that.

'They do think it's a legitimate interpretation of history, their
personal history and the history of where they live, that sees a
great deal of responsibility for the current situation actually does
lie with the British government. Britain's not neutral, they're
not a referee, they acquiesced to lots of things. They may not
have been the active party: but they were the sovereign government between 1921 and . . . what were they *doing*?

'You don't have to go back to the Famine. Sure, grievance
does seem to form a large part of it, and grievance isn't the most
attractive emotion. But it won't do just to dismiss nationalism
as simply a product of an embittered people sitting around mut-
tering, "They took the land off our ancestors in 1609." It's more
real than that. Britain's not only a participating party. They're
the party with the most power, always have been. They're a
powerful, rich state.

'But I don't know how they withdraw, how they get out of
it, without leaving chaos. They'd have to disarm the RUC and
the UDR – the RIR – before they go – and I don't think you
could ask Protestants to face a situation, or any of us, if the
Provos were then left armed. And I don't know how you
would disarm the RUC. If you could answer that . . . that's been
a constant question for British policy, how can they, how could
they, at any point in the twentieth century, face up to the whole
question of unionist opposition, the whole unionist position. I
suppose you go back to 1912 [when unionists threatened to
fight to preserve British control of Ireland]. The problem was
that Britain let them arm in the first place.

'They're now committed to the unionists and from their
point of view I don't see how they can reasonably get out of

it. In many ways they're up a blind alley. I imagine they do want out. I don't see any sound reasons why they'd want to be here. There's certainly no economic reason – and no strategic reason any more. The only reasons are to do with Britain's political standing in the world. In turn that puts more pressure on them to maintain this moral high ground of "we are the referee": which in turn pushes them more and more up that same blind alley.'

Máiréad's views were particularly interesting because she first blamed Britain and then acknowledged what a problem the British face – should they ever decide to withdraw. As others did, she also found herself considering the relationship of nationalists with unionists in the middle of a discussion of attitudes towards Britain. Like a number of people, she admitted she was stumped by the question of how British withdrawal could be achieved without violence – the problem that some republicans have at last begun to consider seriously.

DEBATE

The question of British responsibility, and British intentions, has now become a focus of debate between the SDLP and Sinn Féin, and as such reflects much of the difference in how the two parties see contemporary Northern nationalist identity. On the SDLP side, John Hume has frequently outlined what he maintains is now a British policy of 'moving towards neutrality' and away from commitment to the Union, as evidenced by repeated statements from secretaries of state that Britain has no selfish interest in remaining and will agree to a united Ireland if in future a majority in Northern Ireland so decides. The British must still 'persuade' Protestant unionists that their future lies in an accommodation with the South and with Northern Catholics, Hume says. The argument – with its corollary that Protestant consent is essential for any future arrangements – is obviously central to

Hume's efforts to convince the IRA to stop.

Debate on the subject among republicans, a recent and tentative business, is difficult to follow and clearly slow to develop. It is, however, detectably under way. There has been some suggestion from republican sources that the first accounts of internal discussion caused concern in the IRA's lower ranks because they were 'garbled by the press as though debate was more advanced than is actually the case' – although it seems likely that concern was caused by the mere suggestion that any discussion was under way. After twenty-three years of fighting with the single demand for British withdrawal, the idea that Britain may not in fact be the enemy any longer is bound to be controversial.

MITCHEL MCLAUGHLIN is the republican strategist apparently most engaged in trying to work out a new approach to match the realisation, in at least some sections of the movement he belongs to, that Britain no longer has any selfish interest in staying in Northern Ireland. It was allegedly the incorrect reports of an article he wrote for an internal magazine that caused unrest in the ranks.

'I don't think the British can argue coherently they have a specific reason for staying. In fact I argued that, when they signed the Anglo-Irish Agreement, I submitted a paper to our party. It's a combination of factors now: their own view of themselves and advice maybe they're getting from governments like the Americans that they shouldn't give in to terrorism. Now that can become a hook. But if you're obviously interested in getting off that hook then I think you can come up with definitions that will allow people to talk to each other.

'Certainly, sections of the British establishment have an affinity with the unionist community, and feel they have an obligation to them. That may be a very sincerely held view to some of them, although I've never yet met one that convinced me that was their primary interest in Ireland. I think there is a genuine confusion in Britain about how they handle this situation. And one administration is as bad as another, we've found.

'There is no clear, single, cogent, well-stated reason why Britain's staying in Ireland. I don't think the Brits know why they're here beyond the fact they don't know how to get out of it. Our peace offensive has come out of that. We've addressed those arguments. We've indicated to them, if there's a hook that they're on, if they're pitched into a corner, then all they need to do is inform the republican movement that they need a bit of space to get out of that corner...

'The key political object is to get Britain to say – and they've come some distance to saying it – we've no interest in being here, strategically, politically, economically, if we could get these people to agree among themselves...

'But our problem is we're getting different and opposite signals. Peter Brooke was very adept at saying the reasonable thing but meanwhile we had SAS operations, he developed the whole repressive apparatus, labelled our supporters a terrorist community. At the same time we've had the loyalist onslaught, which the British certainly have a lot of lines into if they're not controlling it.'

MARY NELIS, a Derry council colleague of McLaughlin's, whose political beliefs owe much to the experience of supporting the prison protests that led to the 1981 hunger strike, cannot believe that the British no longer have selfish motives.

'What the IRA campaign is achieving in very simple terms is it's keeping the Irish problem on the British agenda. Do you see if it wasn't? We'd be wiped out of their minds, because as you know, it's not a big priority with British politicians here – the acceptable level of violence, and all that.

'I don't accept that the British have no interest here any more. I think they have a strong vested interest. They want to disengage, yes, but not before they have set up an Ireland north and south that's still going to serve capitalist interests. I also believe that if Ireland regains independence – and I don't mean a neo-colonial state – the Union might break up. And I think the British are acutely aware of that: that they might have a fragmented UK. Scotland and Wales might say, well we're different too and we want our autonomy.'

The contrast between Mary Nelis's views and Mitchel McLaughlin's is clearly not an isolated instance. While McLaughlin and other leading republicans have been dissecting British speeches, Danny Morrison has been in jail. For him there has been no appreciable movement, and the SDLP's policies have not helped.

'I couldn't believe it when John Hume told us at the talks we held with the SDLP in 1988 that the British were neutral! The British are unionists, and the IRA campaign is aimed at changing just that . . . Mayhew [the present secretary of state for Northern Ireland, Sir Patrick Mayhew] rejects articles Two and Three [of the Republic's constitution]. Douglas Hurd recently said that Dublin can have no sovereign say in the North. If they are neutral then they could begin by granting nationalists parity with unionists, allowing the nationalist community the same kind of relationship with Dublin that the unionists have in respect of the British guarantee to their citizenship and identity – joint authority/joint sovereignty. It's not Denmark or Russia that upholds the Union militarily, politically, financially, but Britain.

'Hume would argue that his party's strategy is a low-risk one whereas ours is high-risk. I believe that the SDLP's stance from Sunningdale onwards has encouraged the British to toy with the idea that an internal settlement is possible – although the SDLP position may have undergone a shift with their recent proposals that Dublin be given an executive role in the North. This stance has protracted the conflict more than the refusal of the IRA to lay down its arms . . .

'Meanwhile the IRA believes it has no alternative but to press on and bring British public opinion to push their government to change policy. It can only be stopped when the British objective in Ireland is establishing "peace with justice" – which isn't necessarily the same thing as a thirty-two-county unitary state.

'The only chance of a section of unionism giving an inch will be when Britain changes its policy and puts a question mark over the Union.'

There may still be considerable republican unwillingness to credit Britain with any degree of benevolent neutrality on Northern Ireland. But when prominent figures begin to agree with British secretaries of state, as though repeating the orthodoxy of years, that they no longer believe Britain is chiefly motivated by self-interest, some movement is clearly under way. The arrival of concepts like shared authority or sovereignty between Britain and Ireland, and admissions that the future need not necessarily be in the shape of a unitary Irish state – something other leading republicans have also said – suggest that the painfully slow process of intermittent discussion between Sinn Féin and the SDLP has at least introduced a new flexibility to the traditionally terse language of republican 'demands'.

BRITS IN

Northern Catholic attitudes towards Britain may in many cases have been broadened and blunted by awareness of the difficulties British governments face. From the self-centredness of middle-class Catholics flattered by Northern Ireland Office invitations, to the war-weary who are willing to believe that the British would go if they could but who wish they would show more humility and self-criticism in the meantime, there are few remnants of the old dogmatism. But tentative and contradictory debate in a comparatively narrow circle of republican leaders is a long way from the sort of gut emotion necessary to shift a movement sworn to the crude slogan 'Brits Out'.

Constitutional nationalists have on the contrary worked hard to achieve a British presence that no longer identifies with unionism, however inconsistently and erratically that might be demonstrated by government officials – a 'Brits In' programme. Former taoiseach Garret FitzGerald, who helped negotiate the Anglo-Irish Agreement, maintains in his autobiography (*All in a Life,* Dublin and London, 1991) that following the collapse of the power-sharing executive in 1974:

> John Hume believed that a British withdrawal scenario with consequences for the island as a whole could be pre-empted by a commitment by the two governments to work together to establish new agreed institutions together with a British undertaking to remain in Northern Ireland until these were established. In the meantime others on the SDLP side wanted us to prepare contingency plans for a withdrawal and to discuss them with the British. We refused, however, as this would give the British the excuse they might perhaps want to get out of Northern Ireland, and it was our clear policy to avoid this at all costs.

FitzGerald goes on to recall his own 1974 comment to the visiting Henry Kissinger that in the event of the unlikely, he hoped, 'shift in British policy towards withdrawal from Northern Ireland in advance of an agreed political solution, we would then seek US assistance in persuading Britain not to embark on a course of action that could be so fraught with dangers not just to Northern Ireland but to the whole of Ireland, and conceivably even . . . to the wider peace of North-Western Europe'.

For years now, first as SDLP deputy leader and since 1979 as leader, JOHN HUME has been defining what Britain's role in Northern Ireland should be.

'I've described them as moving into a *more* neutral position on the question of Irish unity. I've often been interpreted as saying Britain is now neutral on Northern Ireland. I was very specific – I said they'd moved into a more neutral position on the question of Irish unity because they said Irish unity is a matter of those who want it persuading those who don't and we, the British, have no position on it. Whereas I think what we need from them is for them to have a position, to join the ranks of the persuaders. I want them to say the divisions that we see in Ireland are to be regretted by everybody, because everybody's paid a very high price, particularly the people of the North, and that Britain would like to see those divisions healed by agreement and by respect for difference, and would use its resources to create the atmosphere in which that feeling of respect would take place. While they're doing that, they should be part of ensuring that whatever institutions are on the ground operate on a basis of total fair play to both. What I'm against is the Provo view of a sudden British withdrawal – because I think that would leave us in a terrible mess which might never be resolved: a high risk of a Lebanon, a Beirut. Nobody's entitled to take that risk.

'What we want is everybody using resources in a peaceful way, healing the divisions. The shape and form that healing takes, or that unity takes, is for agreement between the different sections of the Irish people. At the end of that process, what I see . . . is an Ireland in which both parts have agreed on how they live together, and will also agree on how they give expression to what I'm now describing as their unique relationship with Britain – because it will all be in the context of a Europe in which those relationships are being pooled anyway. We now live in a pooled-sovereignty Europe . . .'

In this scheme of things, I asked, how long would the British link last for?

'I haven't thought deeply about what the nature of the link with Britain should be,' Hume said. 'But I do believe part of the settlement of the Irish people agreeing on their living together would be them agreeing what their relationship with Britain should be as well. Over centuries, the enormous exchange of population between the two islands, the special relationship . . . if it helps resolve the internal divisions of Ireland, it's one we should look at.'

After so many years when Irish nationalists have murdered and died to 'break the British connection', a calm statement by a leader of nationalist opinion that the link should stay is surely remarkable however he has already reinterpreted nationalism – though Hume would no doubt maintain that in this, as in so much else, he is merely reflecting reality. No matter how he underplays it, the commendation of an attempt to institutionalise the special nature of the Irish-British relationship is certainly a measure of how far he feels opinion has already shifted. It is hardly surprising that republicans are only beginning to face up to the implications of regarding Britain in a new light. In spite of prolonged tension in a state of low-level but bitter war, the signs are that attitudes to Britain have already changed considerably. Adjusting to the idea of a permanent, voluntary connection may for some take a little longer.

Northern Catholics' attitudes towards Britain have undoubtedly shifted further as they witness Protestant 'alienation' inflamed by the spectacle of a minority in the ascendant, and above all by the assertions of successive secretaries of state that Britain now has no inalienable commitment to the Union. Increased confidence and status have done nothing to alter the conviction that Catholics will only prosper when Protestants are humbled. The unionist complaint that the strategy of John

Hume and Northern constitutional nationalism has 'destabilised' the Northern Ireland state, essentially by driving a wedge between them and Britain, reassures SDLP supporters and disorients some Sinn Féiners. There must be the makings of a bad joke, however, in the fact that while nationalists relish unionist uncertainty about British loyalty and chalk it up as a gain, some unionists have steadily gathered support to nationalist disadvantage – south of the border.

7

'I don't like their attitudes'

THE SOUTH

'My da talks about "the North" and "the South",' an eighteen-year-old Falls Road girl said. 'Until last year I didn't know what it was the North of. I always thought it was just Northern Ireland, that was its name.'

A sizeable number of those I interviewed, especially the youngest, have never known anything about the South: have learned nothing about its geography or history in school, have parents who know little more than they do, never go there. Others imagined they were in tune with Southerners and now realise they were wrong. There were some who know the place well, have an acute sense of the way Southern society is developing and make no easy judgements, a few who insist that people in the Republic have more fellow feeling for Northern Catholics than Southern media or politicians suggest; a large number who fear that a gulf has opened and is growing. Many detect less Southern sympathy for Northern nationalists than for unionists. This strikes them as fundamentally improper, and yet predictable: although few quoted specific examples from the past, they had inherited a powerful sense of betrayal and rejection by the Southern state. It does not surprise them that the state's Radio Telefís Éireann (RTE) should lionise the Ulster Unionist MP Ken Maginnis, choose to present soft-centred, off-duty portraits of Rhonda and Ian Paisley Junior, and play down loyalist killings of Catholics while emphasising the sectarian aspect of IRA killings – as RTE style throughout much of the Troubles has been widely interpreted.

Over the past five years unhappiness about the drift of Southern sympathies has centred on the argument about articles Two and Three of the Republic's constitution, which assert the right of the Dublin government to jurisdiction over the whole of Ireland while stating the exclusion of Northern Ireland from effective jurisdiction 'pending the reintegration of the national territory'. This has been variously described as a 'sleight of hand . . . [which] demonstrates the de Valera habit of squaring rhetorical circles' (Roy Foster, *Modern Ireland 1600–1972*, London, 1988), and 'an example of de Valera's masterly word-juggling – while seeming to claim the North it actually gave formal recognition to partition' (Michael Farrell, *Northern Ireland: The Orange State*, London, 1976).

The present controversy sharpened when a group of Ulster Unionists secured a judgment in a Dublin court that interpreted the articles as a 'constitutional imperative' on the Southern state to seek the 'reintegration of the national territory' – that is, the annexation of Northern Ireland. The case was launched in protest against the Anglo-Irish Agreement's recognition of an Irish government right to consultation on Northern Ireland affairs. Skilful Unionist lobbying of influential Dublin opinion, depicting the articles in the light of the court judgment as an aggressive claim on Northern Ireland territory, helped focus a small but significant spread of Southern sympathy: the cheerful, gregarious Ulster Unionists Ken Maginnis and Chris McGimpsey became popular figures in some Dublin

circles. 'Too much Ken Maginnis and not enough Belfast city
council,' a Northern nationalist politician told a Dublin
newspaper drily, calculating the effect on Southern opinion-
makers of exposure to the most congenial voices in unionism
without the corrective experience of seeing and hearing
unreconstructed supremacism and sectarianism in the shape of
Belfast's dominating Unionist councillors.

In the South, cross-party support has stayed constant for the
Anglo-Irish Agreement's formulation of a Southern role on the
North – described sarcastically by one SDLP man as suiting the
Republic perfectly: 'a way of being involved without being
responsible'. But the reservation that the agreement infringed
unionists' rights, expressed most strikingly by the present Irish
president, Mary Robinson, who resigned from the Labour Party
in protest, has begun to attract attention. The idea of a new
agreement attractive to unionists as well as to nationalists has
taken root in the South.

As Unionists steadily elevated the articles to the status of a
major impediment to compromise on their part, Southern
opinion has become more vocal in their support. The process
has unnerved some Northern nationalists: the once-despised articles have developed fresh significance. Even people with only
the vaguest idea of what they say have begun to express concern
that the South may bargain them away in some future deal with
Unionists. What was once regarded with derision as a word-
splitting but unmistakable 'recognition of partition' has come to
be regarded as a pledge of solidarity with Northern nationalists,
the definitive statement that they constitute an integral part of
the nation – a nation that de Valera's 1937 constitution took
care never to define.

But there are, of course, Northern Catholics who are only
nationalist 'in shorthand terms', as one put it: brought up
Catholic and deemed to share aspirations towards a united

Ireland until they declare otherwise. Catholics who support the Alliance Party do not share this growing unease about the lack of Southern solidarity: they are more likely to express the hope that new Southern sympathy might encourage Unionists to reconsider their refusal to contemplate sharing political power in Northern Ireland.

There are also those with no strong feelings about the Republic: who see it solely as a rest-and-recreation centre, or who never think of the South at all. After initial hesitation and ritual declarations that this did not mean they felt any less Irish, most of those I interviewed said the South was a mystery to them, and launched into observations as though of a foreign country. A number in their thirties and forties disliked what they saw as the dominant Catholic conservatism – but they were also intrigued by the state's complexity and liked the people. Three spoke of a country they felt part of, finding explanations for Southern attitudes towards Northerners, voicing warmth and clear-eyed assessment.

Those with no qualms about expressing dislike for the Republic, and for Southern attitudes, are the totally ignorant young – and republicans, who see no contradiction in maligning Southerners and damning the 'Free State', as most still call it – though it constitutes the territory they are fighting to be unified with. Unification, after all, would in republican theory sweep away the present Republic and presumably unsound Southern attitudes, as well as the present state of Northern Ireland.

Those who had always believed that some day Ireland would be united – and who can no longer sustain their faith – were the saddest, the most reluctant to admit their lack of affinity with present-day Southerners. Anti-Northern-nationalist, 'neo-Unionist' views are blamed by politicians and non-politicians alike on a small, unrepresentative but well-placed media/ academic/upper-middle-class clique: 'revisionists', in shorthand, or 'Dublin 4', the affluent postal district that houses embassies, RTE, and a large share of leading politicians and media people, and has now given its name to a caricature of its inhabitants.

On a good day, reluctantly realistic Northerners can see hundreds of thousands out there beyond Dublin 4, at one with them in spirit, all Irish in the same way, one people. The rest of the time the knowledge of plain indifference and widespread dislike seeps through. Disgust and a feeling of shame at IRA atrocities explain some of this. But the loyalist bombings in Dublin and Monaghan, which killed thirty-three people in May 1974, have also left a deep mark in Southern consciousness. The attack came three days into the loyalist workers' strike in Northern Ireland, which brought down the power-sharing executive – the joint focus of loyalist wrath was the proposal for a Southern role in Northern affairs through a Council of Ireland. Timed to explode at rush hour in busy shopping streets, the Dublin and Monaghan bombings caused terror: the death and destruction they brought have never been equalled in Southern experience of the Troubles, and the death toll remains the highest for any terrorist action in Britain or Ireland. For much of the past twenty years, however, they have been scarcely mentioned in Southern society except by relatives of the dead – it is hard to avoid the impression of an attempt to blank out the experience. In the immediate aftermath of the bombings, a leading loyalist spokesman said that Southerners had laughed at the suffering the IRA caused: 'But we're laughing now.'

Fear of loyalist reprisals is commonly suggested by Northern Catholics as reason enough for Southerners' distance. That seventy years of partition substantially contributed to different priorities and consequent lack of empathy is harder to admit. It is as though the admission would confer legitimacy on the border and the Northern state by confirming that they have, in fact, split one people in two.

Part of the irritation Northern Catholics now undoubtedly feel towards Southerners is caused by having to stop and consider for the first time what for decades was taken as a fact of life. The South was neglectful, forgetful, not all that interested, true: but the people were 'your own'. Attitudes to the South are not lightly placed on record. People preferred to talk about what they took to be Southern opinions of Northerners, even though those were unpleasant, rather than about their own feelings. Those who were best informed became passionate about one aspect alone: revisionism. Not the academic business of re-examining history, 'revisionist' was instead used angrily to mean 'anti-Northerner' in general and 'Indo-Unionists' in particular – the likes of Conor Cruise O'Brien, Eamon Dunphy, John Bruton, John A. Murphy. 'Indo-' as in the *Irish Independent*, in which O'Brien, Dunphy and Murphy are columnists who have variously identified nationalism, and Northern nationalists, as the most intractable political problem facing the Irish state, and John Hume as singularly guilty because he so influences Southern political opinion. What 'anti-Northerner' means here is 'anti-Northern-nationalist'. The blanket sympathy for unionism which accompanies much of the criticism of Hume is seen as essentially ill-informed, or wilfully ignorant. Rage crosses most boundaries of class and political affiliation. There is little to distinguish the loathing expressed by upwardly mobile lawyers and SDLP politicians from that of Sinn Féin leaders.

The idea of oneness with the people of the South has always been important, but questions have always lurked, just below the surface. The Troubles have meant public confrontation with those questions. At its simplest, the South has lost its chief attraction for Northern nationalist Catholics, the illusion that it was 'home', a friendly, non-Unionist refuge just a few miles down the road where you could 'be yourself' – in the long-lost pre-Troubles days when being yourself was an entirely unselfconscious business. A middle-aged County Tyrone man, not particularly political, who has wavered between voting Alliance, SDLP and not voting at all, summed up his sense of loss with some emotion: 'It used to be that you just drove straight over the border and shouted, up the IRA. There was a great sense of freedom. That's not there any more.'

He was talking about shouting 'Up the IRA' at a time when the IRA barely existed – the gesture meant defiance towards the detested Northern state and a delight at homecoming rather than support for guns and bombs. The IRA has changed: and so, at last undeniably, has the relationship between Southern and Northern Catholics. It pains Northerners to contemplate the fact that the strains are not new. The South has been a sore place in the Northern nationalist soul for a long time.

THE PAST

To anyone who was alive when the Northern state was formed, or born soon after, Southern attitudes have always been a disappointment best left unexamined. In a way the latest wave is easier to deal with than the memory of separation, abandonment by the new Irish state, and decades of neglect by Dublin governments and Dáil politicians, broken up by election time bursts of heated rhetoric about reunification.

The academic Clare O'Halloran in *Partition and the Limits of Irish Nationalism* (Dublin, 1987), charts the contradictions in Southern government attitudes towards Northern nationalist representatives as a mixture of 'resentment and guilt' and the rapid growth of a wish to see and hear as little as possible of them. As the most telling, symbolic example of 'haste to divest themselves of the embarrassing burden of the northern minority', she describes a moment midway through the Dáil debate in 1925 on the boundary agreement – which ratified the final position of the border:

A deputation of Northern nationalists requested permis-
sion to address the assembled Dail. The Ceann Comhairle
[Speaker] was unsure of procedure . . . and left it up to the
House. McGilligan and Cosgrave objected even to the
question of procedure being debated. Cosgrave further
objected on the grounds of creating dangerous precedents:
'An occasion may arise in future in which some of our
own citizens for whom we have a direct responsibility,
may have a case if a precedent has been made in respect
of those for whom we only act as trustees.' Cosgrave's
objections were not challenged in any way, and the
deputation was sent away unheard. The nationalist
minority was thus told, in effect, to address their deputa-
tions to the northern assembly in the future.

Michael Farrell's *Northern Ireland: The Orange State* (London,
1976) describes how in 1951 four Northern Anti-Partition
League MPs and two Nationalist senators at Stormont 'sought
admission to the Dail as elected representatives of part of the
national territory . . . they were refused'.

Northerners reacted to this kind of treatment in various ways.
For older Catholics like the Belfast lawyer PADDY MCGRORY
and JIM, the retired academic in Newcastle, County Down,
there were very different personal adjustments to make. The
declaration of the Republic in 1948 for Jim meant that
Southerners had finally decided the shape of their future state,
and that Northern Catholics would have to come to terms with
the state of Northern Ireland. 'It was the biggest watershed in
my own life. I was in Dublin, at a GAA meeting. They were all
celebrating and I felt very emotional. I went home by myself
and went to bed – it had nothing to do with me. They weren't
thinking about us in the North at all. I think that was when I
decided I might as well try to make something of living in this
place.'

With considerable misgivings, he began to look for wider work experience, more responsibility, and promotion, in jobs that were effectively controlled by the Unionist government. Born in Newry of parents from Tipperary, he had until then been content to take his cue from their total conviction that the Northern state could not last.

Paddy McGrory was brought up on the Falls Road in a similar belief. An all-Catholic childhood world prevented any sense of isolation: his non-political parents referred to 'Northern Ireland' only in passing, as irrelevant and unreal. It was only when he went to Queen's University and began to make friends in what was then a predominantly Protestant student body, that he realised he was living in a British state.

'I went back into my own identity in some confusion, I think, at this revelation that I was surrounded by people among whom I was in a minority, who shared nothing that I had grown up with. After that, what sustained people in those days – I think to some extent it was the feeling of separateness from their own brethren, that they felt the wish to retain this identity. It became very strong in them.

'On every nationalist occasion from St Patrick's Day to Easter week you had politicians thundering from the backs of lorries all over the country about the reuniting of Ireland and their separated brethren and all that – it was heady stuff. They only half meant it, if they meant it at all. But it was accepted as gospel by the generation that grew up in the thirties and forties. I'm sceptical now – but I wasn't then. It was largely the republicans who were sceptical. There were half a dozen guys sitting down there in the lower Falls saying, "Rubbish, we've heard all this before."

'But I went to Dublin feeling a great pride that this was our capital. I would have listened to those Easter speeches and believed... The average nationalist identified with all that, that they really cared about us.

'It was important. Without it, I don't know what would have happened. Either you would have been driven into the arms of the IRA, or you would have become so disillusioned as to say, "Oh well, if that's the way it is, let's *be* British, at least we'll get a job out of it." It had a greatly sustaining effect on Northern nationalism.'

What Paddy McGrory describes as the main effect of separation – a strengthened desire to be identified with the separated – lies underneath many of the most pained attitudes towards the South. A sizeable number want to be recognised as the separated who are equally Irish, whose deprivation and determination to maintain their identity deserves special credit. Those who grew up in the fifties in mainly Catholic environments recall the conviction, more or less openly expressed, that the North's special circumstances required a superior calibre of nationalism: that Northerners – and in this usage, the term clearly excluded Protestants – exhibited a self-evidently truer, stronger, finer Irishness, because it had survived a hostile environment. 'The North began, the North held on, God Bless the Northern man': the refrain of a Thomas Davis verse, written to infuse nineteenth-century rebels with a sense of inherited nationalism, was a popular invocation.

It was clear that MARGARET, eighty, and living in a small mid-Ulster Protestant town, did not enjoy discussing 'the South'. Her mature conclusions on Southern attitudes were terse, understated, and echoed the opinions of several others.

'I never thought of myself as being part of Northern Ireland. When you went across the border, you felt you were in a different atmosphere, relaxed, at home. But now, when I go visiting the South, some of my friends, they don't want to know about the North. They don't want to know us.

'At the outset they wouldn't have been so antagonistic as they are now. You could see the attitude change as the Troubles went on – it started to be "Keep it away from us." I don't think they're worried at all about nationalism. I think it's only the Northerners who are worried about nationalism. Although, mind you, I don't know how much the South ever cared. Before the Troubles I used to think they were quite happy, they weren't worried about us. They didn't show an interest in discrimination, did they? Not a bit.

'I don't think of the Irish government as my government. I think they're afraid to do anything – they're sitting back and waiting for Britain to do something. And some Southerners are just so anti, they don't seem to understand us at all. But then how many of them ever came up here, on holidays or anything?'

ANOTHER COUNTRY?

This last observation was a common theme. Some Catholics clearly resent the fact that Southerners appear to have absorbed too well what was a common Northern nationalist depiction of the state of Northern Ireland as repressed, joyless, dominated by puritan Protestantism. But that was broadcast when Northern Catholics imagined that the South saw them as their own separated brethren, captive in an alien and dour regime. It is perhaps a case of being tarred by your own brush: worse yet, Northern nationalists now find they are blamed by Southerners as having themselves contributed to the intolerance and un- fairness of this dislikable state. The articulate Southern lobby that charges Northern nationalists with sectarianism and general bloody-mindedness – and which implicitly commends their own greater tolerance and flexibility – has provided a sharp political focus for the more diffuse and many-sided Southern dislike of Northerners, and an equally sharp focus for Northern disquiet about the South.

That disquiet is not voiced publicly, where Unionists,

Protestants, might hear, and is not often well thought-out or founded on first-hand knowledge. The controversy over abortion and whether the Republic should legislate against any provision or rely on a constitutional amendment caused ripples and highlighted a number of facets of Southern life: the abortion referendum stirred deep unease right across the spectrum of Northern Catholic opinion. Conservatives dislike Southern liberal, feminist, secularist trends. A County Down grocer, sixty-seven, has warm memories of trips to Clones, County Monaghan, for GAA Ulster finals just after the Second World War, with rationing still in force in the North: 'Apart from the match and the excitement of the game itself, the other great thing was the cooked ham you got.' But now, he says, some of his friends from the South 'give me the puke – I don't expect them to be Catholic-Catholic, but they have for a long time now had this lounge bar society. Materialistic. Like the Gay Byrnes of this world, they have an answer for everything.' What annoys him most is that some on visits North stay with Protestant friends, 'and they don't bother themselves to go to Mass, although the people they stay with would gladly get them the times in the local church'.

The more liberal Northern Catholics, including the many who are no longer 'practising' Catholics, were shocked during the debates on abortion and divorce by the mobilisation of Southern conservative opinion with Catholic clerical support. But neither camp is keen to see such opinions come out in the open, where unionists can get at them. Long years of defensiveness against constant unionist denigration of a poor, priest-ridden South are not easily shaken off. First, and instinctively, most are reluctant to help make a Unionist case. But the abortion debate in particular brought a growing, dismayed realisation that the renewed spectacle of dogmatic and intolerant Catholicism dictating the course of the Southern state does not sit easily with arguments for a new and pluralist Ireland.

HUGH, in his late fifties and brought up on the Tyrone-Monaghan border, considers himself a traditional nationalist and 'fairly conservative Catholic'. He has changed and he believes his adult children are changing even faster.

'All I knew as a kid was that what we belonged to was the South. Portrush was farther away in our heads than Tralee or Galway. You went to Salthill, Killorglin on your holidays. But my kids don't feel like that, and I'm beginning to see it like they do. There'll be dealing about any future all-Ireland arrangement, and the deal might shock the Republic.

'What's bringing this home to *me* now is the discussion of abortion that's taking place in the South and the hypocrisy that's expressed there. It *is* a problem: morally wrong, there's no doubt about that. But it's a fact of life, and it can't be ignored by passing it on to England. I can't square the horror at killing the unborn and the complete lack of sympathy for the murder of the living that's going on up here. That's starting to make Catholic people – like me – not as close to the South as we would have been. We've been disillusioned by the South. They'd eventually take us – but they're making no plans to face up to the pluralist society that we would be demanding.'

Hugh was untypically open. Others 'supposed' the abortion referendum undermined arguments for any kind of unification, but hurriedly pointed to Protestant conservatism in social morality as some kind of mitigation. Southern conservatism need not be a barrier to closer links, they suggested. The most disconcerted were women in their thirties, forties and fifties who saw the whole Southern argument as worrying confirmation that the Republic was in some ways a less attractive society than Northern Ireland, even though they all still saw the North as fundamentally anti-Catholic. But some of these were also the people who were most open in admitting that they rarely thought about it at all – that the South was another country.

COLETTE is from a strongly republican part of south Derry, and grew up thinking of the South as 'the rest of the nation of Ireland – in fact you didn't have to think about it, you were part of it. Dublin was your capital. The unionists, God help them, imagined Belfast was a capital city.' She repeats this early creed now with a rolling of eyes.

A number of her sisters and brothers joined the IRA: three served long jail sentences. Colette 'thought long and hard' and joined the SDLP because 'it looked like it could make a difference'. She dropped out some time ago when she decided the party made little effort in the most deprived city areas, and that in any case, no political solution was possible. She is now forty-four, and the reality of the South as she now sees it has clearly affected her thinking. It is not a state she likes or understands, which makes it more difficult for her to define her sense of national identity.

'Though we go down often – I've a sister living near Drogheda – I don't know if I understand the South. Ireland seems to me a very funny concept at the moment, maybe because of what has happened in the North. In European terms a lot has happened there that hasn't happened here. You can see the money, nicer houses. But then I read about the level of emigration, and I haven't a clue what that means. Is that corrupt government, or can it really not be helped?

'I still see myself as Irish but I may not define Irishness in the same way. I hope this thing that is Ireland will congeal in some suitable form. But just as much as any Protestant I'm absolutely certain I don't want a united Ireland if it means Northern Ireland being absorbed into Southern Ireland ... because of their laws, attitudes to a whole lot of things. I certainly don't conceive of myself as being British. But it's irrational, it's incoherent, my Irishness, because of this.

'I suppose I would like to see Ireland as a whole a better,

more prosperous, more easily lived-in place and I suppose that it really can't be, fully, until the problems are resolved here. I can see everybody has awful traumas: people born into the Protestant tradition but who don't support the UDA any more than I would ever support the IRA – and who are just as confused about Britain as I am about the South. People have awful traumas about coming to terms with where they fit. Basically, I suppose, they just want to live a decent, reasonably prosperous life: and that their views, and them as people, will be respected.'

Much of Colette's confusion about the South was shared by those closest to her in age, many other women and a number of men: shock at the apparent complacency about emigration, dislike of what many saw as a more extreme gap between rich and poor than in the North, and of the South's social legislation. In three ways she was unusual. She visited the South regularly and had a close relative living there. Her attitudes seemed entirely independent of Southern attitudes towards Northern nationalists: and she thought there were implications for her sense of identity – something others did not see, or did not want to think about.

MÁIRÉAD, four years younger and from north Belfast, votes SDLP with great reluctance, as the most acceptable way open to her of registering an anti-Unionist vote. When she describes herself as more nationalist now than at the start of the Troubles, it emerges that this is because she thinks that if it remains British, Northern Ireland will always be dominated by Unionists, and will therefore be an unsafe place for Catholics. Like many others, she visits the South as a holidaymaker, and talks about it as a foreign country.

'In common with many Northerners, I know almost nothing about the South. The extent of our ignorance and our lack of understanding of Southern politics is actually appalling, and I'm as guilty as anybody. Every now and then I buy Dublin newspapers to try and find out what the hell's going on – but I don't understand. So when Albert Reynolds says: "I can do business with the Unionists", I'm left thinking, who's he talking for? What does he mean? I can't believe he really knows about the North. Things like the territorial claim, articles Two and Three, it's a piece of paper to the South. People here would be upset to see it going – but what does it mean to Southern governments?

'We go regularly to Donegal and there are some hilarious conversations. People say, "I've never been in Belfast." But half their relatives live in Scotland, they go back and forth to it all the time through the North. There's a minibus nearly every day between Burtonport and Larne – that's their connection, Larne–Stranraer. Straight through, they don't stop.

'They assume you're Protestant until they know otherwise, so they don't offend you. Then if they see you going to Mass they make remarks about politics, after a fashion. They say it's awful, and they want to offer you sympathy. But whereas many Northerners feel this is our country too, that's not their feeling. We are, definitely, tourists, visitors. Welcome, yes – but that sense that a lot of people from here would have of wanting to stake a claim and say, I'm not just an outsider – you can just imagine them saying hard luck.'

Máiréad has a detached, unemotional way of listing the deficiencies in the relationship between Northern and Southern nationalists: an awareness that ignorance is mutual, and that this has potentially damaging consequences for Northern nationalists. She also has a sharper grasp than many who are similarly detached of the stronger feelings of others: the 'wanting to stake a claim'. Her own awareness that she is ignorant about the state seems to have neutralised long ago any personal feeling of disappointment about Southern unwillingness to claim kinship or to offer closer involvement.

Others are even more dispassionate. STEPHEN, an ex-priest who now lives in London, has thought for years about the attitudes he saw developing among his parishioners in a deprived mid-Ulster urban area. They became steadily more republican, he says, and so did he. But it was a republicanism that had nothing to do with closeness to the real South. Few of them had any contact with it: no cars, no urge to see Connemara or Kerry. He was one of the many who saw the South as primarily a holiday haven for the better-off, expensive and unwelcoming. His own feelings have never had much to do with his political ideas, and he is inclined to believe this was true for others.

'I feel much more comfortable in London than I am in Dublin. Some people say, "I get a great sense of freedom going to Dublin." I don't. I get a kind of sad and sorry feeling. It's that Catholic ethos unbridled, all the conservative elements together. No black people, a very white city. I'm just happier in London. What I saw growing round me – it's not so much nationalism, it was more a political reaction to the experience of imperialism. Why should that be a nationalist reaction? It doesn't have to be. Why should it have anything to do with the South?'

Stephen, however, if pushed, and largely on the strength of an undiminished admiration for the 1916 leader James Connolly, calls himself a republican socialist. So does the 36-year-old Belfast IRA man I interviewed, who thinks, in true traditionalist republican style, that the South is a 'more vicious state than the North.' The executions of IRA members in the Southern state's first two decades are commemorated as meticulously by republicans as any by Britain, but with an extra edge of bitterness. Southern coldness towards Northern nationalists for this IRA man is simply another reminder of how urgently republican victory is needed in the South, as in the North. Victory would clearly mean sweeping away the Southern state,

something republicans choose not to emphasise in public any
longer because it does them further damage in the South.
Unlike the Sinn Féin people I talked to, the IRA man did not
insist that the bulk of the South is in truth pro-republican,
simply distracted by censorship and the effects of partition. Nor
did he suggest that he liked Southerners, or thought of them as
the same people as himself.

'Reunification will be a liberating thing on both sides of the
divide. There's an intellectual poverty in the South as a result
of partition, a crisis within what should pass for the intelligentsia
because of the Northern conflict. The worst spewing by academics is all revisionist – all because of the state's own need for
preservation.

'Sometimes in the South, I can go in for a pint, I'm anonymous, and I join in conversations. People become uncomfortable. The Northern accent brings discomfort, a Catholic
Northerner more so. If it's a unionist, they fall back: "We don't
really dislike you." But to come in contact with Northern
nationalists means confronting the realities of the situation.
There's this cop-out of pretending that there are no Northern
nationalists.

'Conservatism is the dominant force in the South. The Sticks'
[Workers' Party] experiment with working-class politics, parlia-
mentarianism, that left a void in what should pass for the left.
I thought the Greens would do better. Political allegiance in the
South is very much internal to the twenty-six counties.'

Once the contempt about 'spewing' academics was under
control, his tone was distant, almost scholarly. Then I asked
where he saw Southern attitudes tending.

'There may have been twenty years of revisionism, but some
people in the South still know the Brits are bastards. Strong
Fianna Fáil supporters are happy to keep massive amounts of
weapons for you.'

There are moments when opinions about the South and Southerners – not just from this IRA man – sound uncannily like the line republicans once rattled off on unionists and the Protestant community in general: that yes, there is indeed a considerable gap at the moment, strong and possibly mutual dislike, but when Britain declares an intent to withdraw this will melt away in the dawn of a new realism, a new Ireland. In the last couple of years some republicans have made tentative efforts to begin revising that confident assertion about Protestants. But for them, and for others, there is no sign of a rethink on their attitude to Southerners.

For many Northerners, however, dogma has dissolved into confusion. What they feel is one thing: increasing and mutual dislike and discomfort. Colette expressed most sharply what others fumbled: that she felt she was being incoherent and irrational about her Irish identity in not understanding the South, in experiencing 'awful traumas . . . about where [I] fit'. It was a sense of dislocation common to many. Brought up to yearn for the greater part of their nation on the other side of an imaginary, arbitrary line on the map, they now feel little more than lack of sympathy with the inhabitants of another country.

THE BORDER

To Northern Catholics who live along the border from Derry to Warrenpoint, however, the state a few miles down the road or on the far side of the next field is clearly not different, or foreign. Those on the other side are not 'Southerners'. Clones, Monaghan, Dundalk, Letterkenny are where you shop and socialise and perhaps work, where cousins live. You cross the border every day to feed cattle, in some cases every time you go to the bottom of the field behind the house. In the shape of parishes mapped out long before the border, and in the routines of country living, the sense of a community broken up by a

political decision is still strong. The business of border living is
for many a daily demonstration of the nonsense of partition –
and for everyone an illustration of the ambivalence in Northern
Catholics towards the South. For decades there were clear
material benefits attached to living in the North, in a state
created by a British dictate in response to a Unionist demand.
No one could be blind to the advantages, but not everyone is
willing to admit the ambivalence.

BEN CARAHER of the SDLP teaches in west Belfast but was
born in Crossmaglen and still thinks of south Armagh as home.
He has been aware of border ambivalence towards the Republic
for a long time.

'By the early fifties the welfare state had made its impact. On
the one hand you had your Irish inheritance. We didn't think
of ourselves as nationalist. Somebody in Tyrone might have
thought of themselves as nationalist, but in Crossmaglen you
were Irish – which is a difference actually.

'On the other you had a conflict: your identity was Irish,
firm, the political expression of that identity was a desire for a
united Ireland, whatever that meant ... But also there were
advantages to be taken from welfare spending, which ultimately
came from the British connection: the National Health Service,
free education, the eleven-plus. Coming from a family of
eleven-plus passers, getting a grammar school education which
would have been unavailable in the South – this conflict set up
all sorts of tensions and unspoken contradictions. If you brought
it up, there was a sense that you were a sort of traitor. There
was very little welfare spending across the border, no eleven-
plus, no health service. People were aware of the difference:
that you were getting certain advantages just because you happened to be three miles north of that line.

'I don't think people were able to cope with that. The way
they managed was they didn't think about it, or talked about it

as little as possible. What is a united country in those circumstances? What are the consequences for you? Further into
the fifties, the Southern state looked very unsuccessful – the fag-
end of de Valera-ism, unsuccessful coalition alternatives, the
economic dynamism of the Lemass government still to come.
The optimism that generated in the sixties made the relations
of Northern nationalists to the South different again.

'But in the fifties, take places like Crossmaglen and Castleblayney, both very depressed, Crossmaglen with high unemployment always – but the difference was unemployment
benefits and the welfare state. Across the border, round
'Blayney, there was massive emigration. There was big emigration from Cross too but I don't think south Armagh was as
devastated by emigration as south Monaghan – and all of that
certainly caused psychic difficulties for people. It was strange for
the older people to see their children benefiting, going to grammar school. They couldn't say that was a bad thing. The
upwardly mobile benefited most from the welfare state, the
benefits came from the fact that we were a part of the UK. But
anybody who overtly said something like that was considered a
traitor . . .

'There was a feeling of being abandoned and of betrayal by
the South, that they didn't care about you, they'd forgotten
you, twinned by a feeling of letting the side down if you criticised them. From south Armagh, I was very aware always of the
ambivalence of Northern Catholics towards the South.'

In case this blast of realism created the wrong impression
about south Armagh identity, though, Ben Caraher summed up
his own reflection decisively: 'We accepted benefits – but we
still looked for an eventual united Ireland. There's two things
about nationalism that cannot be eroded: one's the fact of it, the
sense of identity, and the other's the political expression of it.
I don't think for people on the border their sense of identity was

remotely affected. Their sense of themselves remained the same.'

He has no illusions about the general level of Northern Catholic familiarity with the South, and no doubts at all about his own relationship with it. 'Maybe more than most Northern Catholics, I have a close working interest . . . I listen to the RTE news, I buy Dublin papers. I even had a motion about RTE's coverage in the North debated at a party conference lately [he laughs] – but it wasn't properly reported by the *Irish Times*. I'm not typical. I know and take an interest in Southern politics: most Northern Catholics don't have an idea. And I certainly do feel the Southern state, imperfect as it is, is the sovereign embodiment of my national tradition.

'For all its imperfections, I'm glad it exists. I'm glad there is an independent Irish state, I wish it well – and I identify with it to some extent. It *does* wound me when its dominant voices are hostile. The feeling I have is that everybody's out of step but me. All sorts of people irritate me in the South: the traditional pious Fianna Fáil republicans with their nonsense about articles Two and Three and the indivisible republic which lives up there safely in some Platonic realm – and the beauty of it is that it can never be made practical, so we don't have to think about it. That drives me bats. The reactionary nature of the Catholic Church and its influence, it drives me crazy. But also the pseudo-sophistication of Dublin 4, which is really a form of pro-vincialism, provincial deference – that irritates me intensely.' He laughs again. 'I rarely come across anybody in the South I agree with, but none the less, it's my place – because it emerged out of the political tradition from which I emerged.

'Most Northern Catholics have a more ambivalent attitude. They want it to be involved in the North, they complain when it's not vigorous enough in their defence. And yet they're also vaguely ashamed of it for being less economically developed than parts of the North. But that's less true now...I just recognise these as facts, I feel no sense of inferiority because of it.

'There'd be no culture shock for me in a closer relationship...there's enough there to feel close to. In that dreadful phrase' – he laughs – 'it's part of what I am. The infuriating nature of the place is a sign of life...'

It was the most reflective and lucid account anyone gave of nationalist ambivalence about the South, though many clearly have similar thoughts. In a way, Ben Caraher's unforced and clear-eyed identification seems to be what allows him to discuss the South as it is and was, rather than how he might have wished it to be – with the frankness of family. Others, less at ease with the complexities of a real place, are more inhibited by inherited defensiveness about a half-imagined South.

For some people, the memory of trying to project a favourable image is still sharp. Paddy McGrory remembers meeting Protestant, unionist criticism of the Southern state for the first time in the 1940s, among fellow law students at Queen's University.

'Part of being a Northern nationalist meant being defensive about the South – denying its poverty etcetera, the kind of thing my new Protestant friends were saying to me. I remember a great counting-up of unemployment benefits, comparing them with the North – they would come in to guys like me with all this. You'd go home and say to your father: "Is that right?" hoping they were wrong.'

Though the contrast of absolute poverty with comparative progress is long gone, the question for some remains the same: how to admit the gap that exists now – between peoples – without delighting the enemy, or without strengthening what is seen as essentially a unionist argument for building up a 'Northern Irish' identity? How to confess alienation from the

Southern state without entrenching the state of Northern Ireland?

The people it is not a problem for are republicans. Partition for them explains everything. The IRA scarcely figures, and certainly not as a major agent of alienation. The twenty-six-county republic is tainted with colonialism because the founding fathers accepted partition, so attitudes towards Northern nationalists are bound to be distorted: the republic's own history has been mistaught by 'revisionists' to make it easier for Southerners to ignore the colonial legacy, the conflict in the North. In this version, there is a great silent mass of potential Southern support for republicans, lost to them because the Southern state has so censored 'the struggle'.

GERRY ADAMS agrees that there is a 'gap' between Southerners and Northerners – but insists that this is superficial. He feels equally at home in west Donegal and Waterford as in west Belfast, he says, because he began hitchhiking and camping around the country at the age of fifteen.

'I think partition has made a gap – but there's no stereotypical Irish person, or there shouldn't be. There are all sorts of differences like there are in any country, like I'll be down at a Sinn Féin function in Connemara listening to native Irish speakers, and there's obviously going to be a wide gap between them and young kids say from the Falls or the Shankill. What partition has done is divide us and prevent the coming together of all that diversity, so that people can be happy with it. What revisionism has done is tell people they can't be satisfied with what they come from. That's putting things you thought of as constants under attack: the effect's like a family trauma, like discovering you've been adopted.

'If you find you cannot commemorate in any meaningful way the history of the twenty-six-county Irish state, if you find that the Irish language and all manifestations not of politics or nationalism but of nationality are under attack – that causes huge traumas. Remember 1966: Fianna Fáil ministers, some with IRA backgrounds, shouldering their way onto platforms; a major drama series about the Rising on RTE; a huge popularisation of the writings of Connolly and Pearse; pageants in Croke Park and Casement and everywhere else – we're all off to Dublin in the green. And then within four short years you're not allowed to sing those songs or play music that wouldn't even be republican – all that is where revisionism has had a political effect, where people can't be contented and confident with what they are.'

And for partition and revisionism, for the deficiencies of the present republic as for the entire violent conflict, Gerry Adams insists that 'colonialism', Britain, is ultimately responsible.

'The whole history of colonialism achieves this: that you touch the forelock to the landlord and then you go round and conspire how to kill his cattle. Or when you meet the Brit on the road, you say how're you doing and yes, there's my date of birth, and then you go off and scheme...

'Graft comes into it, strokes. Even idealism, which once motivated, sometimes to do terrible things, but which motivated earlier Free State governments, where they did make self-sacrifices, is now cynicism. Everybody knows the guards double up as bouncers. Everybody knows the golden circle, hand-in-glove operations that ministers have with big business. It's bad for people. Out of that colonial history there is an on-going question – the conflict – and if you don't do something collectively about that, it's bound to cause problems collec-tively, for all of us. But it's easier to fall victim of ignoring the North – when you add to revisionism things like censorship, disinformation, rampant McCarthyism. I did an interview with a woman who left here in 1970, she came back last year, and she thought she was in a different country. When she went, the

North was a huge story and had to be sorted out. Twenty years later nobody in Dublin wants to talk about it – and who can blame them? If you're thirty-five and live in the twenty-six counties, you will not have heard a republican spokesperson, ever, in your life.

'So how could that person, having been fed a partitionist line – and some of the things that have happened here have been terrible – is it any wonder some might want to stay away from it? But yet you find in opinion poll after poll, on articles Two and Three, no change, people still want to see a united Ireland.'

Apart from the fleeting reference to some 'terrible things', Gerry Adams's analysis of Southern attitudes ignores and implicitly denies the effects of the IRA on Southern opinion, clinging instead to what evidence he can find of a residual Southern wish for unification. Whatever it is that polls identify in Southern attitudes, it is clear that the South does not share the republican vision of a united Ireland. As president of Sinn Féin, Gerry Adams has the acute political problem that the party's vote in the South has stuck stubbornly below 2 per cent. But a practice of criticising Dublin governments and the intelligentsia of Dublin 4 is for Sinn Féin leaders – as for many Northern nationalists – preferable to admitting that time, separate development and above all the violence of the IRA have inevitably left the South with limited interest and goodwill towards the North.

Like the other republicans I talked to, now largely restricted to sympathetic circles when they go South, Gerry Adams's happy reminiscence about teenage hiking holidays is very much a recollection of a lost and wider world. He is also aware that most of the young in Catholic west Belfast have none of his familiarity with the beauties of the rest of Ireland, much less his sense of oneness with people in west Donegal or Waterford.

TERESA, the eighteen-year-old from the Falls who only

recently realised 'the North' meant the North of Ireland, has no idea where west Donegal or Waterford are. Like the Donegal people who travel through Northern Ireland to Larne without stopping, she has travelled to Dublin 'three or four times' to catch planes to France and Spain – on trips organised by charities which for years have taken 'mixed' Catholic/Protestant groups of young people away together in the belief that neutral ground will enable friendships. As she describes it, Teresa drove to Dublin without ever thinking, this is the South, I wonder what it's like? It turns out that she has also gone 'down South' with a youth club several times, on residential trips. The interest in this was being away from west Belfast, not in making acquaintance with the people of the Republic. They 'seemed nice and friendly', but there was no contact.

'It's just all country round you, doing what you want with all your friends. You never see soldiers, never hear shootings. You hear on the news what's happening up here, that somebody got shot, and you don't want to come home. See when you're coming back – driving down the Road [the Falls] towards Beechmount, we used to hate it – just seeing the Road again. The bus goes quiet.'

Teresa had no thoughts about the South, like a number of others in their teens and early twenties. They rarely watch news on television and never read newspapers. 'British' at least means soldiers on the streets and graffiti on walls – but 'the South'? Those who are middle-aged and older may feel surges of irritation breaking through long-established resignation or disillusionment, exasperation when specific IRA bombings suddenly spark Southern outrage and a kind of interest, for example in the peace marches arranged after the bombing at Warrington, Cheshire, in March 1993 that killed two children. There was no such Southern outrage when in the same week six Northern Catholics were killed by loyalists. What about the others who

have died, Northern voices cried, what about Catholic victims
of loyalist violence, children killed by the plastic bullets of
British soldiers or the RUC: why is it only the IRA who attract
such Southern outrage, what about, what about...

'Whataboutery' on this scale tends to be chiefly the reflex
of republicans, for whom the best defence – at least in their
own minds – has always been to list Catholic and especially
republican dead. When the accusations come from the South,
frustration accumulated through the Troubles spills into the
well-rehearsed litany. Others voice some of this feeling in tones
of disappointment: republicans occasionally sound destabilised
by an emotional swirl of rage, isolation and betrayal.

'If you in the twenty-six counties don't want a united
Ireland, just say so,' the imprisoned Danny Morrison wrote to
the *Irish Times* in April 1993. A column in the paper on
Warrington had just extravagantly suggested that republicans
were 'misbegotten, pagan litter'. Morrison's response was to reject the Southern explanation that their protest was intended to
make it plain that the IRA did not act in their name.

No one he knew in jail had 'lifted a gun or planted a bomb
in the name of the people of the twenty-six counties... Don't
use IRA killings as an excuse for truncating your nationality and
identity, the fact that you consider yourselves far too new-
fashioned to be old-fashioned... In your sophistication, your
smugness, your aloofness, your hypocrisy and your forget-
fulness, you are as guilty for prolonging this conflict as I am for
participating in it.'

In many respects contemporary Southern behaviour strains to
the limits the resources of Northerners – including Sinn Féin
and the SDLP – committed to action that presupposed at least a
degree of goodwill from the other side of the border. It leaves
others adrift.

For the young, there are no hang-ups: they simply do not

know the place. The generation between – not old enough to have developed disappointment or formed expectations of the South before the Troubles, not young enough to be as blank and bemused as those born in the last twenty years – can sound dispassionate, even amused, like Máiréad. But for some, what the South means most is hostility.

Northerners from the most troubled areas who have grown up with the Troubles are not disposed to make allowances for the South. ANN, who grew up in Ardoyne through the early seventies, has raised four children on her own while her husband served a long sentence as an IRA prisoner.

'I can't say I don't like Southerners, I'm saying I don't like their attitudes. But attitudes are not people. Attitudes can be changed. A big part of the reason is the media – the ban on Sinn Féin. Sure how under God are you going to get your message across, or how are they meant to know anything about what's happening to us? The things that used to annoy us, that we didn't understand, was how the Free State couldn't see what we were suffering. They could not see what was happening to our people. They never heard the half of it, the shooting that would go on half the night. I don't believe they ever heard about things like Toby's Hall [see pages 10–12] – it wasn't reported at all or they heard something like a man was shot during rioting – even though there was no rioting.

'Then on our honeymoon we went to Dublin and got doors closed in our faces, we weren't allowed into pubs when they heard the Northern accent. And I was really angry at this. I said, my God, when you consider what we all went through, through internment, the whole bloody works – and these people are closing doors in our faces, treating us like total outcasts. Things like that really alienated you. You felt so angry and so betrayed . . . and then you started getting older, reading up on history a wee bit.

'And you said to yourself, what have these eejits been doing for the last sixty to seventy years? Obviously they should have been trying to look after us, after the initial split-up of the state. They'd totally forgotten about us. We were left there and there was no interest in us at all – apart from the articles Two and Three or whatever they're arguing about. That seems to me to be the height of their interest in the North, to make grandiose speeches like Jack Lynch about not standing idly by.

'What came of that? It was just a total let-down. People's expectations were really raised at that time. They felt our saviours are coming: to the rescue!' She laughs. 'People felt brilliant, great, this is the rest of our nation looking after us at last, after all this suffering. And what did they do? They seemed to totally just want to ignore it. They just didn't want anything to do with it. I don't know how they would see it, but that's how we feel – a total let-down.

'It seems to me in a sense that they should be made.' She laughs. 'They can't get away from the fact that we are a part of this island – that I'm Irish and nobody's going to tell me anyway otherwise. We invested too much, I think, as a people, individually and collectively in this country, to be told that we're not part of the nation, not part of Ireland as a nation. And we have a contribution to make to it, a great contribution to make.'

Even a few years ago, Northerners would have been slow to voice anger with the South in such forceful terms. But long-suppressed furies have been loosed by the bogey of being cut adrift, the dread raised by Southern sympathy for unionists and 'the articles Two and Three or whatever they're arguing about', as Ann puts it. 'They should be made' (to care) is a slogan simmering just below the surface. It is not, however, the rallying cry for any campaign that the established nationalist political parties will lead.

POLITICS

The SDLP under John Hume has spent most of the Troubles cosseting a bipartisan Southern approach to the North, maximising the support the SDLP would in any case have received as the alternative nationalist voice to violent republicanism, trying to minimise alienation from Northern affairs by being studiously noncommittal on the Southern political scene. A year after the party was formed, eight years before he became leader, Hume referred to Northern Ireland and the Republic as two 'confessional states, neither of which is worthy of its people . . . [which] contribute to narrowness and insularity' (*Fortnight* magazine, 5 February 1971). Such frankness and objectivity about the Southern state vanished long ago, to be replaced by *realpolitik*.

There are some in the party who have regarded him for the past decade as effectively Southern minister for Northern affairs, the SDLP as the Irish government in the North. It is a view that perhaps owes more to Northern nationalists' need for recognition and status in the South than to reality. Purely Southern domestic concerns – what even Hume irritably describes as 'partitionist' thinking – will always take precedence over Northern nationalist priorities. But however Southern government commitment and energy varies, it is clear that the SDLP's concerns have none the less become an integral part of Dublin policy.

Veteran observers differ only on where to attribute inspiration for the line Dublin has pursued, more or less without variation, through every administration since the early seventies. Some suspect that the most senior civil servants in the Republic's Department of Foreign Affairs – with each of whom Hume has had the closest of working relationships – have influenced him more than the other way around. In any case, the broad outlines of a joint Irish–British approach to Northern Ireland, implicitly putting the objective of unification on the long finger, were already visible as long ago as 1972. By August of that year, four months after the removal of Stormont, Dublin was reported to be confident of being involved in the planning with London of future arrangements for Northern Ireland.

Through each successive Dublin administration since, despite occasional strains, cooperation and consultation with the SDLP has been a constant. The relationship survived the differences exposed by the New Ireland Forum in 1983, when the chief representatives of constitutional nationalism defined aims and principles in public in an exercise essentially geared to evaluate the cost and feasibility of unification. It was to many minds an exercise in political education or self-education, which made plain that unity would be achieved, if at all, only in the most gradual of stages. The then Fianna Fáil leader Charles Haughey, supported by Hume's deputy, Seamus Mallon, held out for the single goal of a unitary Irish state as opposed to the list of options favoured by the other parties and Hume. Mallon eventually declared for an agreed report; Haughey publicly jettisoned it. The subsequent British-Irish negotiations that produced the Anglo-Irish Agreement were conducted by Haughey's lifelong rival, the then taoiseach and Fine Gael leader Garret FitzGerald. Haughey at first derided the agreement, but in office shortly afterwards accepted and worked it. Throughout, Irish civil servants continued to liaise with Hume.

FitzGerald, in his autobiographical account of the Anglo-Irish negotiations, describes telling the British prime minister, Margaret Thatcher, that he did not seek intergovernmental structures to tackle Northern Ireland for the benefit of people in the Republic, but to break the cycle of violence, 'that in fact our people did not want to be involved in the North' (*All in a Life,* London and Dublin, 1991). Five years after the agreement was signed, one of the chief Irish negotiators explained in an off-the-record briefing to journalists that the 'primary

motivation had been to protect the whole island from the
IRA–Sinn Féin menace by two methods: through changes in
security, the administration of justice and the prisons; and by
some form of focus which would allow the minority to focus
loyalty inside Northern Ireland rather than outside'. It was
either a telling indication of the limits of Southern ambition in
relation to the North – or a rationalisation after the event, based
on what Britain had in the end been willing to give.

An early Dublin suggestion for the 'focus' inside Northern
Ireland had been that there should be a Southern 'ministerial
presence' in the North. At one point FitzGerald offered the
quid pro quo of a referendum on articles Two and Three. The
British negotiators declined the offer, and no more was heard
of the 'ministerial presence'. The 'internal focus' shrank to
become the North–South civil service 'secretariat' to service
intergovernmental conference meetings, which still functions,
scarcely noticed, from a base at Maryfield, outside Belfast.

Southern self-interest helped the SDLP to tie the Republic into Northern affairs through the agreement: an achievement
many attribute to John Hume's persuasive advocacy. But
Dublin's assessment of the lack of public enthusiasm for any
commitment greater than the right to be consulted has always
been a brake on the demands the South makes of Britain. The
broad welcome in the Republic for the agreement in 1985
undoubtedly reflected a view that this pointed towards a final
settlement of the troublesome North, with minimal Southern
involvement.

Since then both FitzGerald and Haughey have retired from
politics, and after Haughey's departure, an unsettled and unset-
tling period for the largest party, Fianna Fáil, has given way to
a governing coalition of Fianna Fáil and Labour. The Labour
leader, Dick Spring, is tánaiste (deputy leader) and minister for
foreign affairs, with responsibility for Northern Ireland. Labour

is the SDLP's sister social democratic party: Spring (then in coalition with Fine Gael) was co-signatory with Garret FitzGerald to
the Anglo-Irish Agreement, and has said that he sought the
foreign affairs role in order to seek a resolution of the Northern
conflict. The new order ought to be entirely congenial for the
SDLP – but there is nervousness. Spring has signalled to
unionists that he wants the Irish government to represent their
concerns as well as those of nationalists. Not quite the
'disinterest' and 'neutrality' British ministers have been professing on the North over past years, and which has so unnerved
unionists, but perhaps a move in that direction. The SDLP cannot possibly object: Spring's language has been largely Hume's
language, his definition of Northern Ireland's problem as the
contest of 'two sets of rights' the terminology of the New
Ireland Forum.

Occasionally, however, there has been a hint of distance
between Irish government and Northern nationalism that jars in
Northern ears, the faintest revisionist whisper: as in the statement in a major Spring speech that Northern Ireland nationalists' everyday experience 'reinforced their conviction that
Northern Ireland was created as a rearguard action against Irish
self-determination, or as a contrivance against Irish nationalists'.
An outside observer, unaware that Northern nationalists
imagined Irish ministers to be representatives of the same
political tradition as themselves, might certainly conclude from
this that the minister did not regard 'their conviction' as
his own.

SDLP reactions to the articles Two and Three debate have
been dismissive: the question is a distraction from the real issues,
a Unionist stunt. 'If any Dublin government unilaterally jettisoned them,' said one senior figure, 'it wouldn't affect the central problems, it would simply throw away part of their hand
and reveal that Unionists are not prepared to move.' In April

1993 an Irish official insisted: 'No government here is going to distance themselves from the SDLP, and from Hume in particular.' There would be no movement on articles Two and Three except as part of an overall settlement, he added, and in that regard he recalled that Spring had said no more than that the articles 'were not set in bronze'. But Spring's style occasionally upsets the SDLP grassroots, who are not quite as dismissive as the leadership about apparent threats to articles Two and Three. Being told that they are 'not set in bronze' is hardly reassuring language from a Dublin minister.

Years of Southern neglect and contempt for the old Northern Nationalist Party have bequeathed a deep-seated insecurity that two decades of liaison with government has not eradicated, any more than new nationalist political confidence inside the North has erased suspicion of unionism. JOHN HUME's response to all of this is to lay even more emphasis on the European context any solution must have, and to suggest that a Southern guilty conscience is at the root of the more open anti-Northern nationalist mood in the South. He professes absolute confidence in Spring – but is clearly irked by the degree to which Unionists like Ken Maginnis have made allies, or at least well-wishers, among Southern politicians and opinion-makers.

'If we're seeking agreement on the island of Ireland, that means the South has a major role to play. The North was always a party political issue in the South – attitudes to the North were at the root of the foundation of the South, the civil war etcetera. Our view is that if we're to solve the problem politically and peacefully, divisions in the South are a destabilising factor.

'One of the things that has happened is that the South has been switched off by the violence of the North and doesn't seem to recognise in many ways that that violence has roots in the philosophy that created the South – and that the victim of the past, whatever we describe the past as, the victim is the

Northern minority. What the South doesn't seem to recognise is that Northern nationalism – and by that I mean the Provos, because the Provos are not republicans, they're nationalists – was born in the South. In a sense the leadership of what was called Irish nationalism over the centuries was Southern leadership, and it fundamentally ignored the North in its calculations – and the Northerners were in the front line . . .

'The South is moving away back into, I don't know, the Dublin 4 mentality – "one side's as bad as the other up there". I can even see the newspapers moving away from the whole thing. It really disturbs me. I think politically speaking there is a clear Dublin commitment that will continue, to finding agreement between North and South because the North is the major problem facing the country. And while it remains restless it's costing the South a considerable amount of money as well.'

Belatedly, he tried for a more positive gloss, then fell back into impatience: 'I don't know how widespread this anti-Northern feeling is really – I think it's largely a media, Dublin 4 thing, RTE. It's a guilt complex about the Provos, that's what I think it is.'

Sinn Féin have their own difficulties about articles Two and Three, not least about campaigning in the South where they have little support. As one official put it early in the controversy: 'Why should we campaign to keep a sectarian constitution?' In unforgiving republican mythology, the constitution's author, de Valera, was a traitor who made his peace with an incomplete Irish state, came to terms with partition and drafted a Catholic constitution for a Catholic country. Republicans have never claimed – could never claim – articles Two and Three as justification for their violence.

It is a point they have made so often that defending the articles was always bound to sound uncomfortable. In the end the prospect of embarrassing the SDLP, the perpetual temptation to pick up and run with the latest insecurities on the ground about Southern 'treachery', British perfidy and general caving in to Unionist pressure, have produced a series of half-hearted claims that the articles are important to Northern nationalist identity. But there is a distinct unwillingness to take the argument South, an awareness that it is bound to sound hostile.

Others have no such inhibitions, like thirty-six-year-old Ann, and her early heroine, Bernadette McAliskey, whose angry words on articles Two and Three she now echoes, and who in September 1992 launched her own campaign on the articles with a lecture on her identity at Dublin's Peacock Theatre. The lecture revolved around what she presented as the immediate threat of the South agreeing to delete them as part of a deal with Unionists. If they did, they would be attempting to sell her soul, she declared. They would in effect be 'putting Northern nationalists out of the nation'. Northern nationalists, who already felt 'that you bought your liberty with our slavery', would see it as a final act of betrayal, and a future generation of the IRA would 'vent their wrath' on the South.

'You sell your own soul if you want to – but I tell you this, before you take my soul, you'll take my life. I will not be British. I will not be driven out of this nation. I will not have somebody in Cork or Dublin say to me that my father and my mother are buried on British soil, in the county of Tyrone . . . my national identity is not something for you to barter or trade or sell. It is an integral part of my existence and I cannot and will not live without it. . . I tell you, on the peril of all our mortal lives, don't you even try to put us out of this nation – or we'll leave you without a blade of grass.' She has since made essentially the same speech at republican functions in the Republic. 'We'll burn every blade of grass in your Free State,' she told an audience in Ballyshannon, County Donegal.

There were a number of supporters in the Peacock audience

and a contingent of Irish-Americans attending the Yeats International Festival – of which the lecture was part – who admired Bernadette McAliskey's rhetoric. She received a standing ovation. In the front row, among those who remained seated, was her one-time People's Democracy colleague MICHAEL FARRELL. He is now a journalist, civil liberties campaigner and lawyer in Dublin, having had to leave Northern Ireland under threat from the same loyalist group that in 1981 shot and seriously injured Bernadette McAliskey and her husband. Down the years Farrell has made many of the same criticisms of Southern governments as McAliskey. But he thinks the approach of verbally attacking Southerners fundamentally mistaken.

'Northern nationalists tend not to understand the South. I had to work with people here and talk to them to understand. It seems to me that an awful lot of Northern nationalists, especially republicans, though it probably applies to SDLP supporters as well ... their attitude is sometimes very much a moralistic sort of one – "We are oppressed, why don't you come to our aid?" '

Southerners had their own priorities, he said, in many cases were distracted by economic hardship and misinformed about the North because of censorship. But above all they were alienated by the IRA.

'It's now a very long time since the military struggle in this part of the country – and some Northern republicans don't seem to see that. They make quite a legitimate point that a lot of the activities of the IRA are not very different from those of the IRA in the War of Independence. But that's out of the direct memory of most people here now. And as things have got worse, and as there have been more atrocities, completely indefensible actions and killings of civilians, a lot of people here have got very alienated by them and have a sort of defence mechanism which is to turn off.

'Censorship contributes to that because both Section 31 and the sort of self-censorship that goes on in the newspapers take the violence out of context. Where you simply report another killing in Belfast last night, people here find it difficult to grasp that. They don't know the significance, which streets are which and what this means – whether this is a sectarian killing or an internal feud. Unexplained violence is very alienating.

'But some aspects of the violence you could explain till the cows come home and it would still turn people off: such as killing workmen at Teebane. They don't censor pictures of dead bodies. So maybe the sympathy has been forced deeper down in the psyche. I think it's still basically there. There's still a very generalised understanding that the conflict is one where the nationalist minority has been oppressed for fifty, sixty, seventy years: that the violence is a product of that . . . that the cause is the sectarian nature of the Northern state.'

Northerners tended to see anti-nationalism as primarily directed at them, Farrell thought, but it had local roots. 'The conservative politicians who presided over the slums of Dublin mouthed nationalist slogans. People here feel the leadership of the past has used nationalism to drum up support and ignore social conditions – and they assume nationalism equates with lack of concern for social conditions. Some of the same people are interested in issues like divorce, contraception, abortion. They've seen that politicians who were very strong on nationalist rhetoric were most conservative on these issues . . . at gay rights meetings, say, you find confusion when someone who is seen as strongly nationalist on the North is also strongly supportive of their rights.

'Basically, this state has a dynamic of its own: because it's legitimate, people vote for it, it has its own politics. Quite a few republicans have begun to recognise that. The one thing that distinguishes it from other societies is that it has this unresolved national question, which doesn't dominate everything but is always a nagging irritant. You have to understand that, to understand how this place works.

'The reaction of some Northerners, who don't understand, is to abuse the South, which only compounds the problem – and leaves an impression that Northern nationalists can be very strident and extreme. Demonstrations down here accompanied by marching bands dressed in paramilitary uniforms just frighten the life out of people on the street.'

As one of the leading left-wingers involved in the civil rights movement, Michael Farrell gave republicans what he called 'critical support', describing the IRA as 'elitist' but attempting to maintain links with the mass of their supporters. However, he has for several years now been arguing that IRA violence is increasing division between Catholics and Protestants, is futile, counterproductive and should stop – while also campaigning to enlist Southern opinion on behalf of a number of those convicted wrongly in Britain for IRA bombings.

He has also argued against the South's censorship of broadcasting and the widespread self-censorship of the media, because they so clearly make it difficult for people to form their own opinions about the Northern conflict. MARY MCALEESE shares that view, though she is in many ways at the opposite end of the political spectrum – the most prominent Northern Catholic laywoman, part of the hierarchy's team at the 1983 New Ireland Forum, a Northerner gone South like Farrell but in her case to RTE, Trinity College, and short-lived active membership of Fianna Fáil. She admired Charles Haughey and stood unsuccessfully against Garret FitzGerald for election as TD in 1986.

She went to Dublin in the mid-seventies. Now Director of the Institute of Professional Legal Studies at Queen's University Belfast, she looks back on her years in the South with a mixture of fondness for a society she sees many virtues in, and frustration at the attitudes she met – primarily among senior colleagues in RTE.

'I had been born and reared in Ardoyne, knew it inside out: lived in Andersonstown, knew what it was like. It was a degree of authenticity you're not likely to meet every day of the week in Dublin. But I found slowly but surely that I became silenced by two things. One was the glazed-over look when you started to talk about the problems in the North and in particular when you started to recite the things that happened to you personally. The second was this business of constantly being labelled as a Northern Catholic from a place like Ardoyne. You ran the risk, if you opened your mouth on the subject, of being labelled a fellow traveller with the Provos.

'Martin, my husband, and I felt, looking back, that our lives in Dublin had been a very shocking experience. We had left Northern Ireland because of the bigotry here: both our families had been victims of that. We both have a phenomenal love for the Republic, however – Dublin isn't the Republic and revisionism isn't Ireland. But I went there first when Conor Cruise O'Brien was in the ascendant – and if ever anyone was a culture shock, Conor Cruise O'Brien was to me. Here was this extraordinarily arrogant man, in the process of revising everything that I had known to be a given and a truth about Irish history – and who set in motion a way of looking at Northern Ireland that we are only now beginning to grow up and grow out of.

'It was a myth, destructive, took the truth and ran away with it, revised current Irish history in a way that allowed a kind of apologetic Catholicism to develop, that ran away from confronting the dark side of Northern Ireland. There are things that have got to be said, without running the risk of being called sectarian – or being called a Provo, which is exactly what happened to me in the Republic.

'I had a dreadful time with the Workers' Party, people who now hold very prominent positions in RTE – whose idea of coming to the North was to talk to Unionist politicians whom they cultivated in a really obsequious way, to talk to other Workers' Party people, and then come back to Dublin and tell what was happening in the North. I'd go round my family, Andersonstown, my aunts, talk to people I knew living there.

'The classic example of the kind of clash I had was when Bobby Sands died. A member of the 'Today Tonight' staff argued before the funeral that all the evidence suggested there would be more camera crews than people. I said the Catholic population had been and would continue to be radicalised by the hunger strike, that people who never in their lives would have considered voting for Sinn Féin were finding themselves drawn by their umbilical cords into this. And of course 70,000 people marched behind the procession. What happened in RTE as a result was that a reporter, a most apolitical person, who brought back an interview with Father Des Wilson, who essentially said what I had been saying, was accused of being a Provo. It was a case of killing the messenger because you don't like the message. That bit of the Republic I found very hard. I think that almost created the syndrome of the apologetic Northern Catholic: the atmosphere in which if you did not become apologetic about the IRA, you were in serious danger of being written off as a Provo.

'Some of that was politically motivated, whipped up by people who had their own political agenda. But some of it I think was simply because I was a Northern Catholic from Ardoyne, my family had lost our home, our business: having actually physically suffered during the Troubles. People didn't want to know that. Nobody wanted to face up to it, and I think still don't really, to the ghastly meandering war on their doorsteps. They would have preferred if I with my personal witness had gone away. And because I refused to, their way of dealing with me was to stick me in a box and label it: maniacal nationalist, ultra-republican – neither of which I was.'

The Republic for Mary McAleese has never been the unknown. Her father came from Roscommon, she spent much of her childhood there, and with her own family spends her life 'as though there is no border, flying up and down to Dublin and the West, loads of friends in both places'. The 'bad days' in Dublin were followed by a spell in a County Meath village, where she saw 'the wonderful side of life in the Republic . . . a deep-rooted spirituality, a great prayerfulness'. And yet she is as wounded by Southern attitudes towards the North as the many who know less: maybe even more so, because in so many ways she feels affinity with the South. The experience of being treated with suspicion and hostility has helped change her ideas about her own identity, and, she thinks, those of others.

'It's different from twenty years ago – there are new layers of identity, Europe, overlaying the old. But in a way it has to be a suspended judgement. Part of our identity is just sitting waiting, in cold storage. A lot of things I thought were my identity, growing up, were to do with thinking of the Republic as a spiritual homeland, before I knew what the place was. Then going there and discovering it wasn't all I thought it was, and yet was more than I thought as well . . . for a lot of Northern Catholics of my way of thinking, experience of the place has adjusted their view of the Republic very much. To that extent our identity has been tempered. But how exactly that develops now is a matter for conjecture, for as long as the constitutional shape of this country remains unspecified. It's in a state of flux: it's a matter for debate.'

BRIAN FEENEY admits to no such uncertainty. As a high-profile SDLP representative he is accustomed to explaining confidently how the party has worked closely with the Irish government to ensure that the Irishness of Northern nationalists can never be ignored again. He thinks of Dublin as his capital city, is interested in Southern society and politics, has no doubts about his own Irishness. He is also sharply conscious that the interest is not mutual.

'The general election in '92, the referenda on abortion and the right to travel and information – all that – my friends and myself looked upon that with envy because it reflected a real political nation that people were fully part of and arguing about. Some friends were down canvassing for the Labour Party, because they see them as a party that will break the mould and usher in a new, modern society – and they want to be involved in that.

'At the same time, there's a sadness, a counter-balance: that those same people in the South really don't care about anything that's going on up here. For example, there hasn't been a TD in Belfast since Peter Barry, certainly that I know of. Usually some would come to the SDLP conference – but they stay the minimum time. And none know the situation on the ground. TDs do not know the North. It strikes me especially because British MPs are regularly here for briefing sessions. The Northern Ireland Office organises it: they go round the political parties, and I'd give briefings to ten to twelve at a time, a couple of times a year.

'I feel regret, that nobody in the Republic reciprocates our desire.' He laughs 'That it's all done grudgingly, because it's a duty – and they keep reiterating this. There's this desire here among nationalists to be part of something. And really now, to be honest, in that respect it's the exact mirror image of the unionists who desire to be part of Britain and say for God's sake protect us and save us.

'There's the same desire to say to the Republic: look, my kids play Gaelic football, they're going down this weekend to play in Castleblayney or Carrickmacross, they share exactly the same ethos as your kids, something that is intangible. But it is not reciprocated. I fully realise that. Nevertheless the regret is still there.

'Think about the '92 election: we had no part to play in the emergence of a coalition, I don't know anyone in the Republic who before they put their 1, 2, 3, or 4 would have said, now I wonder what effect this is going to have on the future of talks in Northern Ireland... the shape of government we get here, the way these referenda go. You would have been led away gently by two men in white coats if you had suggested that. They want to know, naturally, is the hospital going to be kept open, is there going to be more money for school books, what about school uniforms? It's extremely difficult to get people interested in something which doesn't affect them – which affects Cavan, Monaghan, Donegal, Louth, the faraway border counties, not anywhere else... It's simply an effort all the time to try to persuade an Irish government to give time to the problem, because their electorate doesn't want them to.'

But he adds, forcefully: 'I don't think that amounts to an identity crisis – it's not like the unionists in relation to Britain in that way. I don't think anybody in the Republic denies that Northern nationalists are Irish. There's an emotional attachment in the Republic, when teams go down to Croke Park and teams come North. No one will say they're not Irish. They all sound the same as well and they have the same sort of background. They don't care equally, no. But the problem for the unionists is that people in England say, "Come on, *you're* not British, just listen to you" – by which they mean you're not English.

'There is a difference in kind between the two: the English would call unionists "Paddies", whereas Southerners feel Northerners are the same people but they don't want the trouble associated with them. They don't want them dragging all their dirt and tin cans clattering behind them, messing up the society that they're getting together.

'Everybody's very nice to me in the Republic; they sympathise: "Terrible time you've been having." They don't give a damn. They don't want to do anything, and they're not going to pay anything. And why should they? How is a politician going to get an electorate interested in something which is going to cost them money, which may get some of them killed, and which is not going to put bread on the table? It's a luxury.'

Like others, he cheers himself up only to be cast down again, realism and optimism warring.

'I don't know how long the mutual identification will go on for. I know there are Northerners who don't play GAA etcetera, have few links with the South and more with England. But then so do people in the Republic watch English TV, read the *Sun*. It doesn't make them English. I know the most deprived have the fewest links, the young, and there's a lot of ignorance and resentment. They think the South should have done something and they don't care, so sod them.

'But really, it's ignorance. I remember taking students away on a field trip to Kinsale and there was a student, a Sinn Féin supporter, a very bright fella. The first morning there he came over to me and said, "Do you know something? Nobody knows you down here." I said, "It's brilliant, isn't it?" He said, "No, I don't mean that – you know all those statements you make in the *Irish News*, nobody reads them here." I said, "I know that." He said, "Do you? I went into this shop and said have you got the *Irish News*? The man said of course we have. I said well, I can't see it. He said what do you mean, we've got the *Irish Times*, the *Press*, the *Independent* . . . but he'd never heard of the *Irish News*!"

'I said, "So what?" The guy said, "Well I thought . . ." He was stunned. Very intelligent, and totally ghettoised. He thought he was living in a thirty-two-county Ireland that somehow the British had stopped gelling, coming together. He thought there were lots of people in Kinsale dashing out and buying the *Irish News*... those sort of guys in west Belfast grow to resent the people in the Republic, who don't pay the slightest attention.

'When Peter Barry was in Belfast, he arrived at the office we had then on the Falls and he was besieged. Danny Morrison etcetera were round him saying to him, come with us, we'll show you what it's like on the streets. They weren't really abusing him, they wanted to confront him with a number of issues where the Anglo-Irish Agreement was failing. But they wanted him: and that was unrequited desire too. There was the object of their desire, and they wanted to grab him, and show him. They didn't love him, but they wanted to show him how bad things were. And he was the last one to come up.

'I think there's enough interest at the top to maintain joint authority as an aim. The Republic's less well-off because of the North, the violence: their finances are skewed by the need for guards and soldiers on the border. So if they're involved in taking decisions... they'll be talking about another place that's not part of the Irish state. They're not going to interfere, demand radical things. And they're not going to pay for anything. They'll be talking about another place and helping run it with another sovereign government...'

Máiréad is a few years younger than Brian Feeney, dislikes him as a political figure, and resents being forced, as she sees it, to vote for his party by the absence of a more radical alternative and by the desire not to lend support to the IRA. But she and he sounded many of the same notes. The difference was that she felt no identification with the South and saw real everyday links between Northern Catholics and Britain as a puzzling contradiction. In the end, she found she was indeed describing an identity crisis, and had no inhibitions about saying so.

'What do we want? Where do we belong? What's our relationship with the South? To the British, ultimately? People
start, and they're absolutely lost. They say, "Well, you know
now, I've no relatives living across the border, all our ones
would be in Liverpool or London – so I wouldn't know
anything about the South, I don't know if I'd like to live down
there or if I'd have anything in common with them." They
have no feeling that people across the border really do understand or care about them, or would even bail them out in a
terrible emergency. In one way Northern nationalism is shot
through with absolute contradictions. If we articulate clearly
what we're talking about in being a republican, say, it means we
want an all-Ireland solution. And yet if we sit down and divide
that up, and say what does this mean, I think most people will
say, "I can't really see the possibility of that happening. How can
that possibly come about? You can't make the South link up
with you!"' She laughs. 'It's clearly the case that Southern
nationalists would have to be pressurised to accept that – it's evident they don't see that as their responsibility.

'So we're saying what we want is an all-Ireland republic, we
don't really know what that republic means any more, don't
know what the attitude of the South is to that, and for most
people their family connections are with England rather than
with the South: I *do* think that constitutes an identity crisis in
many small respects, and it amounts to a big thing in the end.'

The theme of the South's unwillingness to 'link up' was as
common as the complaint that there was no interest. What was
remarkable in Máiréad's assessment was that she so naturally did
exactly that: assessed in an objective way her own feelings
towards the South and drew conclusions. The old and middle-
aged dislike admitting how strange the South is to them today,
how alien. After all, this was the unionist refrain down the years,
and still is: that the South is 'a foreign country', nothing to do

with the North. The solution frequently means tailing away at
the end of a sentence: 'They just don't care...' The more
republican finish on an upbeat note, though occasionally
it seems more determined than assured: 'The sympathy's
there...and we're the same people, whether they like it or
not...'

Some are blank: for them there is no North, no South. At the
border they fall over into the same nothingness that many
Southerners think starts at Dundalk.

Repeatedly it seemed in interviews that we were pulling back
from the subject of how attitudes towards the South and the real
relationship between Northerners and Southerners during the
Troubles had affected a sense of identity. The South was always
a sore place, and for many is now a strange and hostile place.
But for many, measuring degrees of foreignness is much too
close to declaring that the rift is final: separation from the South
all over again, and this time by mutual consent.

8

'Contact with hearts and minds'

THE CHURCH

'I think the Church has handled things very well. The Troubles and the civil rights movement forced change upon them. Everybody was caught on the hop, including the nationalist political leadership. And the Church, an organisation which seemed ill-equipped to deal with all of that, has achieved enormous successes. Without compromising their political attitude at all, without playing the populist card by shouting "Free Ireland, a United Ireland", without harping on discrimination – those kind of things – they have been able to keep in with the people. A lot of the change has been cosmetic, as it has been everywhere else: the vernacular in the Mass, guitar-playing priests. But they have kept faith with young people.

'Some people are surprised at the numbers who don't attend Mass, but I'm always surprised at the numbers who do – and get married in the church, and celebrate baptisms and first communions. Very quickly it seems to me that young people of seventeen and eighteen who are radical-minded, within ten years have become Mr and Mrs X with the children at the Catholic school, and they're fundraising for the school and for church functions . . .

'Obviously the Church was in a position of strength. Twenty years ago, they had a monopoly of power in the Catholic community. But as an organisation they certainly changed remarkably successfully. They're as strong now as they were then, as influential. Perhaps more so, though in a different way.'

The testimonial does not come from an elderly parish priest, off the record and making a tongue-in-cheek assessment from the privileged and clear-eyed heights of age. The Church has not changed that much: STEPHEN is an ex-priest, and an ex-believer. For the past few years he has lived in London but he comes back often to visit family and friends. Perhaps because he has made a new life for himself he is neither bitter nor obsessed, unlike many in a similar position. From an unusual standpoint, with humour and only the occasional temptation to discern a grand plan where muddling through seems more likely, he evaluates how the clergy have responded to the many pressures of the past twenty-five years, and what as a result the Church in Northern Ireland means to its people.

Properly speaking, of course, there is no such thing as 'the Northern Church'. Dioceses straddle the border, as in the Church of Ireland, and a high proportion of priests, particularly those over fifty, were educated at Maynooth and have classmates in parishes all over Ireland. Yet there is no doubt that Northern Catholicism was a Church of the ghetto and still bears the marks. Stephen talked with great openness, but for the sake of his family in a small Northern town he dreaded identification. South of the border, where the overwhelming Catholicity of society permits the display of widely differing strands of Catholic behaviour along the whole spectrum from fundamentalist to radical, it may have become unsurprising to hear former priests speaking publicly about their past. There is no such casualness in the North: segregated, shut-in Belfast is a hundred miles and a world away from the fizz and frivol of Dublin pub talk.

Several Northerners I interviewed aged sixty or over remarked with some disgust and a degree of amazement on how 'people gawk and gabble' on RTE chat shows, as one put it, about the sexual affairs of 'the clergy': priests who fall in love and leave the priesthood to marry (Eamon Casey, the Bishop of Galway fled Ireland in 1992 after a woman revealed he was the father of her teenage son). Obviously they watched these programmes with some fascination, but equally obviously they could not quite comprehend what they saw as a scandalous Southern openness about family skeletons. A minority faith behaves differently.

The role of official Catholicism in defining and sustaining Northern Catholic identity is widely recognised as having been central since partition until at least the late fifties. For a community that disliked and felt alien from the wider state, the parish became the main civic unit: two of the oldest people I interviewed recalled that 'the local parish priest was the centre of every important gathering'. In the absence of political organisation and because Catholics felt no allegiance to the entity of Northern Ireland, the Church by default was the acknowledged chief source of authority and social coherence in a 'state within a state'. It says something about the past two decades of development within the community that the same description is now borrowed, to fit a much narrower grouping, by the imprisoned DANNY MORRISON, Sinn Féin's director of publicity until his arrest. He used the term to distinguish between Sinn Féin's support and the SDLP's: 'our constituency being a state within a state'. The phrase no longer suits the Catholic community as a whole – and the Church's role has evolved accordingly.

To Stephen, it is clear that 'they've played the conservative card. People twenty years ago chose conservative politicians. Like the Church, they had to cope with the sudden questions the civil rights movement threw up and they weren't geared for radical change. So it wasn't that the Church had to hold onto a radical flock. They probably correctly assessed just how far the flock would go and were able to not just play the conservative card but actually work towards a conservative position. And they've held onto the people and their loyalty. I think that must be agreed by anyone who's come through the whole thing.'

Like many others, he examines clerical behaviour in mainly political terms: and with a certain amount of distaste for the way the institutional Church – meaning cardinal, bishops, and priests in pulpit and confessional, preaching on Sundays and reported in the media – has 'played the conservative card'. There is a general agreement that what has dominated leading clerical minds in Northern Ireland over the past quarter of a century has been the threat posed by civil disorder and political upheaval to the Church's standing in the community, and that a prime ecclesiastical concern has been to maintain and negotiate alliances that will safeguard its position. Stephen readily admits that this is no different from past Church policy in Ireland, or elsewhere in the world – or from the policy of any other powerful institution.

Churchmen dislike such worldly terminology. They insist that theirs is not devotion to temporal power: their mission is 'to build the kingdom of God' – though the most frank admit that there is no distinction between the two. There is a wider clerical admission that the existence of an IRA more deeply rooted in their flock than ever before, and the emergence of Sinn Féin as the political voice of republicanism, have posed major problems for them.

Priests must minister to a community in which thousands have been killed and many more have suffered greatly – but this is also a community which has generated many killers and much suffering. The institutional Church has had to grapple with its own internal ambivalence about the use of violence in defence of the community, in the name of a political cause, and by the state. In the turmoil of 1969 when Belfast Catholic districts were attacked by Protestants and the RUC failed to protect them, priests in a number of places turned as they did in the twenties to local people to defend their churches. They found themselves relying on ancient IRA guns. In 1969 to 1970 several priests were involved in setting up the vigilante groups that came under the umbrella of the Central Citizens' Defence Committee (CCDC) and included members of the old IRA, soon to split into two separate organisations, the Provisionals and the Officials, though at this stage their role was solely defensive. Senior clergy took control soon after the CCDC was formed: leading figure left-wing republican Jim Sullivan was forced out.

It was a period of great tension and confusion on the streets. In May 1970, as the Provisional IRA began to emerge, the Northern bishops issued a statement declaring that a decision by an individual or group to 'deliberately provoke violence' would be a 'betrayal of the Catholic community – a stab in the back'. This was clearly meant for Provisionals thought to have helped organise street clashes between Catholics and the British army. But a month later a CCDC group including local priests invited Provisional IRA men to a thank-you tea after they had spent a night firing on loyalist crowds trying to burn down St Matthew's church in Short Strand – three Protestants and one of the defenders were shot dead.

The days of a purely defensive IRA are long gone, and the desire to dissociate Catholicism from violence by Catholics is strong: the Vatican demands it, there is a perception abroad that this is an inter-Christian religious war, and the Troubles are more than two decades old. As has been the case for generations, the IRA ignores denunciation from the Church but is indisputably drawn from their flock: its very existence is a 'grave scandal', senior clerics say. But official Northern Catholicism has had difficulty finding a clear and consistent message on militant republicanism. It relies instead on a few strong voices, who between them have preached a mixture of faith and politics in varying styles, and with varying degrees of persuasiveness.

The common thread has been the Church's traditional bottom line of obedience to the properly constituted civil authority – which has built-in limitations. This is a Church rooted in a singular way in Northern society, at the centre of a community whose identity was denied and which for decades experienced discrimination. More fundamentally still, it was the Catholic community that during the establishment of the Northern state in the 1920s suffered disproportionately from sectarian violence, in which some members of the new state's forces were implicated. The community withheld their allegiance from the state, and even that section now largely participating in it is far from completely reconciled. Twenties memories revived in 1969, and still walk. The present cardinal has urged Catholics to join the RUC, while two other leading clerics have expressed fears that RUC members and soldiers may be involved in collusion with loyalist paramilitaries. One of those clerics has also called on Catholics to give the police information about republican violence. The attempt to assert authority, defend civil order, and balance condemnation of the IRA with criticism of security force abuses has been a constant strain on the Church's credibility.

Priests on the ground have had more mundane problems. From the essentially middle-class framework of clerical life, they have to maintain contact on what should be an intimate level with people whose experience is starkly different: dependent on state benefits, in families strained and often broken by the pressures of poverty, endemic unemployment, and the additional stress of the Troubles. People throughout Northern Ireland say that a number of priests have struggled to adapt and update traditional clerical behaviour: others, not all of them the older generation, seem fossilised.

COLETTE was born in a small south Derry town, one of eleven children. Before they began to think about nationality, the family grew up aware that they were Catholics in an unfriendly wider world. The Church was part of the fabric of their lives.

'I was part of a majority community within a very small area, a tiny enclave of the town, but surrounding it were all these Protestant places, bigger and more powerful. You thought of yourself as a Catholic first, of course, because in a small town everything happened through the parish. Going to Mass, to the chapel, that was your social life. Everybody around was Catholic – for most of my young life I never met anybody who wasn't. All the activity, all the points of reference came from the Church: Catholic schools, the parochial hall, ceilis, carnivals to raise money for this and that, variety concerts, plays – a priest ran the drama society. The first time you were allowed to go out on your own with no grown-ups was to October devotions in the chapel. Walking home with your friends in the dark, that was quite exciting.'

For Colette, the Troubles shone a new light on this childhood Church. She started to teach in north Belfast, on the Shore Road. The migration of Catholics intimidated out of nearby Rathcoole had just begun.

'Pre the Troubles was pre Vatican Two, wasn't it? And that's what priests by and large brought with them into the Troubles, that they couldn't deal with the people. They were old, or they were coming through Maynooth and they were still being taught in the old style: "We perform the mystery and you watch."

'Then there came the big transition, the upheaval of the early Troubles. Whole communities on the move, people moving to areas where priests didn't know them, where they didn't know who to visit. They hadn't the will anyway – because the priests only went to people in respectable houses where they were sure they could drink out of the cups. Do you remember that? They came to our house – I mean, we had no money, but the children went to grammar schools and we were very respect-able. They picked the people they went to. Those who needed them most, people who could have done with advice from someone with a bit of education sometimes, they were the people they least knew. They shooed them away in case of contamination. And when those people started to move, people who might have had dirty houses, priests didn't visit them.

'Priests said Mass and if the people wanted the priests they had to go to them. They didn't see themselves as missionaries at any time. The idea was, God teaches that you go to Mass every Sunday, you come to us. And there was no argument. There wasn't a large enough educated class to argue.'

Over the past ten years a more profound class division has sharpened the contrast between the role of the Church in the most troubled areas and among the comfortably off. In the most affluent areas, parishioners describe Church-run schemes to 'twin' them with the most deprived: the idea is apparently to build solidarity and generate encouragement and entre-preneurial skills. It has been an awkward business, several said, which for many heightened a bitter contrast between their lives – but they felt that at least the Church was showing awareness of the divide and forcing the better-off to open their eyes to conditions a few miles from their comfortable homes. Others in less wealthy but comparatively untroubled parishes said they felt

priests ignored the Troubles. One woman said she'd like them
to mention every violent death: 'But they mention none, not
one – not even when inside the same short time a Catholic man
was shot dead on the side of the road by loyalists no more than
a mile from the church and a Protestant man was killed by
republicans in his own home. It looked like retaliation. Wouldn't
you think there'd have been a sermon in that? It's as if we were
living in County Meath.'

The criticism is the opposite of that in the troubled districts,
where priestly condemnation of republican violence has often
brought walkouts, and sermons on violence committed by
police or soldiers are combed for evidence of Church partiality
towards the forces of the state. Externally, the Catholic hierarchy is attacked for anything less than unforgiving denunciation
of republicanism. Internally they are criticised across a range of
viewpoints: 'You've had forty shades of green all wanting the
Church to say their thing, and you've also had a few shades of
blue [meaning pro-Union views],' says one senior cleric tiredly.
'It's been very difficult.'

CHURCH AND STATE

Most internal unhappiness about the Church's response to the
Troubles has come from the green rather than the blue – and
as the weary cleric said, it is a green of many shades. What unites
the greenest republican and some of the mildest constitutional
nationalists is a conviction that Church leaders have traditionally
been reluctant to challenge their secular counterparts, the 'temporal' authorities of the state: an opinion apparently common
among priests who are stationed in trouble spots, though they
are loath to be quoted. 'Turn off that tape,' said a man who has
held several sensitive positions, 'and I'll tell you what I think of
the bishop.' It was a routine that became familiar – on each of
the occasions when an interviewee wanted the tape recorder

off, they had something harsh to say about a senior cleric.

What this man thought was that preaching the gospel faithfully should 'make you unpopular with everyone, including the authorities, and I don't know that our Church leaders have been willing to be unpopular with the authorities. They haven't minded the Provos not liking them – because that improved their standing with the leaders of other Churches and with government officials.'

Catholic Church relations with the state today in Northern Ireland are by anyone's standards considerably warmer than in the past. The hierarchy had a well-established accommodation with the Stormont Unionist regime: distant, but adequate for the purposes of both sides. The American sociologist Richard Rose, who conducted the first of the large-scale attitude surveys in Northern Ireland in 1968 in the last few months before the Troubles began, summed up the bishops' stance: 'In short, the officers of the Catholic Church in Northern Ireland are disaffected but not rebels: they refuse support but give compliance to the regime.' Rose also noted that when civil rights demonstrations began, the hierarchy approved of the movement but priests were not in general openly involved in marches, and that Cardinal Conway had publicly expressed concern about an 'ultra-left and neo-Marxist' element in the civil rights movement: these were 'usually lapsed Catholics', in Rose's words, 'who threaten the authority of the Church as well as that of the Stormont regime' (*Governing Without Consensus: An Irish Perspective*, London, 1971).

In 1971 when Cardinal Conway met the then Unionist prime minister, James Chichester-Clark, it was the first such meeting in fifty years. Over the past twenty-five years, by contrast, there have been countless encounters between bishops, priests and Northern Ireland Office ministers.

These have occasionally been strained, as during the prison

hunger strike period when Cardinal Tomás Ó Fiaich and Bishop Edward Daly met Margaret Thatcher and on several occasions the then Northern Ireland secretary of state – 'the unspeakable Humphrey Atkins', in Bishop Daly's words – to plead unsuccessfully for official flexibility. But in recent years relations have been increasingly cordial. For several years now in Catholic areas of high unemployment the Church has been the chief operator of British government job schemes, a development sponsored by the present cardinal, Cahal Daly, in his previous position as Bishop of Down and Connor.

When Stephen concludes that the Church is perhaps more influential than before the Troubles – though differently – he is summing up a whole range of relationships: with the people, with the state, with nationalist politics, and with other Churches. Some of these have been more difficult and less satisfactorily negotiated than others, even in the eyes of the faithful. Stephen would have preferred to see more warmth between priests and people, and he thinks, like the cautiously critical cleric, that the hierarchy courts state favour in an unscriptural fashion. He is the first to admit that this has not diminished their importance to the community.

'They have the majority of the people still attending, respecting the Church. There may be some criticism of their political point of view, but the Church most definitely matters to the political parties, to the SDLP and Sinn Féin. The SDLP fits neatly into the Church's agenda. And Sinn Féin, if you like they're an unruly member but they certainly aren't outside. Many of them attend Mass. They still agonise over what the priest says from the altar, they insist on burying people in the Church.'

The perception that the Church's 'political point of view' includes an unwillingness to offend the state – as well as closeness to the SDLP – is widely shared. The first worries priests more than the second, but is scarcely voiced. The only sizeable study of Catholic clerical attitudes in the course of the Troubles (Gerard McElroy, *The Catholic Church and the Northern Ireland Crisis 1968–86,* Dublin, 1991) lists the clerical protests of the early years that went farther than the bishops of the day were prepared to go: a press conference in November 1972 called by 65 priests in the diocese of Down and Connor to protest at 'military violence . . . in the poorer Catholic areas' of Belfast; a statement by 387 priests in November 1971 which claimed that the internment imposed in August had led to brutality and torture, and was intrinsically immoral. A priests' association called on the bishops to back them. The association's secretary, who went on to repeat the call publicly and to make other criticisms of the hierarchy, was ordered by his bishop to give up his post as a university lecturer and move to a country parish as a curate. He left the priesthood.

Those were extraordinary times. The period from 1970 to 1973 was the time of greatest friction on the streets between Catholic civilians and the British army in particular, and internment raised communal feeling to a level unparalleled until the prison hunger strike of 1981. But as recently as 1986 Gerard McElroy polled all 628 Northern priests – 232 answered him – and 43.1 per cent of those who replied agreed with the statement that 'the hierarchy has not done enough to criticise various forms of state violence'. It is not a sentiment they make known to their superiors.

The number of public dissenters from the hierarchical line long ago dwindled to a tiny few. Since 1975, with no more than three exceptions, priests have not publicly challenged the bishops on political affairs – or on any other issue. The three exceptions are Des Wilson of Ballymurphy, west Belfast, Joe McVeigh, of County Fermanagh, and Pat Buckley: the last-named is a Southerner, whose clashes with the hierarchy might have happened no matter where he was. Father McVeigh's

public statements consist in the main of the accusation that
the hierarchy is sympathetic to the British and the enemy
of republicanism. Father Wilson's differences with the institutions of his Church are longer-running and of a wider order:
he has most consistently complained about the lack of internal democracy. With Father McVeigh he has published
several open letters to the hierarchy, castigating them for attacking republican violence instead of tackling the root of the conflict, which he and Father McVeigh define as 'the British
presence'.

For almost twenty years Des Wilson has worked as a community educator in Ballymurphy: Cahal Daly's predecessor
stripped him of parish duties, Dr Daly allowed him to say Mass
in public again, and for the past ten years he has functioned as
a priest but without the constraints of parish responsibilities.
Like Father McVeigh, he refused to be interviewed. He feels
bitterly isolated, both as a priest and as a citizen of Ballymurphy,
he said, and for much of this isolation he blames the media
North and South of the border who have 'marginalised and
silenced the nationalist people: they were not there when we
needed them'.

Stephen watches from a distance and concludes that the
Church can afford to tolerate this level of dissidence. 'They
have their odd radical priest like Desi Wilson – that was a very
confident move to reinstate him. I think it's very sad for him
that he couldn't break away and have a different kind of life. But
he's not damaging the Church, is he? And Father McVeigh,
publishing books and things about discrimination against
Catholics – nobody's going to object to that too much.' It was
a judgement shared by others. 'It suits them fine to have Des
Wilson in Ballymurphy,' said one woman. 'And why not Joe
McVeigh in Fermanagh? Useful enough – speaks for one element of the flock.'

VOICES OF AUTHORITY

For many years now, statements with the weight of Church authority on the morality of republicanism and the conduct of the security forces have been routinely offered by no more than two or three members of the hierarchy: by the cardinal, Cahal Daly, by the Bishop of Derry, Edward Daly, and by a priest with extraordinary access to the media, the Reverend Denis Faul. Father Faul is forceful in condemning the IRA, and simultaneously catalogues abuses by the British army, the RUC and the UDR (now the RIR).

The most individual voice has been that of Cahal Daly's predecessor, Tomás Ó Fiaich, who both made Father Faul's type of complaint against official violence and condemned IRA killings – but never with the same mechanical care to weigh one against the other. Like Cardinal Ó Fiaich, Father Faul talks of 'British' soldiers with regularity; but what lent Dr Ó Fiaich's tone weight was his position, and his emotional delivery. When an unarmed republican supporter was killed by a soldier at a border checkpoint, the cardinal said from the pulpit at the funeral that he had been 'regularly abused by the British army at the highly fortified checkpoint where he was shot dead: he was constantly stopped and searched to the eve of his death. In these circumstances many find it hard to believe it was a complete coincidence that the same young man should then be shot to death.' Then he widened the charge, in a way no other senior Catholic cleric has done before or since:

> Since John Gallagher was shot dead in Armagh city by British security forces in the opening days of the Troubles, the record of these forces in the diocese has been quite deplorable. To add insult to injury, it has just been revealed that the only serving British soldier who in all these years has been called to account for the murder of

an Irish Catholic, sentenced to life imprisonment, was released from prison inside three years and is now back again serving with the British army.

John Gallagher was an Armagh man in his fifties, shot in a crowd by B Specials who were never charged. The soldier prematurely released was convicted of the murder of a roadie for a pop group, shot on the Falls as he ran away after the two apparently exchanged insults. Cardinal Ó Fiaich's sermon pleased many Catholics concerned that the unaccountability of police and soldiers for the use of illicit force has been eclipsed by the IRA's record. The words from the pulpit made British officials nervous. Protestants who had long ago forgotten the shooting of John Gallagher heard a Catholic prelate with an Irish name from republican south Armagh suggesting that, in the very district where the IRA has killed most soldiers, it was 'British security forces' who were most at fault. Republicans were delighted. Such storms of controversy broke regularly over Tomás Ó Fiaich's head: according to friends, he was hurt and often bewildered. In the last few years before his sudden death from a heart attack, his public utterances were fewer, and guarded.

There could not be a greater contrast than that between the voluble, gregarious Dr Ó Fiaich and his successor, the bookish and prim Dr CAHAL DALY. His was the name that switched off the tape recorder. A profile shortly before his installation in 1990 as Archbishop of Armagh (by Ed Moloney in the *Sunday Tribune*, 28 October 1990) described Dr Daly's criticisms of the security forces, in the words of 'an associate', as 'delayed, measured and occasional'. It was noted that by contrast he had recommended with enthusiasm that Catholics should join the RUC and opposed the MacBride campaign in the USA which lobbies for firmer anti-discrimination action in Northern Ireland.

After more than ten years of eloquent denunciation of the IRA, Dr Daly became Bishop of Down and Connor in 1982. When he liaised with the Northern Ireland Office to establish government-funded job schemes under Church control, in the name of tackling Catholic west Belfast's high unemployment rate, republicans declared that the Church had become an agent of 'British counter-insurgency'. The move made the Church one of the largest employers in the area and unnerved some clerics. One senior figure worried that 'it made us look like an arm of pacification'.

Dr Daly also has a fully developed argument on the path to political progress. It bears considerable similarity to that of the SDLP leader, John Hume: republicans add up the prelate's public stance and denounce him in return as pro-British and pro-SDLP. The cardinal is confident that he speaks for the faithful, and responds to republican criticism by returning the attacks. What does he feel about being called a 'Brit', the ultimate republican insult, and what does he feel about the accusation that his leadership of the Church has helped to 'marginalise' a section of Catholic political society?

'I'm amused by it. It's absurd. Yes, it does worry me that people say they are excluded from society and politics and that the Church is part of that process – but I sometimes wonder if they're self-excluded from genuine dialogue with others. That generates a sort of desperation. I wonder if it's because their ingenuity and intelligence have been too concentrated on their military survival – that they haven't really done enough deep, informed political thinking to see if theirs are realistic and feasible political objectives.'

He denies that his is a political message. 'There are two views on what the long-term future of Ireland should be – they cannot self-evidently be settled by violence – and we can only get into a situation where rational political debate and discussion can take place, and mutual accommodation can come about, if we get institutions in the short and medium and perhaps the longer term that each can identify with and neither feel alienated from.

'As a Church person I have no right to express a view. But there is no other way morally but to support the constitutional political process. We cannot proceed normally unless there is some explicit and constitutional and institutional expression within Northern Ireland of the Irish identity: that's the pre-requisite of an internal settlement. Full and equal respect for both traditions, for unionists with their British identity and for the Irish tradition. Then you could create conditions in which there could be normal political interchange and an agreed future in the longer term.'

Dr Daly's distinction between his personal political opinion and the view he feels called to deliver as a bishop is lost on the multitude. Those who approve of what he says are in no doubt that it is the moral and proper stand for the Church to take; those who disapprove blame what they take to be his politics. Since his installation as cardinal and his move to Armagh, however, there has been a change in the dominant tone of Cahal Daly's public statements – as several veteran insiders predicted would happen when the new man in Armagh discovered that rural republicans were among the most respected in his congregation, not the 'corner boys he thought they were in Belfast'. One ageing priest commented drily, reckoning that this would be a 'bit of a culture shock for Cahal'.

When the IRA blew up a bus carrying Protestant workers at Teebane Cross in January 1992, killing eight men, the cardinal visited their relatives, expressed horror at the scene, and spoke on radio of the 'few evil men in each community who hold the whole community to ransom'. He was asked if those responsible were members of his flock, and he said they were not. The IRA lived in a 'blinkered situation, in such narrow, confined circles that they simply do not know the depth of revulsion which there is for them right across the whole Catholic community' – all fairly characteristic.

But when asked how he accounted for Sinn Féin's electoral support, Dr Daly said votes for political parties were 'very much a matter of tradition, emotion, concern with local community politics rather than great national issues'. There should be ways of dissenting from this or that element of a party's programme. People had a moral responsibility to ensure as far as they could that their votes would not be 'misinterpreted for nefarious purposes'. This applied to more than the Sinn Féin electorate, he said. Though this kind of statement will not erase the memory of his time in Belfast, it is an altogether more diplomatic and complex approach to the republican voters in his congregation.

Although some SDLP supporters dislike the cardinal's style, no prominent party figure has anything less than praise for him. BRIAN FEENEY says his anti-IRA speeches are intended in the main to demonstrate to the wider world that IRA violence is not Catholic violence and 'to give the Catholic middle class a verbal armoury against republicanism'. He adds with characteristic frankness that 'as far as making contact with the hearts and minds of IRA/Sinn Féin supporters in places like Coalisland, Derry and west Belfast, they have no effect whatsoever'.

THE CHURCH AND THE PARTIES

SDLP members maintain that theirs is a pluralist, secular party. Republicans jeer that the party is no more than a retread of the pious old Nationalist politicians of the forties and fifties. But the relationship between Church, Nationalist Party and people was entirely shaped by the circumstances of another age.

A story from the mid-fifties told and retold in our family, and familiar to many others, involved the parish priest presiding over the selection convention who ceremoniously wound up by writing out a cheque to pay for the candidate's deposit. The candidate began with a stammer to propose a vote of thanks. 'Sit down you eejit you and shut up,' said the parish priest. Though it was certainly recognised that this was boorish behaviour, the point was the futility of contemporary nationalist politics, not in any sense criticism of the Church. Clerical intervention in elections was always regarded as dependent on the interest of individual priests, not at all as coordinated or centrally directed.

Where once local priests stood in for nonexistent political organisation, the SDLP is now the respectable voice of the community. It inherited Nationalist Party votes, and in many places much of the old closeness of Nationalist Party politicians to the Church, but for all that their interests are in many ways identical, it is a different party, as the Church is a different Church, both of them adjusting to shifts in the Catholic community as a whole.

Some SDLP people, cheerfully acknowledging their origins, recall a north Antrim branch formed wholesale from former Nationalist Party stalwarts which forwarded a list of names to the new SDLP headquarters. 'They hadn't quite got the idea that we were to be a new type of animal. There it was, up at the top, after Chairman, Secretary and Treasurer: Spiritual Director the Reverend So-and-So – the local curate.' A number in the party know that closeness to the Church does them no harm in the community; others would prefer that was not so. The official line from both Church and party is deadpan acceptance that there is agreement on a correct and proper path for Catholics to follow politically – but a proper separateness.

But it would be difficult not to notice how nice they are about each other – and I have yet to meet the SDLP equivalent of former Sinn Féin councillor BRIAN MCCAFFREY in deepest rural Fermanagh, who said that it is well known locally that he does not go to Mass: in fact he thinks the voters respected him

for his openness. They know, of course, that his rift with the
Church is in part because of its pronouncements on politics.
Rather than being considered a freethinking immoral atheist, he
therefore got credit for being in the tradition of republicans
anathematised by the hierarchy through the centuries – some of
them, like de Valera, famously pious upholders of the Church
in their later years. On the other hand the most indiscreet of
SDLP people, some not at all religious in private life, become
paragons of discretion when asked how they think the bishops
have responded to the Troubles.

'They are what they are. Even asking how the Church has
performed during the Troubles suggests that religion has
something to do with the problem, which as you know well it
hasn't,' sighed one usually more forthcoming source. The same
person went on to commend churchmen for 'doing their job
and hammering it home that the IRA has no moral justification'.
Another concluded that 'as far as possible they have delegiti-
mised the campaign of violence – there's little room for ambiguity. And they've managed to do it without making martyrs,
which is a feat.'

The approval was for the general tone of clerical pronouncements at the top, not solely for the particular contribution of Cahal Daly. Repeated denunciation of the use of
violence, and of apologists for violence, has made clear what the
officially approved attitude is to Sinn Féin. Constant praise for
the moderation and morality of the advocates of constitutional
nationalism indicates where the Church's blessing lies. What
diversity there is in priests' opinions may be detectable in their
own parishes, but rarely breaks cover. 'They have their sneaking
regarders, like the rest of the community,' says one dry observer
– covert republicanism has never been admired by Catholics of
any opinion.

It is almost impossible to convince curates and parish priests alike that their opinions will be anonymous and they may speak freely. Several told me they would like to discuss a Catholic sense of identity, but they were afraid they might 'mishandle' politics. The solution for many seems to be a middle course: they say as little as possible about politics in their pulpits and nothing outside them except in private conversations. Generalised denunciations of violence may leave the impression that priests favour the SDLP rather than Sinn Féin. But often people remain unsure what their local clergy think.

The 1986 survey of Northern priests' opinions found that 87.9 per cent expressed a voting preference for the SDLP to only 3.9 per cent – just nine priests – who said they would be 'most likely to vote for Sinn Féin in a general election'. The finding led the researcher to wonder 'how an almost exclusively anti-Sinn Féin clergy can retain credibility among a large section of the Catholic community'. The many nervous jokes I heard about 'sudden transfers' (to less pleasant parishes) if they were quoted 'out of turn' prompted the suspicion that the survey might as easily reflect dread of self-revelation – even anonymously – as orthodoxy.

Whatever the real situation, republican bitterness at what they see as unanimity between priests and the SDLP is a measure of how much the Church still matters to Northern Catholics. Outsiders may be more struck by the fact that the Church tells the IRA to stop and is ignored. Republicans insist that their 'sound' voters are loyal and undeterred, but they regard clerical condemnation as part of the web of official or 'establishment' opinion that they maintain has restricted their appeal and damaged their standing. It was striking that three leading republicans in interviews cited their mothers as having been greatly distressed by sermons on the iniquity of the IRA and of those who supported them by voting Sinn Féin.

The IRA man I spoke to was particularly incensed. His

mother 'lights candles, goes to Devotions, daily Mass, does the whole business – and Cahal Daly told her she wasn't a Catholic because she voted Sinn Féin, which is grossly insulting given her historical experience. It's arrogance, pure arrogance! I would never dream of attacking her beliefs. And to say that to thousands of people!'

GERRY ADAMS, the Sinn Féin president, was MP for west Belfast during Cahal Daly's stint there. Though leading clerics would have tagged him a communist when he became prominent in the late seventies, he is also republicanism's most public Catholic: an assiduous Mass-goer, conspicuously prayerful. When he comments on Church leadership, it is always as a member of the Church: 'It's my Church as well as Cahal Daly's,' he says. His response to ecclesiastical wrath is to characterise it directly as overtly political – and as an attack on republicans' rightful sense of identity as Northern Catholics.

'What has affected Catholics most in terms of alienation from the Church on the national question is that British ministers give off to them, the press gives off to them, TV and the British media give off to them. I know this is a very subjective view – but they're on the receiving end of whatever happens and there's nobody up there sticking up for them. And then lo and behold, when they go round to the Church, the Church is giving off to them as well. To be a Catholic is still a political thing: it identifies you as a Fenian, a Taig. People are killed for being Catholic, or they can't go certain places without that danger. And they have an affinity with the Church which has to do with its history in Ireland, echoes of the penal days, punishment by death for being a priest or a bishop – the Church was part of people's struggle.

'It's also group solidarity. If you're from a small parish, and you're living with loyalists all around you, the Church isn't just spiritual or religious. It also becomes an important identification. If you don't get succour there, it mightn't be just so bad; but if you get condemnation, denunciation, when you're looking for a bit of understanding – it's that which has caused alienation.

'The Church has certainly been much more outspoken against militant, physical force republicanism in the last twenty years than it ever has been about the British presence. They say they speak in such firm terms against republicans because so many of them "come from our flock". But the RUC man in charge of the operation where Sean Downes was killed was a Catholic, and there was none of that language used to him, no call for him to remove himself from that organisation. He got something like an English liberal's lecture on proper police crowd control from Cahal Daly – not a sermon which was critical on theological grounds.

'There is a section, and Cahal Daly personifies it best – Father Faul less so because his feet are much more firmly on the ground and he lives and works with the community – and that is one that's absolutely outraged that people like those in Sinn Féin should be in positions of public responsibility or representation. There's a snobbery: they are quite appalled, and I think this is in part why the hierarchy attacks us in such harsh terms.

'I don't altogether group Father Faul in this, though I do think that when we were all wee Catholic boys and girls being tortured and beaten up and hadn't any great political thoughts of our own, he was less strident too. I think the hunger strikes changed Father Faul. The Church sees the rise of radical republicanism as threatening their control.

'I think it was the experience of most people of my age at grammar schools that we were being groomed. Certain people finished that grooming, and became bishops, parish priests, leaders of the SDLP – and other "responsible" positions. You hear all this talk about "responsible" leaders: homilies by the cardinal to Catholics that we should be involved in campaigns like housing because if we don't the men of violence will fill the vacuum. That's a most unchristian reason to be involved in any just cause. There's an aspect in all of this in which the Catholic establishment looks for "safe" and "responsible" figures. And at least among some of them there's this snobbery: that these Sinn Féin people haven't been trained in our schools to be in positions of leadership.'

For all that Gerry Adams addresses himself so directly to his own supporters' grievance about Church strictures, he raises echoes of unwilling agreement elsewhere: in particular on the class issue, in the suggestion that republicans challenge the Church's preferred social structure as much as they do the Church's moral teaching. The association of lay 'respectability' and Catholic clergy is familiar to many, most strikingly in reminiscences about poor childhoods in which it was obvious that those with professional status or 'a bit more money', like local shopkeepers, were the important members of the parish.

Many are angered by republicans' insistence on their own Catholicism. 'It maddens me,' one young County Down woman said. 'Over and over again they hear the Church saying it's the word of God that you shall not kill, and if you do you can't call yourself a Catholic. They keep right on murdering, and then they say, "We're Catholics too."'

According to the Catholic Church's 'just war' theory, the six conditions that determine whether a war is 'just' are: (1) a just cause; (2) force must be the only way left of affecting change; (3) there must be a properly constituted authority to direct the action; (4) there must be a feasible goal; (5) the means must be appropriate to the end; (6) reconciliation must be sought as the ultimate end (*Violence in Ireland – A Report to the Churches,* Dublin, 1976). But the Church has difficulty making sense of its 'just war' theory in Northern Ireland terms, and enough people are aware of the inconsistency to give Gerry Adams's argument at least a grudging nod. The picture of a group constantly scolded from on high also brings recognition. Many orthodox and dutiful Catholics who regard the bishops' word as law also worry that the tactic of sermonising from a distance has been counterproductive.

For Adams, the constant emphasis on republicans' membership of the Church is a clear response to what he knows his supporters want him to emphasise. His notably careful treatment of Father Faul springs from the same impulse. Many IRA supporters blame Father Faul for helping to break the 1981 republican prisoners' hunger strike. But he attacks republicanism in a way that acknowledges their membership of the same community as himself. This matters to Gerry Adams, whose own challenge is to locate the Sinn Féin he leads, and his own brand of modern republicanism, within the mainstream of Northern Catholic identity.

In the late seventies I remember asking a senior republican who had been standing silently in the middle of the praying crowd at an IRA funeral, if there was not something odd in a movement that liked to use Marxist language conducting ceremonies complete with priests and the public recitation of the Rosary. 'We're no mugs,' he said, 'you're not going to find us making the same mistake the Stickies made.' The unsuccessful electoral history of the openly atheist-Marxist Official republicans has been more complicated than that, but his point was clear. There is a sharp republican awareness that open attacks on bishops are all very well, even expected of them – but loyalty to faith and religious affiliation is an integral part of Northern Catholic identity, too deep and instinctive for debate, and must never be even implicitly slighted.

THE TIGHTROPE

In the Church's struggle to reflect different facets in the

changing identity of Northern Catholics – which is what statements about the IRA, the state and violence revolve around – Father DENIS FAUL is a major figure, an institution in his own right. Although a headmaster in Dungannon, County Tyrone, he is effectively a full-time commentator, issuing unsolicited statements at a rate of one or two a week and perpetually available for interview in print, on radio or on television. He talks fast and fluently and always with the same intensity, rattling out confident assertions across an apparently unlimited field. His is a more direct and pugnacious approach than that of the bishops. He is not, however, a public critic of the hierarchy, and he juggles furiously to ensure that his criticism of official abuse or violence should not be taken as justification for the IRA: an expert on the tightrope that the Church negotiates in making public comment on the Troubles.

No one is more aware of the community's conflicting impulses: middle-class desire for stability and order, resentment among the poor, the strains within republicanism between social conservatives and radicals, shared memories of loyalist aggression and suspicion about security force collusion, an un-diminished and even strengthened sense of Irishness alongside distance from Southerners and dependence on a British social welfare system. 'The Dungannon priest', as the media style him, has commented on them all.

The odd thing is that Denis Faul is not himself a Northerner, at least not in the sense of being born within the state. He went to boarding school in Armagh and has spent his entire adult life as a priest in Northern Ireland. But he comes from County Louth, just south of the border: the same countryside as south Armagh linguistically and culturally, as he points out enthu-siastically, and yet part of the independent Irish Republic. Of all the public clerical voices throughout the Troubles, Denis Faul is most given to talking about what 'Northern' Catholics think and want. Tomás Ó Fiaich spoke of 'Irish' Catholics, Cahal Daly speaks of 'Catholics', as though to blot out the support for unchristian violence among his Northern Catholic flock. Father Faul says repeatedly, and with no inhibition about making political assessments, that Northern Catholics do not want unification, they want equality and justice inside Northern Ireland. They do not want to lose their 'British benefits and educational scholarships', they do not want the border to go. Though these are statements of fact, not criticism, there is more than a hint in Father Faul's tone of disapproval for the degree to which Northern Catholics have been seduced away from pure, nationalist disaffection by 'British benefits'.

He speaks of 'Northern' Catholics, but always of 'Irish' Catholicism. This is threatened from two directions: by a growing secularism and materialism, and by the IRA: 'They ask Catholics to live a lie, to plot to kill their neighbour, it destroys the meaning of the Mass and Holy Communion, they're a threat to decency – and this present generation of IRA men have taken up opposition to the Church and in particular to the bishops.' Denis Faul, a wry and humorous man off-duty, without a trace of pomposity, sees himself as a shocktrooper on both fronts. His 'mission', and he talks in such terms, is to maintain the faith by demonstrating that the Church will 'stand up for the poor Catholics of Northern Ireland', the group he clearly feels are still most true to the traditional faith, and to traditional nationalism.

In the kind of clerical argument Gerry Adams characterised as unchristian, and that Father Faul makes totally without self-consciousness or apology, he says that the Church must speak for Catholics 'at the sharp end of injustice and sectarianism' – or lose souls to 'the Provos' by allowing Sinn Féin to consolidate an underclass vote. Modern middle-class Catholics, a rapidly changing group he does not understand although undoubtedly middle-class in origins himself – mother a teacher, father a doctor – are not so close to his paternalistic heart.

He is as committed to campaigning against liberal changes in the Republic's social legislation as he is to his full portfolio of Northern issues: he opposed the introduction of easier divorce to bring Northern Ireland into line with the rest of the UK, and travels South to speak at anti-abortion meetings after a day's teaching and making statements on Northern affairs. His was the only clerical voice raised when free contraception became available through the Northern Ireland health service, courtesy of an SDLP minister for health and social services in the short-lived power-sharing executive, the avowedly atheist, socialist Paddy Devlin. Where in general the Catholic Church coexists in the North in near-silence with the kind of legislation it has fought off in the Republic, aware that it had no option and in part consoled by the social conservatism of Unionism, Father Faul's distaste for the secular and British Northern state is scarcely concealed. He does not hide his conviction that what he calls a 'Catholic lifestyle' is threatened by the very existence of a secular state, and by the proximity of other Christians, that is, Protestants, who have a different concept of social legislation.

'You can have tea parties and you can have chats and you can have talks but there are certainly very definite differences in the style of life, and you have to be insistent on the Catholic point of view coming forward on Catholic family morality and contraception, abortion, medical ethics and divorce and those things.'

Down the years Father Faul has denounced the British army, RUC and UDR treatment of Catholics, the judicial system, anything that looks like collusion between the security forces and loyalist paramilitaries, discrimination against Catholics, integrated education, the Northern Ireland Office for its support of integrated education, middle-class Catholics who send their children to Protestant schools, the extension of British abortion law to Northern Ireland – and republican gunmen. With the Armagh priest and former prison chaplain Father Raymond Murray he has written numerous pamphlets; their early catalogue of injuries sustained by internees helped to propel an Irish government case against Britain to the European Court of Human Rights. In 1969 he criticised the judiciary of the time as in nationalist eyes essentially composed of Unionist placemen rewarded for discrimination against Catholics. There was a Unionist outcry and Cardinal Conway called the criticism 'unwarranted'. Father Faul was silenced – 'for about a fortnight,' he says impishly.

While he churns out statements, he also finds time to phone police stations for people with relatives arrested and held incommunicado under anti-terrorist legislation, and makes complaints on behalf of those who say they have been ill-treated by the security forces. It is the kind of pedigree that induces republican politeness and restrains their wrath, in public at any rate, when Father Faul also helps Catholic fugitives from the IRA to leave the country or publicises their complaints about IRA beatings and threats.

Many Catholics long ago reached the conclusion that the institutional Church sees Denis Faul, unimpeachably conservative in doctrinal issues, as a safe channel for indignation perhaps too undiplomatic for a more senior cleric to voice. In recent years, with NIO administrations increasingly soliciting his advice, particularly on prison protests, Father Faul has developed his own style of diplomacy, on several occasions publicly offering British government representatives congratulations on their fair dealing. He has in recent years encouraged the prison authorities to stand firm in their policy of integrating republicans and loyalists, maintaining that this is the only way to break the paramilitary organisations' control over prisoners affiliated to them.

The response of the Church as a whole to the Troubles preoccupies him: and the role of the bishops at the outset of the Troubles still bothers him. Where Cahal Daly and Eddie Daly try to distance the Church from nationalism, Denis Faul thinks 'the Catholic religion is not passed on in a vacuum . . . the context has traditionally been the Irish nationalist context – we were fortunate in Ireland that the attack on the Church by the reformers coincided with the attack on Irish independence and the Irish state, and the two went together'. He makes no comment on the senior clerics' style, but the difference is marked. When he recalls the Church's role at the start of the Troubles, he regrets that the hierarchy did not demand more of the British government, in particular the dissolution of Stormont as soon as soldiers were put on the streets.

'Cardinal Conway was a very good man and a cautious man. He was afraid if he did that, Paisley would shout "Rome Rule". . . It meant the Unionist government became identified with the British army, and that created the Provos. You had the Falls curfew, Bombay Street and the lot – and then of course you had Bloody Sunday. . . There was a failure of leadership there. Why didn't bishops, senior politicians, get together and insist?

'There was this thing that you didn't go out and demand. You kept the head down. It's easy to be wise with hindsight – but whatever opportunities the Church had, it had them at the beginning.'

Father Faul is admired by colleagues who are themselves terrified by the very idea of making a public statement – perhaps the best indication that the Church fills a need by leaving him free to act as both vent and spokesman. But it was nonsense to suggest Father Faul had been 'licensed', said the cautious senior priest, whose criticism of the bishop emerged only when the tape recorder went off. 'Nobody could license Denis. There's room for crusaders all right, and he's an admirable example. He would have been branded a Provo in his day, and was never a Provo.' It was a telling afterthought: the very consideration that most deters others from speaking out.

In his regrets, as in his patent nostalgia for a simpler past when a smaller, more devout middle class stood four-square beside the Church, and IRA men did not challenge bishops with the articulacy of present-day republicans, Father Faul would probably admit that he is a wishful-thinking reactionary – not a description he regards as an insult. This glum assessment that the Church 'missed its chance', however, suggests a lurking fear that even the most frantic effort since, like his own exhausting campaigning, can only pick up pieces, and that the Troubles mark a transitional stage for Northern Catholics during which the Church has done well to conserve so much power and status.

But there is also in his inimitable style something of his origins. When Denis Faul regrets the inordinate caution of episcopal behaviour in the early Troubles, the prevailing tendency to 'keep your head down' and when he recalls Cardinal Conway's governing fear of provoking loyalist violence against Catholics, there is surely more than a trace of Southern, freeborn-Irish disdain for the defensive style of ghetto Northern Catholicism.

Bishop EDWARD DALY of Derry – commonly referred to as Eddie or Ned, an affectionate familiarity few bishops earn – has been the fourth most public face of the Church over the past twenty years. No one forgets, least of all you suspect Eddie Daly himself, that his appointment was the most direct response the Catholic Church has made to the Troubles. Once he was the youngish priest waving a white handkerchief as a desperate flag of truce towards the paratroopers firing into the crowd on Bloody Sunday. He gave interview after interview, plainly sincere, bewildered, anguished. Next he was whisked away for a course in communications. In 1974 he became a bishop.

'That was a clever move the Church made,' says Stephen the ex-priest. 'Ned was never *episcopabilis,* as they say – he was a very good priest, very popular, cared for the people, went on civil rights marches – but he wasn't being groomed for anything.'

In a sense his public stance as a Church spokesman might be said to fall midway between those of Denis Faul and Cahal Daly. He deplores police and soldiers' disruptive searches of Catholic areas, has condemned various fatal shootings by soldiers in Derry, called on Catholics to give information to the RUC and frequently denounces the IRA. He has also held a series of talks with Sinn Féin leaders in Derry over the past two years, interrupted when he had a minor stroke in early 1993. Cahal Daly welcomed the talks as an attempt to bring about an IRA ceasefire, though he has himself repeatedly declared that he will never speak to Sinn Féin, 'not even in a pastoral capacity'.

The cardinal expounds at length on the need for nationalists to recognise the validity of the British, unionist tradition: Bishop Daly has developed a personal and public friendship with his Church of Ireland counterpart in Derry as part of a policy of building civic, cross-community pride in the divided city. His public image is softer than that of Father Faul, though he has been a campaigner in his own way: primarily in the cases of the Birmingham Six and others jailed in England, and in reiterating the innocence of those killed on Bloody Sunday. Speaking about the effects of the Troubles on people's opinions, he said, 'Our current Northern identity has been shaped to a significant extent out of a sense of shame at things done in our name, not with our consent or approval – and also at things that were done to people whom we would consider our friends, attacks we would perceive as attacks on our whole community:

Bloody Sunday, yes, and the murder of Danny Cassidy recently in Kilrea [a Sinn Féin worker, killed by loyalists, whose friends said he had been threatened by police] and everybody washed their hands off it: the fact that there are people who do the most terrible things almost with impunity.'

Where Father Faul is endlessly specific about allegations of collusion against the security forces, for example, Eddie Daly makes allusions then passes on to more general statements of religious teaching. He is clearly unhappy with some aspects. The Church's 'just war' theory he described in a Catholic magazine in 1975 as 'vague and ambiguous in the extreme . . . almost every two-bit revolutionary has his own version of it. We need far greater development of the theology of the morality of violence and of institutional injustice and of the theology of the just war. It is a crying need in the Churches today.'

He says now, 'These years have been very difficult for the Church here. Each element wishes the Church to support its point of view. As a bishop I have always felt that my duty should be to preach forgiveness, tolerance, charity, and through my work to exemplify the search for a political solution through non-violent means. But the Church is perceived in different ways. My perception is naturally from the inside, very subjective.'

Unusually for a senior churchman, Eddie Daly admits mistakes, the admission pointing up how difficult he has found it to strike the right note under stress. 'I have said a few things I regretted, usually in the immediate aftermath of some atrocity when a journalist stuck a microphone in front of me at a time when I was very upset emotionally. At one stage early on I described somebody as Satan which I should not have done.'

Recalling visits to the H Blocks in the Maze prison during the 'dirty' protest, when republicans dressed only in blankets smeared excrement over their cells; and remembering meetings with various NIO ministers when he and Cardinal Tomás Ó Fiaich 'tried to speak sense to them', he wonders whether they should have been 'tougher with Thatcher before the devastating hunger strikes began. However, I do not believe that anything we might have said or done would have changed her mind on that issue... We spent many days and nights on that mission. We were both quite exhausted at the end – we tried and sadly we failed.

'One of the problems about taking a very strong stand in situations like that is the fear of retaliation on someone else or of one's words being exploited by one group or the other. I remember once issuing a very strong statement critical of the army and the following day a number of soldiers were murdered. I am sure that ambush was set up long before I spoke. However, some people blamed me and what I said for the murders. I experienced great remorse after that, and on many other occasions. I have also experienced situations where the British have quoted from my statements in their propaganda or carried out extensive raids after some statement of mine.'

Derry's smallness has much to do with Bishop Daly's image. Perhaps even more than Denis Faul, he identifies publicly with the Catholic community: where Father Faul declares that 'Northern Catholics' think such-and-such, Eddie Daly habitually says 'we'. He has always been approachable: the combination evokes affection. When he recommended that Catholics should give information on violence to the RUC, the slogan 'JUDAS DALY' with the phone number of the bishop's house appeared on a Bogside wall. It was washed off within hours.

The most public test he has faced has been the question of how IRA funerals should be conducted. When shots were fired on the steps of a Derry church by an IRA colour party, Eddie Daly imposed restrictions on the next paramilitary funerals to take place. There was a lengthy and mutually embarrassing stand-off: the IRA have since been careful to keep their ritual to a minimum inside church grounds.

Eddie Daly says now: 'The paramilitary funeral is one of our major problems . . . when there are several television crews jockeying for position, a packed church and people distraught with grief and anger and a degree of uncertainty about what precisely happened or who did it or why, or whether the deceased was actually a member of an organisation or not – it is very difficult. It can be daunting and sometimes frightening for the priest. He has to cope with huge crowds, an intimidating army and police presence, he may have had to spend the previous two days and nights with the family helping them to cope with the sudden grief, he will have been under pressure from police, army, paramilitary organisations about the route of the funeral, he will have been hounded by the media for quotes and the text of a homily. He may well have to jot that down at half seven in the morning after being up all night and then those words will be parsed and analysed for all kinds of hidden and subtle meaning.

'Then in a crowded church under television lights he has to follow a set of guidelines from the bishop about flags and emblems in the church and grounds – in front of a highly emotional and often angry congregation – and every move he makes is monitored. He is very conscious that he will have to minister and live in that parish tomorrow and the next day and the months ahead after all these others leave. And very few of the people present can be expected to have the courage to take his side in a public manner if and when he is challenged in these circumstances. He is on his own and knows he is on his own. I have enormous admiration for the manner in which so many priests have conducted themselves in these very different pastoral situations.'

It was the most telling account any cleric managed of what the Troubles mean to many priests, the public and visible challenge of their own ideas about politics, brought into sharp focus by the Church's requirement of them. Awareness of their visibility in a society with a strong streak of anti-Catholicism is a massive inhibition for Catholic clergy. Even if the hierarchy had not made it plain that statements should be left to them, the widely shared Protestant perception of a pan-Catholic alliance spanning IRA, Sinn Féin, the SDLP and the Catholic Church would deter most from making any public statement on potentially contentious matters.

IRA funerals cause furore enough: even though most priests clearly accept that those baptised Catholic deserve a Catholic burial, they are plainly embarrassed by the publicity, aware that the occasion presents to the world the spectacle of the most sharply opposed elements of the Catholic community in close proximity and apparently engaged together in a sacred rite.

During the hunger strikes, a wave of emotional anti-Britishness and support for the prisoners carried thousands who would never have marched in an ordinary IRA funeral procession onto the streets of Belfast for the funeral of Bobby Sands. Though few wore their clerical garb, there were priests among them. Discretion, fear of censure and of 'giving scandal' deterred display – but the public spectacle occurred in any case.

One of the hunger strikers, Raymond McCreesh, was from south Armagh, the brother of a priest. The funeral was conducted in Irish by the dead prisoner's brother: scores of priests, there to show sympathy to a bereaved colleague, processed up the aisle in full vestments to Communion as the choir sang a traditional Irish hymn. It was a beautiful sunny day. I remember one old priest coming back down the aisle, beatific in the sunshine and the sound of Irish, eyes shining. Gerry Adams knelt near the back with his young son, then both went to

Communion, tweed jackets neatly ironed, hands joined prayer-fully. The lines of priests looked on. Through a side window the congregation could see uniformed girls and boys, young Fianna members in black berets with saffron handkerchief masks around their mouths, waiting among the gravestones to form up behind the coffin. The hills of south Armagh were soft and blue in the background. A film director might have thought the combination a touch unsubtle. Soon after Communion, Adams left the church to give directions outside, and the priests arranged themselves in white soutaned rows to follow the coffin with its uniformed guard.

It was of course to some degree a fiction. Funerals by their nature impose togetherness on the ill-assorted. But one tele-vision audience was not disposed to be detached and judicious. Tension between the two communities had rarely been higher, and a few days earlier and a few miles away, the IRA had killed five young soldiers – their tribute to the dying Raymond McCreesh. Unionists blazed with rage at the sight of prominent Provos and priests by the dozen in close proximity by his grave. The funeral for any priest's close relative would have seen a similar number of priests, a point made sharply to me by several practising Catholics who read the report I wrote, and disliked what they took to be unnecessary emphasis on the ranks of mourning clerics and the impression of unifying Irishness. They were also acid about the spectacle of Gerry Adams taking Com-munion: the final embarrassing touch and quite deliberate, they thought; though by all accounts he does so regularly, varying the churches he attends to protect himself against would-be loyalist assassins.

For him, as for many others, there is no difficulty in reconcil-ing religious practice and political belief. They take as justifica-tion the conditions the Church has refined and re-refined as their 'just war' theory. 'The Provos by sleight of tongue can bring themselves within it', says MARY MCALEESE. 'I know people who do it. I hear them: tremendous Catholics, all form, up at the altar, beating the kids out to Confession, great exponents of the Catholic school system – who vote Sinn Féin. I say: "How can you do that?" And there's no problem for them. Just war, they say, even the Church, they say, Christ Himself... I say it's not Christ, it's man trying to rationalise God into his own miserable mediocre littleness, the same God that thought black people were second-class citizens. Not *the* God.'

Mary McAleese is the only Northern Catholic laywoman to have a significant public profile based at least in part on her religious beliefs. Her access to bishops and Church authorities generally – as a lawyer who has advised the hierarchy on abortion and divorce legislation – is fairly unusual for a lay person, and almost unique for a woman.

'The just war theory for sure causes the Church problems. It's not addressed. I know Cahal Daly attempted to do that, but frankly every time you enter that dialogue, your words are music to the ears of the Provos. And yet, I don't think anyone who purports to speak on behalf of Christ has the right to say "I won't talk". They've got a gospel to preach.'

She is entirely loyal to her concept of the Church, praises the cardinal as a 'very forthright and principled man', and says she would not want to 'knock the clergy because they're going through a tremendous valley period'. But she is unhappy about the dominant tone in Church teaching on the Provos.

'You never hear from them the voice of forgiveness. The person we associate most strongly with forgiveness was not a churchman at all, but the father of a girl who died in Enniskillen. Are they afraid to say it? I think possibly they are. I'm quite happy to say this because I've said it to the cardinal face to face, told the bishops it. Their message is too like the messages of all the other politicians – "scum, maniacs, not human beings". It's not the language of the Christian who has to love unconditionally. If I was hearing that about myself, I would shut myself off further and further, I wouldn't listen.

'I think the Church should have dialogue with the Provos. They are the people who are literally keeping hell going in this community...the very fact that almost all of them are ethnic Catholics means that somewhere along the line they were baptised in the faith. If the faith means anything, there ought to be something there to work on. It's a work of evangelisation, work for clergymen that Christ sent them on this earth to do. The people in the churches are irrelevant. They're in the bag. They have to concentrate on the ones who came like little shining beacons at Confirmation – what the hell happened?'

It is perhaps a measure of how difficult the Troubles have been for the Church that even one of their most ardent defenders should make such a fundamental complaint about their teaching. Essentially, Mary McAleese demands that the bishops abandon political concerns, undue sensitivity to unionist opinion, attempts to influence the British government. They should, to her mind, turn first to pure evangelism: 'Are they afraid to say it?' she asks, as many others do who are equally devout but more timid. 'Turn the tape recorder off,' said a sixty-year-old County Antrim woman, so she could tell me how wrong she thought Cahal Daly was in refusing to talk to Sinn Féin.

THE SCHOOLS

SEAMUS MALLON, the 57-year-old SDLP deputy leader, was formerly headmaster in a Catholic primary school in County Armagh. He says there is 'no mystery about the place of Catholicism in nationalist identity. This was a small community and the Church was close to it, because it had originally been a peasant community – which I don't mean pejoratively, I mean close to the land and it was therefore close to its institutions. The only institutions it had originally were the Church and the local schoolmaster. They were its only recourse.

'The Church has been a very positive thing, in that it is greater than Northern Ireland, part of the whole island, of Europe and the world. That lent an element of ability to think outside the immediate context. The counter-element was that you had a Church as totally defensive as the nationalist community was. It had to defend its position, especially in terms of hospitals and schools, and as a result it tended to become too authoritarian in its approach. That has started to give way now.'

In recalling the days when priest and schoolmaster were the only communal figures of status, Seamus Mallon recalls a central and enduring alliance, one from which his party still derives strength. For much of its existence the most distinctive strand in the party's membership has been a core of teachers from Catholic schools: a conservative, cautious and frequently devout group, part of the most communally active element in the old Catholic middle class before affluence and diversity of occupation spread. Many are principals, as Seamus Mallon was.

The common ground between Church and senior teachers, as reflected in the SDLP, is on middle-class Catholic values: the desire to present a Northern Catholic identity that is moderate politically and uncompromising on the basics – which include separate Catholic schooling. A Church tenet worldwide, separate schooling has an extra layer of meaning for Catholics in Northern Ireland. For most of the Stormont Unionist years, it was the one area of stable, salaried employment that was entirely Catholic-controlled. It offered a sphere of influence that could reflect Irishness: it was, above all, not Unionist, not British.

The relationship between senior Catholic teachers and the

Church has not been without strain. Clerical management could be dictatorial, and principal teachers tend to be authoritarian themselves. A number of people said they had left teaching because they so disliked clerical domination of management and of senior positions in second-level education – now considerably diminished. For many years, until 1968, perhaps the greatest strain was that in the name of preserving the 'Catholic ethos' the Church refused an offer of increased government funding and insisted on raising half the finance for capital expenditure and maintenance of their schools, in Sunday collections and special fundraising drives, from the disadvantaged Catholic community. A Fermanagh teacher, still concerned not to publicly offend the Church five years into retirement, thought 'the insistence on separateness by the Church was a combination of things: suspicion of the Northern Ireland education authorities – and who could blame them when there were so few Catholics in the department or among the inspectors – and a tendency to believe the best way to preserve the Catholic ethos was to exercise power in the hands of the local parish priest. This was sometimes not in the best interests of education,' he concluded sedately.

There was always an outlet for some irritation through the main Catholic teachers' union, the INTO (Irish National Teachers' Organisation). INTO resolutions repeatedly urged the Church to accept proposals for funding from the Stormont government, first made in 1944, which would have brought their schools closer to the provision for the state sector without infringing their separateness. Of the deals the Church struck and those they refused, a present-day SDLP politician says: 'Unionism was very kind to them.' There are many teachers now retired who are convinced the hierarchy for twenty-four years refused an offer of increased funding with the establishment of 'four and two' management committees – four Church nominees, two from local government – not because they feared Unionist interference in schools, as they claimed, but because it would have threatened clerical control by putting Catholic lay representatives on management boards.

'It was the four they were afraid of, not the two,' says one retired principal. 'They'd have had to put a couple of lay people in there for each school. But of course those would have been yes-men. And the irony of it was that the Unionist local authorities they said they were afraid of, they ended up often putting Catholics forward as their nominees.'

In the past year the Church has finally negotiated full government funding at the cost of still greater lay representation. This might be seen as belated clerical trust in what the bishops have always boasted of – the devotion of their Northern flock to separate education – or belated recognition that they must relinquish some clerical power.

They still exercise powerful constraints. In April 1993, a teacher in a Catholic primary school gave the *Belfast Telegraph* – significantly, in nationalist, Catholic eyes primarily a unionist newspaper – a copy of a letter from the Church's 'diocesan advisers' on behalf of the 'bishops of the North'. It ordered teachers and principals throughout Northern Ireland to stay away from new religious education courses – on a syllabus produced by the main Churches working together – to be run by the state authorities for specialist teachers in all schools. The teacher told the newspaper that this was 'antiquated bigotry' designed to stop contact between Catholic and Protestant teachers and discussion on 'Christian development'. A warlike statement – but anonymous.

The bishops' injunction puzzled a number of religion teachers; though not others, who interpreted it without hesitation as the voice of unchanged and unchanging authoritarianism. The tone might certainly have come from the hierarchy of past decades.

All Catholic schools should know that at the heart of the
Catholic school system is the fostering of the Gift of Faith.
Religious education is the core subject in this process. In
Catholic schools it is taught catechetically [through the
official Catechism or catalogue of Church dogma]. For
this reason the Catholic bishops of the North have asked
us to inform our schools that they consider the Diocesan
Advisers to have the sole responsibility for the RE in-
service training in the Catholic sector.

Principals and teachers are not to attend the courses
provided by the Education and Library Boards. These
courses take the non-denominational approach suited to
the controlled [state/Protestant] sector.

Although in the lengthy series of meetings to produce the
agreed religion syllabus the bishops had already reserved the
right to give additional denominational instruction, the old
reflex of separateness is clearly still strong. The lessening of
authoritarianism and defensiveness that Seamus Mallon discerns
has some way to go.

Many are still grateful for their Catholic schooling and
recognise that its failings were to a large extent those of the
times. Others felt stifled by a force that dominated their school
days and their community. VINNY MCCORMACK at forty-seven
is still angry about the snobbery and violence he saw at school,
and the way the Church chose to direct a poor and downtrodden community. Now a university lecturer, a veteran of
ever smaller left-wing parties, he is one of the comparatively
few people to campaign consistently since the civil rights movement against discrimination in employment. He grew up in
Derry.

'I was born in Bogside, two hundred yards from what's now
Free Derry Corner. What dominated us in Derry was not
nationalism, but Catholicism. The Catholic Church had iron

control over the community: I remember thinking the streets, roads, houses, even the sky was Catholic – there was nothing around us that wasn't. I went to school first to the nuns, then the Christian Brothers, then St Columb's, which was priest-dominated.

'Most couldn't get work, and the Catholic Church in the fifties and early sixties didn't seem to care very much – in fact it seemed to suit them, that their flock were dependent on them. I don't want to let the Unionist government off the hook by saying this, it was their prime responsibility. But the Church didn't try to get the state to face up to their responsibility.

'I never remember any single issue relating to social justice spoken of from the pulpit or at school. The education I suppose was good of sorts, but lacking. The Catholic Church thought it was providing us with everything we needed: we were not encouraged to use our critical faculties so we would not reflect on what had happened to us, and who was responsible for it. Instead the attitude seemed to be that to suffer produced a certain amount of dignity, that a person was not responsible for unemployment. Certainly, there was no great shame attached – and that was a good thing. But what this bred was a kind of fatalism, that that's the way things were. It was all God's will.

'When we went to St Columb's, the grammar school, we were told in the school's chapel that we were a cut above the boys we had left behind. The president, who was the bishop's cousin, told us quite explicitly that we ought to dress and behave in a different way because we were made for greater things. I think we were meant to service the Catholic community by being teachers, possibly lawyers or doctors. But social justice, no, no talk of that. Equality of any sort, no. Instead we were reminded of our lowly origins.

'I remember the jeering litany of one teacher to a friend of mine, a kid of thirteen, in a classroom at St Columb's. How it

started I don't recall, but the theme was how you knew you
were working-class. 'Do you wear a greasy cap? Do you walk
greyhounds? Do you smoke butts?' Just getting at the boy,
goading him. The teacher went on to be the headmaster of a
secondary school in County Derry.

'The other point about the Church in those days has to be
its violence – and it's linked to this snobbery. There was certainly very little corporal punishment in our home. But the
punishment and the personal humiliation from the nuns, the
Christian Brothers and the teachers in St Columb's was of a different order and was clearly assault. Since I was a pretty small
guy, it was relatively mild . . . but I remember very strongly the
savagery with which others were treated. I've spoken to a
number of Protestants over the past years and they've said, "Oh
yes, Protestant schools engaged in similar things." Having
listened to their stories, I actually don't believe they did. It
wasn't just physical – there was a ferocious humiliation and
destruction of the personality. And because of the way in which
young Catholics were treated, ritually and daily, in those
schools, I believe that the Catholic Church has some responsibility for the violence in Northern Ireland.

'We were socialised into a very rigid Catholic identity – there
was no escape from it. It was assumed that all of us would go
on to University College Dublin, as the Catholic university. My
first minor spark of rebellion was to decide to go to Queen's in
Belfast. Very few contemporaries did, but to me coming to
Belfast seemed to offer a liberation. I was a fairly timid kind of
guy, and Belfast frightened me. But I felt suffocated in Derry.'

The evocation of a community totally Catholic and totally
sealed off from a hostile wider world was much repeated by
others, though never so vividly. For someone who does not
believe, who dislikes the Catholic Church so fervently and
whose entire adult life has been coloured by secular, left-wing

politics, Vinny McCormack's concern that his criticism had let the Stormont regime off lightly was a telling anxiety.

He is now researching the psychological impact on his generation of religion and education. His denunciation of cruelty and snobbery from teachers is a common feature of reminiscences – and clerical violence was mentioned by half a dozen interviewees, two of them leading republicans. One, in his early thirties, said he often notices statements denouncing IRA violence in his local paper from a former teacher, a priest, 'somebody who wouldn't stop at one or two whacks on the ear'.

'As a boarder I saw some fairly radical cases that today wouldn't be tolerated, it would end up in court. The thing that stood out was their willingness to just use pure thick wit and violence to get their own way. That would have been the start of my resentment of the Church.'

He did not claim that clerical violence fed republican violence, or was a model for it. But he seemed not to hear how his description of using violence to get your way fits the IRA, the organisation he now gives allegiance to.

Father Faul sweeps aside the accusation that Catholic schools of the past were seedbeds of violence: there was no more corporal punishment in schools than in families at the time, he says. For him, the school's role as a prime agent of Catholic teaching is unchanged, and he is as ever more blunt on the subject than bishops tend to be – and more overtly nationalistic: 'The schools represent power for the Church, both in Northern and in Southern Ireland – the power to influence the people. People accuse us of being in the business of brainwashing children. Well, I make no bones about it: we are.' The Church was therefore bound to oppose integrated education, he said, as a government-sponsored movement 'to get rid of Catholic schools'. The schools had another function: 'They are the channel by which the nationalist/Irish culture is brought to the people. Interest in Irish music, Irish games, Irish history, all those things are kept alive in Northern Ireland and channelled very successfully into the Catholic community by the schools, which insist on Irish and insist on Irish history.'

Father Faul says what others think, but also in some cases what others reckon is outdated. The Catholic school system was only ever a channel for Irish culture where teachers had a personal interest in Irish language, music and history and who were encouraged, or at least not hindered, by their clerical management. Belfast SDLP member Brian Feeney remembered how in his primary-school days cramming for the eleven-plus had already in 1957 squeezed out Irish history – in the overt cause of producing a bigger and more successful Catholic professional class. The Irish language he learned was on the level of commands to sit down, stand up and close the door, an experience familiar to many others in Catholic schools in the fifties.

Catholic schools are not only a channel of faith and in some cases, of Irish culture: they have also traditionally been the community's only agent of upward mobility. Increasingly, the two roles seem set to conflict. Recent research shows increasing emphasis on the sciences, and comparatively less on the arts subjects once disproportionately favoured in Catholic grammar schools (what the study's author, himself a Catholic, calls the 'old Catholic/classical/humanities ethos'). One principal told him: 'If I were you, I wouldn't put too much emphasis on the Catholic ethos bit. It's fast fading in the face of increased middle-class expectations' (Dominic Murray, *Standing Advisory Commission on Human Rights Education Project 1989–92*, Belfast, 1992). Parents and teachers bear out the study's finding of a 'response to market demand', reflecting a drive for educational attainment ever more strongly directed at enabling Catholics to participate at higher levels in the administration and economic life of Northern Ireland. In more affluent areas many further suggest that when there is any clash between arts and science time-tabling, Catholic schools tend to drop Irish first. Several people told me that they found outright hostility among other parents to the teaching of the Irish language in school. It seemed clear to them that the schools were making no counter-effort.

Some see in the attitude to education of the new middle class yet another reflection of a redefined Northern Catholic identity, what is perhaps the first questioning of the old automatic equation of identity with Catholic schooling. There is a perceptible and apparently growing trend for affluent parents – orthodox and even ostentatious Catholics in other ways – to send their children to Church schools at primary level, then to prestigious Protestant grammars. Yet again market demand has a knock-on effect. In one of the most comfortable districts, parents report that the local Catholic primary principal is obviously accustomed to people wanting to transfer to the nearby state grammar, one of Northern Ireland's best-known, rather than to the overcrowded, though academically successful, Catholic rival a few miles away. 'There's no shock – he expects it,' said one slightly bemused mother. 'What's happened to the doctrine of "Catholic schools for Catholic pupils"?'

Her husband totted up the neighbours who sent their children to the various excellent Protestant schools in the area, singling out several wealthy businessmen as conspicuously supportive lay members of the parish: fundraisers for building projects and diocesan charities. 'Big-time Catholics, and generous – the bishop has good cause to be grateful to them.' He wondered sceptically if their status as fundraisers exempted them from what would in the past have been strong clerical pressure to conform. It was a scepticism about the Church's identification with the wealthy that is as innate and traditional as the loyalty of the poor.

Like the SDLP man who wondered whether the children of

the new rich would still believe in a modernised nationalism, as
their parents do, several priests have begun to question the commitment to Catholicism of those they once considered 'pillars
of the Church': the 'professionals' who were expected by virtue
of their greater education and social standing to give good
example to their inferiors. A universal concern – 'materialism
has always been the enemy of the faith,' sighed one middle-aged
priest – it is also in Northern Ireland yet another facet of an
identity in transition.

As ever, Denis Faul voices what others will not. 'It's a bit
of a shame that Catholics who came up the ladder on the back
of poverty, chastity and obedience [the vows of priests and
nuns] and got a very cheap education for themselves from the
Christian Brothers and the nuns, then send their children elsewhere. They're more concerned about their accent than their
religion. They haven't stopped practising, no – not yet. But the
Catholic school system needs the support of the wealthy: their
money, their influence and their moral support. It's an awful
pity.' Even the frank Father Faul, however, had no comment
on the lack of clerical censure towards these renegade rich. The
Church clearly recognises that they would be as likely to secure
obedience in this instance as on contraception.

Open, indeed severe, Church disapproval has instead been
directed at parents who send their children to the integrated
schools that have begun to spread in Northern Ireland over the
past ten years (although they still educate under 1 per cent of
pupils). In spite of the integrated schools' public and repeated
declaration that they are Christian rather than secular, Church
representatives consistently decry them as secular.

The preservation of power and influence plainly motivates
institutional Catholic opposition to integration. But the desire
for separateness and the hostility to integrated education, among
both laity and clergy, suggests a fear of political and social

assimilation – and loss of identity – as much as any purely theological concern. In one rare off-the-record encounter with journalists, a leading Northern bishop mused aloud about the motivation of the integrated education movement: 'What is it they're trying to achieve? I wonder. Some kind of blend?' The word 'blend' was pronounced with what looked like mingled suspicion and disgust.

The sentiment was echoed by people of widely different backgrounds. The SDLP's BRIAN FEENEY, a lecturer in the Catholic St Mary's teacher training college, thinks the Church's plain dislike of integrated education – and of mixed marriage – is a popular attitude, which he shares.

'Church attitudes have become more politic on mixed marriage, maybe, but it's still dislike at the bottom, a reflection of what people want, as segregated housing is. Separate schooling too, although that's a worldwide canonical injunction – here that has to do with identity. Catholic schools are a feature of Catholic identity which is positive and ought to be preserved – and Protestant schools are too. In a society in which their identity has been attacked in so many ways, it's important for kids to gain confidence in who they are and what they believe. The alternative is a nothing.'

The IRA man I interviewed was extremely rude about the present cardinal, Cahal Daly, for the most part on the basis of his attitudes towards republicanism. He added: 'He opposes anything that would damage his power base, for example integrated education.' So did this mean that he by comparison supported integration? Not at all.

'The basic ethos is to turn out nice West Britons, the same as the core curriculum that's now being introduced through the Catholic maintained schools. [He meant the NIO-sponsored programme Education for Mutual Understanding, which emphasises common experience and tradition.] The education system is fully locked into the broad British counter-insurgency programme, as part of the Hillsborough [Anglo-Irish] Agreement.'

Stephen the ex-priest, like Brian Feeney, links mixed marriage and integrated education as instances of the Church refusing to change or compromise – and is similarly convinced that in both cases this is popular because the Church's stance is seen as bolstering identity. It is not a position he finds appealing.

'Look what they've given way on, by comparison. The special position of the Church in the Southern constitution – scrub, no problem. Articles Two and Three: no problem, Cahal Daly thinks they should be changed. But Catholic schools, mixed marriage: hold the wee sinews of power and sectarianism tight as a drum, eh? It's popular, it's the Church standing up to Protestants, reminding the flock that they are the one true Church and even though for political considerations the Church might like to compromise . . .

'They've maintained the identity, all right – and they've increased sectarianism. They've reassured their own people of their identity and the importance of it – and there's a large chunk of anti-Protestantism in there. It's "we are the one true Church" all right, and a fear that the kids will mix only too well.'

'THE FAITH'

Examining the record of the institutional Church and authority figures like bishops is considerably easier for most people than discussing their own faith, or lack of it. Seamus Mallon offers a crisp summary: 'The Church is one of the elements of stability in an unstable situation. It's provided a refuge, succour in suffering and death, in periods of great agony. Religious practice matters to people: things like novenas and pilgrimages are thriving – and that's why.'

In any Catholic area, particularly the crowded urban districts, the manifestations of piety Seamus Mallon mentions are immediately obvious: notices in shop windows advertising 'Vigil at Melleray [a monastery in County Louth], coach, breakfast included'; posters with flight details for Medjugorje, the site of supposedly Marian visions in the former Yugoslavia which has a particular following among Northern Catholics; the mammoth novena each year since 1971 at Clonard Monastery, in the Falls.

For the past few years, Northern Ireland's one evening paper, the *Belfast Telegraph*, has for the first time carried small stories about the Clonard novena, but only the avowedly Catholic *Irish News* and *Andersonstown News* convey any sense of the scale and exuberance of devotion on show. Every day for nine days in June there are ten sessions of prayer in the huge old monastery church, the first at 7 a.m. In June 1993, about 18,000 people attended daily.

People overflow into the square at the front of the church, a more varied crowd than in most ordinary Sunday congregations: young men pushing prams, young women in carefully ripped jeans beside elderly women with scarves on their heads, a scattering of the neighbourhood's most derelict drunks mooching around the fringes. Children play quietly among adults who stand, heads bent in concentration, a tannoy carries sermons from visiting clerics, and anonymous petitions, the mundane and the tragic mingled, are broadcast by priests from the pulpit into the nearby streets where bunting in blue and white (Mary's colours) runs from rooftops to the pavement: 'For my wife, that she may be able to stop smoking: for peace in our land and an end to the heartbreak of so many, Catholic and Protestant; someone dear to me who hasn't long to live, that they may come back to the faith; dear God, if it is your holy will, please get my husband a job before he loses his mind; for my youngest son who's in jail for nine years, may he return to his religion; in memory of my Tommy, shot dead at his work.' The petitions are a 'sociological record' of life in Belfast, the novena's coordinator said last year. A Presbyterian deaconess spoke at the final 1993 session, the first Protestant preacher. Several hundred of the congregation stayed on from the previous session to hear her: Clonard is proud that some Protestants attend the novena each year and that others send petitions.

'There's people go to the novena who'd never darken a church door the rest of the year,' says one young Falls Road woman. 'And a lot go there on a Sunday because maybe in the church near them the priest does nothing but give off about the organisations [republican paramilitaries] or he goes on about teenage pregnancies all the time. Clonard, they're more spiritual. They give you a good feeling about yourself, and you want to pray. I don't know if it's the Catholic faith at all brings them in, proper religion. It's just, people need a break from all this here. Hymns, singing, everyone together, it's peaceful, there's an atmosphere. And there's a lot of faith in the nine days bit: if you go every day and you never miss and you pray hard for a special intention, you'll get what you pray for. I don't know how many do, but they keep going back anyhow.'

An older man thought there might be 'more magic involved there than religious faith – but then what's faith? I think the Troubles have kept more in the churches than they've driven out.'

Colette, who blames an old-fashioned Church for its unreadiness to handle community turmoil, looks back now from her south Derry farm at her years teaching in north Belfast at the start of the Troubles and the changes since. 'I've friends still in the city, and in Derry and Craigavon, and what they describe is just disintegration of urban Catholic society: like all over the world but with the pressures here contributing. The paramilitaries help: the clubs, access to cheap alcohol – I sound like a nun now, but you can see the damage. It's as primitive as this, as attitudes to contraception and divorce, men in jail or on the run and the marriages break up. The kids are going to primary school where they're taught the Commandments and they know that mammy has a boyfriend, their daddy's out now and he's living down the road with another woman and their big sister's fifteen with a baby. So endless mothers and fathers and brothers and sisters are being specifically decried as breaking the Commandments. The point is that people didn't leave the Church because they made a positive decision to. It's just that the Church didn't make room for them: the social circumstances in which people live don't fit the ideal.' But Colette did not want to discuss her own 'loss of faith', her reasons for no longer attending Mass. Like many others, she is as sensitive of identification on this subject as about her political attitudes. Someone in her family would recognise the story of how she stopped believing, she said. Her father, fifteen years later, would still be hurt.

Being a Northern Catholic means inheriting an inextricable tangle of religious, political and social influences. Poking about for the ends of the various threads is a self-conscious business most have little taste for, particularly when it comes to discussion of their own attitudes to religion or those of their families.

Prominent lay Catholic Mary McAleese is an exception. Her habit, for example, of sprinkling conversation with unself-conscious references to 'spirituality', both her own and that of Irish society, is alien to many shy Northern Catholics – a characteristic they would think of as American, Californian. She has no trouble fixing her religion in the context of Northern Catholic identity.

'I grew up with the idea that my faith was not welcomed in Northern Ireland,' she says. 'But Ardoyne was dominated by the

Passionist Monastery, and you know how they go about, dressed in these long flowing robes and with big wooden crosses round their necks. It was a matter of pride to the people of Ardoyne – not just the Catholic people but the Protestant people as well that these men could wear their priestly garb. It wouldn't have been true outside it. But in Ardoyne they weren't spat at, they were treated with enormous respect. It was always a great source of pride to me as a person from Ardoyne – and you don't realise how clericalised your view of the Church becomes, living in that kind of environment. I owe an awful lot to those men. . . I remember going to Dublin and being amazed at the anti-clericalism then rampant there.'

Though Northern Catholic religious practice has undergone many changes familiar elsewhere, many believe it still has distinctive aspects. Mary McAleese is sure there has been a ghetto Catholicism, heavy on devotionalism. 'And it's still very strong. Mainly on account of people having suffered a great deal, their devotion is enhanced. But world changes, openness on sexuality, women, the breakdown of the class structure, have all affected the way people look at the Church as well.' Still the old customs cling, of thought and practice.

She herself is an example of ghetto Catholicism, Mary McAleese says self-mockingly. On a visit to Paris she was invited to a reception to meet the man due to take over as rector in Ardoyne: she looked in vain for someone in black and was introduced instead to 'an extremely handsome man in double-breasted French suit, a soft greyish-blue, Italian shoes, perfectly coiffed, with a wee discreet cross. "I'm Father Eugene," says he. "You're what?" says I. "Are you the one's going to Ardoyne tomorrow? I hope to hell you've a black suit – I hope you're not going in that there." The man was mortified, he said he hadn't had a black suit in years . . . and what did he meet when he got to Ardoyne? Two and a half thousand people just like me. He had a tough time. A friend's mother was buried a few weeks later. I asked who said the Mass. "Oh, him with the suit."

'I never knew myself to have any views on clerical garb, that I was conservative on matters like that. I don't know where it came from. But it wasn't just brute ignorant prejudice on my part. I think it had a lot to do with the fact that I took a great pride that our priests could walk freely through Ardoyne, wearing their clerical garb, and that it was a kind of witness.'

PADDY MCGRORY, another highly articulate lawyer, is none the less more typical of believing Catholics who are not accustomed to discussing religion in personal terms. He says simply that when he was growing up in the thirties 'the Church was a very significant part of life for every Catholic: it pervaded the home, the school, reached deep into the psyche. And even people who regard themselves as having lapsed who were reared as Catholics, there's something there that never leaves them. True everywhere, of course. But here – where everything is bottled up and intensified, both politically and religiously – feeling that you were in a minority, and in some cases a despised minority, it brought out a resistance in you that became part of your personality. And I think it's still as important, all-pervasive still. Practically all Catholics tend to identify themselves as Catholics, in a way many Protestants don't.'

The idea that Northern Catholicism has a particular 'steel' to it, a quality of determined enduring piety, is one that many people mention – most of them over fifty. But many who are younger also believe that falling attendances at Mass, and a general tendency towards what Paddy McGrory calls with a grin 'à la carte Catholicism' – the widespread silent abandonment of Church teaching on contraception, for example – do not mean a significant decline in faith. The old may talk sadly about the death of 'respect for the clergy' – though as many in their seventies and older seem equally critical of priests. When the children of the modern, television age are dismissive of priests and bishops, they use a global language of irreverence. They are, however, not much less likely than their parents to marry in church (as Stephen the ex-priest noted to his own surprise), scarcely less disposed to have their children baptised, and not at all less likely, according to their own admissions, to want a Catholic burial for their parents and themselves.

'The parish priest thinks it's 15 per cent that don't go,' says a young curate in a sizeable town, 'but I can tell you it's more like 40 per cent.' Sunday Mass attendances may have slipped badly in the biggest urban areas and fallen in other towns, the pattern of Catholic education seems to have a few new wrinkles here and there, unquestioning adherence to papal pronouncements on contraception may now be as rare here as anywhere else. But commitment and devotion to Catholicism as a religious practice, as spiritual sustenance, are very strong and very important to a wide variety of people.

Contrary to what some might think, there seems little to suggest that living in a society with freely available contraception and which allows divorce has made Northern Catholics in general any more permissive than their Southern counterparts. Perhaps the very smallness of the community, and the lack of a decent-sized city with the protection of anonymity have much to do with it. It seems beyond argument that the long separateness of Catholic society from Protestant has helped preserve old codes: and Protestantism is also socially conservative. There is no easy, tolerant, wider society to aspire to or be tempted by.

But the Catholic birth rate in Northern Ireland has been in decline since 1968. Contraception, however, is not a subject for open and general discussion. Social conservatism is one reason. In a society obsessed by the balance of population between Catholics and Protestants, there is also a powerful self-consciousness about Protestant jibes that Catholics intend 'breeding us out'. Women with large families, orthodox and dutiful Catholics, talk resentfully about doctors' attempts in hospital to urge them towards sterilisation: it is generally assumed that the advice, or any comment, comes with an anti-Catholic slant.

Others have found the orthodoxy in their own community painful. In Strabane a 53-year-old woman described how she first discovered that other women felt as she did about endless pregnancies.

'Somebody started this wee group in the estate, a crowd of women sitting down to have a yarn and a look at their lives, though no one called it anything fancy. I remember a woman saying we were allowed out to it because the men said it was only a women's group, it would do no harm. But one of the things we found we talked about was birth control – none of us had any understanding of it – and childbirth. It was the first time I discovered that other women were like myself, scared out of their wits of having children. People automatically think because you have weans every year that you're not, you know, scared.

'For me, now, it wasn't the priests that were hard, it was a layman. After I had my seventh, I was only thirty-four then, it was one of the local priests first mentioned the idea of birth control to me. "What age are you now, Kathleen?" he said, "and you have seven children. I think you should have a wee rest to yourself. Who's your doctor? Go down and talk to him and tell him I sent you." And the doctor was a good Catholic doctor, and he sort of looked at me and then he explained to me the safe period and in the next breath he said, but because of your irregular periods it'll be very difficult to work it. Never a mention of the pill, it probably wasn't in his vocabulary and certainly it wasn't in mine. I had three more weans, and then I just stopped having children. I never used contraception. My body must just have developed its own natural form of it.' She laughs.

A significant number of older people are censorious about what they see as a spread in Southern permissiveness and lax practice of religion. But in the interviews that underpin this book, as in observations over the years, there is the sense of as much variation of belief in the North as by all accounts is evident among Southern Catholics: a solid strand of piety ranging from the reticent to the charismatic; a swathe of non-believers from teenage to late forties and a bit beyond; a general suspicion that the Church's battle on contraception has been lost, with divorce not far behind; and a growing number of women, young and middle-aged, who feel that the Catholic Church worldwide, particularly in its teaching on women priests, ignores and slights the female half of its congregation.

At forty-three and from the perspective of west Belfast SHEILA is convinced that clerical attitudes to women and to working-class community groups have much in common. In both cases, she says, the effect is to 'disempower'. Adult education gave her the tools to break away from the orthodoxy of Catholic schools as well as a sense of worth and individuality. It is an experience common to many others, especially women.

'The Church at key points just failed people. Looking back, you can see where it sucked power in: its activism in community groups and provision of jobs – I see that as insidious – and when it comes to women's groups that's on top of the way women are second-class inside the Church in any case. Groups I've been involved with, you have the experience of little pockets of nuns being set up to run things alongside and they get the backing instead. The strong network of community groups is a feature of the experience of working-class nationalists, and increasingly unionists. People are well able to be responsible for resources, but the Church, the Churches

generally, have become a conduiting mechanism for government money to local schemes. Disempowering, for their own
selfish ends.'

According to those who are among the most committed and
participant of lay Catholics, only a very few raise institutional or
doctrinal issues in any church setting – but then, opportunities
for discussion have only begun to become organised on
anything like a wide basis. People who seem to be lively,
interested Catholics complain that they still feel there is no local
forum where they can question priests, for example, about
parish matters: they know there are some new parish councils,
they say, but not in their dioceses. Few, it seems, have ever
discussed their faith or the institutional Church outside the
circle of family and Catholic friends; and many are inhibited
there.

Much of Northern society, after all, is highly segregated in
housing and at work. The exceptions tend to regard religion as
no more fit for 'mixed' conversation than politics. For many of
the young, who mix in the centre of most sizeable towns in
casual and superficial ways, the question does not arise. 'Which
church?' asks a west Belfast teenage boy – joking, but with
meaning – in response to a question about how the Church has
come through the Troubles. Neither he nor any of his friends
had been to Mass since their mothers had last been able to
make them go at twelve or thirteen. But it was not something
they talked about, he said, echoing older people who are given
to adding that they discuss their doubts neither among Catholics
('because they'd talk about you'), nor when Protestants are present ('because you wouldn't give them the satisfaction').

The defensive element in Northern Catholicism is apparently
undiminished as yet by growing political and economic confidence. 'You couldn't even laugh at Bishop Casey because
you'd be letting the side down,' as one highly politicised and

sophisticated man put it. 'There's a sort of mutual defensiveness. Protestant political tradition has oppressed Catholics, but yet is afraid of Catholics and so is defensive. Catholics in turn are afraid, so there's a "let's not let the side down" kind of thing. Whereas the South, now ... they're capable of at least intellectually discussing the various strands.'

But he could not be quoted on the subject of religion by name, nor in any disguise that might be dismantled, because he teaches in a Catholic school in what he called 'the depths of the conservative countryside'.

Inside the Northern Church generally, among both laity and clergy, and even among many who no longer have any religious belief but who were 'born Catholic', there persists a strong consciousness of a shared faith, or at least indoctrination, in a religion that is accustomed to frequent attack. Former Northern Catholics may have all the flair for exuberant blasphemy and anti-clericalism of their counterparts elsewhere, but anti-Catholicism is a powerful check. Awareness of hostility whether open or concealed, crude or polite, from political enemies who were until comparatively recently all-powerful, has always protected the institutional Church from open and damaging criticism by its own members, and to some extent still does. In Northern Ireland, criticism from within the fold has always been understood as providing ammunition to 'anti-Catholics' without.

'Lapsing' has become common enough for community censure to have lost much of its force. What counts is that you are still willing to be identified in terms of your origins, especially if you stand vigilant against open or covert incitement of anti-Catholicism. 'Falling away from the faith' is one thing. Denying your religious origins and therefore your own identity is another. The institutional Catholic Church in Northern Ireland profits, and is aware that it profits, from the bonds

made early and reinforced by family and the community between a sense of self, isolation in an unfriendly state, and
Catholicism.

9

'No going back'

IDENTITY

Once, 'Northern Ireland' was a term many Catholics refused to use. To speak or write the name would have recognised the existence of a state they denied the validity of, even though that was where they lived their lives. Who were they? Not 'Northern Ireland Catholics', certainly: that would have suggested acceptance of minority status and smacked of the reservation. There were people I interviewed who objected to the phrase 'Northern Catholic' as a collective term and as a definition of themselves – because they thought that in itself it signified acceptance or 'recognition' of partition, and more particularly of British attempts to portray political difference as no more than sectarian squabbling. They were, they insisted, 'Irish Catholics', no different from Catholics anywhere else in Ireland – but they preferred the simple description 'Irish'.

Even today, many still automatically say 'the North' rather than 'Northern Ireland'. Though the South has become more and more clearly an unknown quantity in the past two decades, there is still a conviction for many that minority status is no more than a state of mind. In their hearts they know themselves the northern branch of a major tribe, separated, unwanted, but of the blood. In very much the way that Protestants speak fondly and possessively of British heroes and literature, and with as little encouragement, indeed often to equal if covert derision from those they implicitly claim as fellow nationals, Catholics think of themselves as heirs to a wider culture: no mean people, for all their street-fighting reputation in Dublin and London.

Fussiness about terminology used to be underpinned by all the institutions of the Catholic 'state within a state'. Until the late sixties the *Irish News* unfailingly referred to 'the six counties' and 'the six-county Cabinet', as a way of demeaning the status of the Stormont government and to deny the reality of the state. The Unionist prime minister was 'Mr Terence O'Neill, the Northern premier' rather than Captain O'Neill, as he styled himself. By 1968 O'Neill had at last become 'the Northern Ireland premier, Mr Terence O'Neill'. There was a pervasive Catholic derision of unionists who used British army titles: it was seen as an attempt to aggrandise themselves in civilian life, but also as a means of insisting on the Britishness of 'Ulster'. The term 'Ulster' never failed to provoke: a generation grew up on lectures about the lost three counties. Each niggle had a unionist mirror image for reinforcement. 'The Ulster people' is still used by Unionist politicians to suggest an undifferentiated unionist populace; Catholics who talk of themselves as Ulster people are invariably intent on the point that they share a regional identity and history with Cavan, Monaghan and Donegal. It is a rule of thumb that the more a term annoys the 'others', the longer it persists. In the *Belfast Telegraph* and the *Ulster News Letter* the Republic is still 'Eire': '36p Eire', says the *Telegraph* masthead, insisting on the foreignness of a separate country.

But it is no longer easy to be pedantic about terminology. The modern compulsion to reflect on identity has given many people difficulty – much as thinking about the spelling of a word makes the proper spelling begin to look not quite right. Terms of self-definition used automatically for years begin to spin and shift under scrutiny. For decades before the Troubles, simply being a Catholic in Northern Ireland was identity enough: as one observer put it, 'Just being a Catholic is a political act.' The state was Protestant and Unionist. Being born into the minority defined you as nationalist, republican, disloyal in thought if not in deed. For some, there was a blacker realisation: that partition redefined Northern nationalists as unionists, that Northern Catholics had effectively ceased to exist as part of a political entity, had ceased to have a political identity that counted. *You* were Irish: Northern Ireland was British. People born and grown to adulthood before partition in a thirty-two-county Ireland still thought of Dublin as the capital and believed the new arrangements for the six counties could not last.

Children grew up to view the machinery of government, dimly and at a distance through the barricades of church, school and home, as alien and hostile. The level of hostility and the way it was expressed varied, from near-total withdrawal to violent protest. In every decade some attacked the state with bombs and bullets: blew up public buildings or tried to, shot policemen. For its part unionist Northern Ireland set out by exclusion, by harsh legislation, by electoral manipulation and by discrimination, to ensure that this disaffected and dangerous minority remained a minority, and a powerless one. Emigration by both Protestants and Catholics had always been high, but the Catholic rate settled at around 60 per cent of the total.

The mass of Catholics sank into resignation and inwardness. Protestant state for Protestant people, so Catholic schools for Catholics – doctors, lawyers, shopkeepers who 'were your own': what had been custom before partition became dogma. The reinforced segregation of the Troubles, as documented in recent statistics, is no more than the most recent manifestation of a historic pattern, as in Dungannon's Scotch Street and Irish Street, Carrickfergus's Irish Quarter West and Scotch Quarter West. Even in those areas where they lived side by side, it was possible for Catholics to lead most of their lives – as Protestants did – through their own institutions. There are towns throughout Northern Ireland where the main street has a 'Protestant' side and a 'Catholic' one: Protestant-owned businesses down one side, Catholic on the other; and there are many who make considerable effort to transact as much business as possible inside their own community.

'There were twenty to thirty years when there was nothing,' a 67-year-old south Down man says of political organisation. 'The community was mainly rural, remember – and as for priests putting forward nationalist candidates, well, they never seemed to be involved at the grassroots. The Nationalist Convention was as mysterious to ordinary folk as the Papal Consistory. It wasn't until you got the *Irish Weekly* or the *Frontier Sentinel* that most houses would have known there *was* a convention and you heard who the candidate was, and people just went out and voted. There was no vehicle for putting views forward – that was just the way it was.'

Insistence on the niceties of non–Britishness, non–unionism, helped fill the need for a self-respecting political stance. It was not enough to have separate schools, sports, shops, drama groups, choral societies. There was a concern to protect this distinct identity, bolstered by Catholicism as it was before Vacitan Two, that in many ways mirrored unionist exclusivism.

'The Queen's University of Belfast', named after an English Queen, was clearly a British foundation, with a Protestant-dominated faculty and student body. So even as late as the early sixties Catholic grammar school leavers were encouraged instead to go to Catholic teacher training colleges or, in the case of those who could afford it, University College Dublin. The

Duke of Edinburgh Award Scheme might very well be aimed at building up adventurousness, physical and mental stamina and a sense of public service in the young, but the name was enough. The scheme did not find favour with Catholic schools: indeed, it has only recently begun to appear in Catholic areas, chiefly for youth training schemes.

The death in 1992 of the veteran Belfast dance teacher Patricia Mulholland brought disguised references in the *Irish News* to an ancient quarrel within the world of Irish dancing. People over fifty remember that because she took a troupe to perform abroad as part of a British team – which meant that at some point they danced under a British flag and stood for 'God Save the Queen' – she lost her outstanding credentials as an Irish-dancing teacher. Even then, this orthodox reaction struck some as excessive. There was a kind of pride – I remember it – in seeing what was thought to be an Irish art form wedded to an internationally recognised classical dance style. When Miss Mulholland developed an 'Irish ballet', there were parishes and schools that invited her to put on concerts in their halls, though she was boycotted elsewhere.

Where their parents did their best to ignore the reality of neglect by successive Dublin governments and almost prayerfully insisted on their oneness with people in 'the South', Catholics in Northern Ireland in the nineties have had to admit the gap between piety and reality. And the effect of media usage during the Troubles, if not new thinking, has made us all sloppy. 'Northern Ireland' still is for many, especially the older, and for nationalist politicians, 'the North' or 'the North of Ireland'. Either will do. 'The North' because it begs the question 'north of what?', 'the North of Ireland' for its proud ring, its invocation of inviolable, spiritual unity. When I interviewed four young people on the Falls, however, they all talked unselfconsciously about 'Northern Ireland'. Even the most

purist republicans will occasionally stumble into 'Northern
Ireland' rather than 'the six counties' without remembering to
put disdain for the term into their voice.

'Irish' is the first word most Northern Catholics reach for to
describe their identity: and even that is a Troubles development. MARGARET, brought up in south Derry and settled for
almost fifty years in a small, mainly Protestant County Tyrone
town, has memories that stretch back over more than seven
decades.

'You didn't think about being Irish, you *were* Irish. It was
only after the Troubles started you began to think about it.
Before that, you were just Catholic, and you were in Northern
Ireland, and you weren't part of it. So, yes, you were nationalist
too. Or republican. But you didn't stick the "Northern" in first.
Of course we were Northerners, and proud of it, proud of the
North. It was the North fought on against the English until the
Flight of the Earls.'

We ended up agreeing that the terms themselves are of the
present: Northern nationalists, Northern Catholics, Northern
Ireland Catholics: the media's need for shorthand has produced
a whole list of titles people never gave themselves in the past
because they had no need for names. They knew very well who
they were. External attempts to reclassify them – by compulsory
oaths of allegiance, by the question 'Are you loyal?' at job interviews, the Union Jack and the British anthem at the most hum-
ble of public functions, standing for 'God Save the Queen' in
the cinema – were resisted, by the least and the most republican
alike. A few sacrificed jobs rather than 'take the oath': their
names and histories were recalled for years with considerable
respect. The masses evaded the issue, automatically, with a sulky
doggedness. There was no glory involved – many remember the
process with irritation at their own preoccupation, as much as
at the pettiness they ended up reflecting. 'You were expert in

judging how long the final kiss in the film was going to be, so you could get out before "God Save the Queen" started,' a seventy-year-old man remembers. 'You never saw the screen fade.' The custom of playing the British national anthem lasted into the Troubles, presumably until locally owned cinemas died out. At Catholic functions, there was always a sense of daring about playing the Irish national anthem, forbidden under the Special Powers Act: patriotic, and elitist pride for some in singing it in Irish, which the masses did not speak.

At her age, Margaret has little interest in picking over names and terms. The Republic to her is variously 'the Free State government', 'the South', sometimes 'the Irish government'. Like many others, she has been wounded by Southern attitudes and thinks of Southern politicians as in the main uninterested, unhelpful and occasionally hostile. British governments she speaks of with no heat: 'But they're not tackling it.' She feels sorry for Protestants, who have been 'let down by the British'.

'We didn't realise civil rights was going to create such a backlash, really . . . but I suppose that was inevitable. There had been troubles every ten years, but this was more than that from the start. I can't see an end except there'll have to be compromises all round. I suppose it's made me more broad-minded. I'm not fussy on the nationalist end at all: if we got equal rights and equal recognition here, I could live with that. In the long run, I think there'll have to be a united Ireland, it'll be a long time frame but it's inevitable. And there'll have to be some kind of arrangement between people here to be going on with.'

The most significant development for Margaret has been in her own community. She can remember the attitudes of her parents, and grew up among resigned and cowed people, who thought of 'Northern Ireland' as a temporary phase but were convinced they could do nothing to bring about change. Recalling the petty details of that time as well as the larger issues, what most strikes her about Catholics today is their assertiveness. 'They've got up off their knees,' she says repeatedly, 'and they're not going back.' A sense of progress and confidence has brought her to the point where political structures are no longer an obsession. Many others, especially those over sixty, have the same ability to be relaxed about the future. Taking a long perspective is traditional in this community, after all. Sustaining Northern Catholic myths in the Stormont days never included a local version of 'next year in Jerusalem'.

'Northern nationalist' continues to be a shorthand tag many accept for themselves. But definitions of nationalism are becoming looser and more various by the day. The first shift during the Troubles was perhaps made when those who supported what once was termed 'physical force republicanism' – that is, the IRA – and who had always referred to 'nationalists' with scorn as temporising, compromising 'constitutionalists', began routinely to describe themselves as part of, indeed as the leaders of, the 'nationalist people'.

Women in particular, and some men, say that although they have little or no interest in an Irish nation-state, they are forced to describe themselves as nationalist because they think a British unionist-majority Northern Ireland will always be sectarian: meaning biased against Catholics. Nationalist for them means anti-Unionist and non-British, rather than positively Irish in any way that suggests affinity with the South or Southerners. Those with a public role or who are political activists in general offer more precise definitions: or, in most cases, what they say are redefinitions of their original positions.

The willingness – even eagerness – to admit to change is recent. Even a few years ago, 'redefining nationalism' was suspect among many Northern Catholics, widely equated with 'revisionism', which was taken to mean being anti-nationalist in general and anti-Northern-nationalist in particular. But debate in the wider Irish context is well-established. The 1983 New Ireland Forum in Dublin, which included the full range of constitutional nationalists, helped restore nerves shaken by the revisionist onslaught, according to several participants.

MARY MCALEESE, who was part of the Catholic Church delegation to the forum, maintains that it was particularly important for nationalists who had been 'using these terms, "republican nationalism" and "a united Ireland" as if we all knew what they meant, to come together and reflect on their view of national identity: and especially then, because constitutional nationalism was in danger of dying from the effects of silencing, the impact of revisionist history. This was the point at which nationalists started to get their voice back. They were being emasculated on two fronts: by revisionists saying nationalism is dead and gone, an outmoded nineteenth-century phenomenon, and the Provos saying we are super-nationalists, the true voice and the only voice. The forum was the planting of seeds: there's all this talk now about joint sovereignty. It gave a latitude to the Irish government or the SDLP, and a flexibility, that hopefully in the days to come will bear fruit – a backdrop against which to argue and debate.'

SEAMUS MALLON maintains that the Forum's reflections on nationalism have led to new thinking among republicans. 'Any reading of their statements shows they're now talking about a staged approach, meaning federalism – or if you look at Gerry Adams's statements, meaning much less in the initial stages: a "period of transition", which might be defined in generations.'

For Mallon, the question of redefining nationalism is a delicate business, though he accepts the need for redefinition.

'The danger is that it's the aim of many in this country to delegitimise nationalism. It's a very legitimate political philosophy, proud. It's dangerous to query its legitimacy – if you do that, you confuse people very substantially.

'There's a danger in creating an uncertainty within people about their beliefs, which they're pursuing through the democratic process – telling them they're irredentist etcetera – you're not doing the political process any good. People have a right to respect for their most deeply held views.'

But Seamus Mallon supports and participates in the debate on new formulations of nationalism that SDLP leader John Hume is generally perceived as leading: as ever, Mallon's role is to voice the fears of the more traditional, then assuage them by insisting that the essence of identity is not being abandoned.

There are external factors to encourage debate. The break-up of the USSR and the spectacle of bloody nationalist conflict in eastern Europe frightens many. John Hume's insistence on the inevitability of European Community movement towards greater political union can sound unduly optimistic, but his denunciation of 'sterile territorial' nationalism, in conjunction with his resistance of Unionist demands for a diminution of Irish involvement in Northern Ireland, has steadily pushed republicans towards their own new forms of words. The attraction of a European identity to many Northern Catholics, the potential of a wider stage to allow different identities to coexist as equals, a theme trumpeted and shaped by Hume, caught Sinn Féin off balance. Its once-total opposition to the European Community has dissolved without fanfare, amid statements from prominent spokespersons on the ways in which closer European involvement may in fact help provide a way forward.

Similarly, when in October 1992 Hume dismissed the possibility of an 'internal solution', describing Northern Ireland as 'an unnatural political entity' irreformable in normal democratic terms, it became more difficult for Sinn Féin to claim that his anti-nationalist speeches had been preparing the way for SDLP entry into a new arrangement within an unchanged United Kingdom context. In May 1993 his agreed statement with Gerry Adams used language generally identified with Sinn Féin to claim the right of self-determination for the Irish people 'as a whole', but also made the point Hume has laboured for years, that this self-determination can only be given effect when there is agreement between unionists and nationalists. Hume saw this as another stage in the effort to convince republicans that unionists can never be coerced into a united Ireland, and that the IRA campaign is futile and counterproductive. There is some evidence that at least a section of the Sinn Féin leadership has been working over the question.

MITCHEL MCLAUGHLIN, Sinn Féin's Northern chairman, says that his own 'Irishness' is of crucial importance to him, but that he has always thought of himself as a 'socialist republican with an international perspective' rather than as a nationalist. Consideration of what he meant by nationalism led him directly into how he thought nationalism could accommodate unionists.

'In terms of Irish nationalism, Irish democracy, I would see the need for the next three or four generations to arrive at political arrangements which would allow those of a unionist tradition to live in an Irish democracy and with nationalism, without being compelled to be a part of that nationalism.' Unionists could be convinced, he said, 'that their perception of a relationship with Britain could be accommodated within an Irish democracy. That's how I now define my Irish nationalism: what I'm looking for is a democratic structure that allows people of different political persuasions to coexist. I had a much narrower view of nationalism than that – but now I see it as an inclusive definition.'

McLaughlin refuses to be more specific about arrangements that could so accommodate unionists. Would there be a link with Britain to express their British identity, for example?

'The structural links with Britain are being redefined daily as part of the European project – there are a lot of things I disagree with John Hume about, but I think that Europe does affect people's perceptions of relationships in the island of Ireland in a positive way. No doubt there will be people in the North who will cling desperately to their British passports – but within the framework of Irish national democracy, as a result of negotiation, people can hang onto their British passports as far as I'm concerned.'

There are clear echoes of John Hume in McLaughlin's time frame of 'three or four generations' to work out new political arrangements, and in his deliberate vagueness about structural links that might include Britain in a European context. The hint of dual citizenship is an additional frill. It is all a considerable distance from traditional republican thinking: but also conducted at arm's length from the role of official spokesperson – this was an interview to discuss his personal views on identity. There have been signs that Mitchel McLaughlin's willingness to elaborate on republican theory, though clearly a licensed position, unnerves other republicans. At one point in 1992 IRA prisoners, endemically wary about being left out of new thinking, feared from media accounts that he was canvassing the possibility of a ceasefire. GERRY ADAMS leaves the teasing out of possibilities to McLaughlin, and reserves his public position as Sinn Féin president by dealing in more folksy terms with questions on nationalism and identity.

'I don't think national identity is anything to do with nationalism, necessarily. It's important in this country because the national question is unresolved. We define the Irish nation too narrowly. There isn't a Fine Gael Irish citizen, a Sinn Féin Irish citizen. To be Irish has to be a mixture. There are some Irish who are unionist and who play in Orange bands; there are some Irish who are unionist and do things which I politically don't agree with, including maybe the fact that they won't even accept that they're Irish.

'I do think it's impossible to be a nationalist in the political sense without having the position – though you might do nothing about it – that the British shouldn't be here, and we'd be better off on our own, because that's the very essence of what nationalism is about. But one can be an Irish citizen without all that. To be Irish is to be born on the island of Ireland. When the national question is resolved, then we can all have our diversity of attitudes, religions, hang-ups. At that point, nationalism would not need to be expressed in a political sense. For now it's a major political question. When that's settled, it'll be possible to be nationalist in a broader sense like other more settled nations.'

In contrast to Gerry Adams's insistence on the thirty-two-county reality of Irishness, many of those 'born on the island of Ireland' but north of the border are openly preoccupied with the particular circumstances of being Catholic in Northern Ireland. Of those who admit their sense of identity has changed – and many maintain that essentially it has not – almost all agree that they have been most affected by how they now feel towards the South, Britain, and Protestants.

When they try to separate and weigh elements of identity, in effect many are discussing how Irish Catholics, Irish nationalists, evolved into Northern Catholics. First they adjusted to a new, narrower identity but flinched at recognising it: then they steadily emerged from their confined 'state within a state' to develop a still separate and still changing identity, in a society that has increasingly adjusted to accommodate them. For many people, argument about how 'nationalism' should now be defined is not a pressing question. There is a high level of politicisation among Northern Catholics. But for most that means relating political developments or lack of them to their own lives, rather than discussing abstractions.

Southern attitudes and unionist behaviour have both

influenced how SINÉAD thinks of her identity. What is striking is that in spite of living in Catholic west Belfast, her attitudes seem unaffected by the presence of the British army. She is more preoccupied with the threat she feels from a Protestant majority, physically and to her sense of identity, than with the British presence. Sinéad votes Sinn Féin because they refuse to accept a 'second-class identity' for Northern Catholics, an idea she keeps returning to.

'The South is not the same as us now, they're not the same type of people. When people have a cause they're different. If we had a united Ireland, that would change us too and it would be handing the Protestants a cause. They think they have one now, but I would say they haven't. They're just out to make us think we're still second-class citizens.

'The South doesn't care about people up here really. I'm still Irish – it doesn't mean I want to be like them. They're all right as people, they've got economic problems, yes, but it's an OK society: I wouldn't mind being part of it. I wouldn't mind being a bit worse off if that was the price. Because, basically, I'd like to be Irish rather than being in the middle. And that's how I feel now, that I'm somewhere in the middle: I'm not British, I'm not Irish, there is no identity there.

'Protestants say they're British. I don't think they believe they are, in the sense the English are – and *we're* not Irish in the sense an Irish person is. The difference is we realise that and Pro-testants don't. We know we're not Irish and we can't be, until . . .

'I don't think Protestants could ever be fully British. But I do believe Catholics here could be fully Irish if the British withdrew and things settled down. There's more of a difference between Protestants and the British than between Catholics and the South. If you go to England, you see that. You know you'd have to live there forever to be part of them. Whereas when you go down South, they're different, yes – but I can imagine becoming like them. We could sort of blend in.'

It was a telling example of the contortions many Catholics go through when they begin to examine something that once was a given. Sinéad, twenty-six years old, speaks with more frankness and ease than older people. Declaring that she felt in the middle, that there was 'no identity there', could have sounded tragic, but did not. She is a young woman, confident, enjoys life, and says she has thought 'quite a bit' about the difficulty of finding a political solution that can accommodate Catholics and Protestants. But none exists, she concludes. 'I don't believe in the politicians. In a lot of ways I wish we had politicians like the Unionists. Ian Paisley, now – it doesn't matter what, he will not give in. That's what we need.' From someone who had said earlier that she voted for Gerry Adams and supported Sinn Féin as 'the nearest thing to a party which will stand up for us', this was slightly shocking: a suspicion that Sinn Féin might in the end compromise too?

As for the meaning of her 'Irishness', Sinéad was vague about its elements. She listed a love of Irish-speaking Donegal, Catholicism although she rarely goes to Mass ('but it's always part of you') and the Irish language. But there had to be 'a tie between the language and the fight here, if you like – not to be treated as second-class citizens'. Politically she had not changed at all, she thought, except to become 'more rational – I wouldn't be saying I want a united Ireland and I want it right now. I think there still has to be a united Ireland some day. If you feel you're Irish and you say anything else you are settling for less, you're treating yourself as a second-class citizen. I still believe I *am* Irish and should have the right to have others who are Protestant accept that – but they won't.' And that seemed to be the meaning of second-class citizenship: not discrimination, but what Sinéad sees as the coercive denial of her political identity.

She was scathing about Catholics who accepted, even welcomed this. In one school she attended, the majority were middle-class, she said, 'and they thought they were British, they said you're a British citizen, it's a British government. But they would be Irish if that was an easy thing to be. That's the thing about Catholics I don't understand – they tend not to mind, they won't stand up for themselves. Protestants still feel it's their state. But middle-class Catholics can happily live in Northern Ireland as it is now, say things are terrible and get on with their lives. There are probably more Protestants that want to be British than Catholics who want to be Irish – and that's sad.'

The perception that middle-class Catholics accept Northern Ireland's present status and are tepid about 'Irishness' is common, and repeated with similar scorn in working-class districts all over the North: in essence it is the old taboo about 'selling-out' – shared in the Protestant community, where signs of deviation from traditional loyalties are as suspiciously charted. There is a dread common to both communities that the other will somehow suborn their members, and an equal concern to show that modernisation, or redefinition, does not mean any diminution of essential differences.

In clinging to the idea that Protestants have a greater identity problem than Catholics, Sinéad speaks for many other Catholics of all ages and circumstances and from different parts of Northern Ireland: 'at least we're not that confused' is the unspoken, slightly consoling message. Her anxiety about continued second-class citizenship, and her awareness of being part of a threatened minority, are on the other hand concerns voiced most by those who live surrounded by Protestants. It is put most sharply in Belfast: by people from Short Strand, Ardoyne, New Lodge and the west of the city.

But others come from places that have as distinct, if different, regional preoccupations. Fermanagh Catholics have a reputation

for being old-fashioned nationalists, still resentful of having been
penned in on the wrong side of the border even though the
county has a nationalist majority and obsessed above all with
'getting the vote out' for a 'unity' candidate to prevent their
representation by a Unionist MP. In even the smallest cross-
section of ages, gender and background, however, it is as easy
to find a variety of Fermanagh views as it is elsewhere. One
woman born near the border with Donegal described her own
early views as 'mad republican and fierce Catholic'; she is now
a non-voting agnostic. In 1968 she was twenty, marched for
civil rights and 'flirted with socialism'. Now she lives in
Armagh, working at night in an old people's home and bringing
up three children on her own as well as studying for an Open
University degree.

'I think Northern Catholic identity is in a state of flux. The
certainties of the sixties that I was brought up with don't exist
– not for me, and maybe I'm projecting it, but not for other
people I know. I think the vast majority say to themselves "I'm
Irish" but don't necessarily mean "anti-partition" – even that
word dates you now. It belonged to the fifties and sixties.

'People feel they have no control over what's going on in the
streets any more. They haven't for a long time. They're so
burdened by it: in order to deal with it, you just get on with
your own life and don't think about identity. Because your
identity is caught up with acts which you totally disapprove of
but for which you're blamed. Maybe in Derry or west Belfast,
say, there are larger areas of consciousness about questions like
identity, that sort of thing. But then there are group pressures
there too, and community pressures.

'There's a bottom line, a general conception that Northern
Ireland's a dead duck and that it's just a matter of time. There's
no short-term solution and everybody thinks the British are going to go. People don't use words like "the Northern Ireland

state" any more, or even "the six counties". Maybe they'd say "the province" now – can you imagine? Even "Northern Ireland". When we were growing up it was "the six counties" and no mucking about.

'It must be something to do with direct rule too. There isn't a government: you're in a vacuum. So you keep your head down and do the best you can and hope that it all dies down. There's no choice.

'And when it comes to Irishness, identity – I've grown up. When I was eighteen everything was black-and-white. Brought up in a border town, in the fifties campaign, of course I was anti-border. Mad republican is the only way to describe myself at that stage. Now my priorities are different. I don't see nationalism and identity as linked. I see identity as to do with how you relate to other people. The differences between Irish/British, male/female, they're none of them so important. I have very strong political views to do with the way people live: I dislike the way they're manipulated, like in the whole Bosnian affair, by pulling on their strings.

'I still have all the strings that can be pulled – but I can decide now, do I go with this one or not? I'm a lot less compulsive, maybe a lot less spontaneous.'

In the emphasis on the personal, this is perhaps a line of thinking more common among women than men. But in retreating from a narrow and primarily political definition of identity, and from contemplation of the Troubles or any of the dilemmas connected with the conflict, this woman is undoubtedly one of many. The notion of direct rule as somehow nonpolitical, more vacuum than government, also had echoes of others who talked about Britain as almost irrelevant. It was quite clear, however, that in putting her old concept of identity aside, this woman had not decided she was now British. She prophesied both the end of the present state of

Northern Ireland and British withdrawal as inevitable and natural. And when discussing the Catholic Church's opposition to integrated education, unflatteringly, she said she still recognised that Catholic education had 'ensured we maintained the identity, and were able to get to the stage that at least in '68 we had the civil rights movement'.

HUGH, the 59-year-old businessman, SDLP supporter and devout though questioning Catholic who criticised the economically successful Catholics who 'put nothing back into the community', admits that he does not talk politics to his affluent Protestant neighbours in south Belfast. 'We talk about nothing. Because you feel if you're scratched far enough, you're a nationalist and further down you're republican and if it really got bad you're a Provo: and they're in exactly the same position. They're Alliance, and then Ulster Unionist, and you know that if it came to it, they'd be DUP and if it really went bad, they'd be UVF. There's that in us.'

Like the Fermanagh woman, he had reservations about the separate school system, but believed that Catholics in the days of the Stormont Unionist government needed to be separate. 'We wouldn't have kept our identity in a system where we'd have been looked down on. We needed separate education in which we were told we were the best.' As he says this he laughs.

He thinks Irishness 'is in continual flux. It was hugely anti-Britishness, and it certainly isn't that any longer. To me it *was* a united Ireland, a different language, culture, sport. But I'm changing now. For a start the simple solution of an all-Ireland is impossible to achieve without continual bloodshed and it has to be recognised that a quarter of the people have a different tradition. And what the Provos have done in the name of Ireland, the South won't accept any part of. We're not perceived as first-class Irish by the Republic, we're second- or third-class, and it's getting worse all the time.

'I sometimes think this is part three of my life. Part one was living on the border, nipping up and down to Dublin and hardly coming near Belfast. Part two I came to Belfast and worked, and I grew to like the place. Part three you start thinking again about Ireland, and Irishness – and you realise you're neither fish nor flesh. You're not part of the Britishness and you're not part of the Irishness that goes as far as the Provos. And you're also not part of it, because if you want to be fully Irish you have to live in the twenty-six counties. That's who *they* award Irishness to.

'It was great when it was all simplistic and you sang "A Nation Once Again" – but then you find that history has given you the wrong story on "A Nation Once Again". So we don't know whether we're coming or going. But whatever damage it has done to us, it has done more damage to the other community. Now we have to reinterpret, and maybe realise we can live together. We're going to be Irish, in some way or other. They *may* be British and hopefully they'll get a bit Irish, or something.'

For an articulate man who clearly enjoys talking about ideas like identity, it was a weak conclusion. But like almost everyone, Hugh cannot see a solution. Like most others, he has been affected by Southern attitudes, by what he sees as progressive British disengagement, and by a growing perception that the power balance between Northern Catholics and Protestants is tipping significantly towards Catholics. As the old united Ireland mirage fades, it has also become possible to contemplate 'living together' in Northern Ireland on a new basis. From the security of a comfortable home and sizeable income, Hugh is influenced equally by what he takes to be increased Catholic confidence and diminishing Protestant assurance, an unflattering comparison that is almost unanimous.

Where he falters is in contemplation of his own identity – and in assessing how Protestants will adjust. The familiar dismissal of

Protestant identity as more damaged than that of Catholics clearly brought him no comfort. For once, it sounded more like a factual assessment than an excuse for self-aggrandisement. His own sense of Irishness had not been voiced with any great assurance. An open, direct man, he did not try to hide behind a screen of cultural Irishness, though he speaks Irish and has a scholarly interest in Irish history and literature. None of that seemed relevant to his consciousness that courtesy of the border, the IRA and Southern detachment, he was now 'neither fish nor flesh'.

Hugh spoke more personally about his shaken sense of identity than most Northern men tend to. In many ways, he sounded the same notes as a considerable number of women, whose ability to be remarkably open about loss of certainty and about doubts about the shape of future identity seemed directly related to the semi-detached views most had about both the main nationalist parties, Sinn Féin and the SDLP. They were not silenced by the notion that admitting doubts about identity would make nationalists sound as bereft as unionists, something Northern Catholic men, even the most frank, often seem stricken speechless by.

In the case of community worker MÁIRÉAD, her analysis of a shaken Northern Catholic sense of self is the product both of her own experience, and of her observation of the people she has worked with in north and west Belfast. Northern Catholic identity is 'strange', she thinks.

'The idea that it's only Protestants who have an identity crisis on their hands is not true at all – *we've* lost our sense of exactly where we're rooted, but the necessity of facing up to that is papered over by day-to-day realities. You can define what you're *against*, you're part of a group that is essentially the victim of injustice. *That* becomes the core of identity.'

WOMEN

Perhaps, although trapped by circumstances into voting for particular parties, women feel little loyalty to a political system that has shown little interest in them. Sinéad and a few others remarked on the number of young women involved at grassroots level in Sinn Féin, though they all reckoned that at leadership level republicanism was essentially as male-dominated as constitutional nationalism. But outside the small world of feminist groups, there is not much enthusiasm for debate on the absence of women from Northern political life. Instead many invest energy and ability in community groups, which for some have come to substitute for political organisation.

It is widely recognised by younger Northern women, at least, that among feminists the attempt to build a broad-based women's movement has repeatedly foundered on the clash of political identities. The historian Margaret Ward ('The Women's Movement in the North of Ireland, Twenty Years On', in *Ireland's Histories – Aspects of State, Society and Ideology,* edited by Sean Hutton and Paul Stewart, London, 1991) noted drily that in 1980 during the Armagh women prisoners' protest a small lesbian group broke up on the issue of whether its members should be supporting the prisoners: 'They found that lesbians could be unionist or nationalist [too]'.

Repeatedly during interviews, I had the impression in talking to women that they were in general more curious than men about how Protestants felt now over a range of issues. This did not mean they were any less concerned about a return to Unionist domination.

COLETTE, forty-four and brought up in a republican family, a teacher in Belfast at the start of the Troubles and now living on a small farm in County Derry, says she has begun to identify with the North – but not with the Northern state.

'I feel a strong dislike to say the least for the hardline Protestantism of the DUP, say, but I feel the same antipathy towards the IRA and Sinn Féin. Protestants who are my friends for years, women mostly, some men: people are people ... I don't think of them as a different nation. Since things like the divorce referendum in the South, I think of Protestant women in particular as the same breed as me, I think of myself as less Southern Irish and more Northern Irish. I feel I know very little about the Republic and a lot I don't like.

'And yet, the Northern Ireland state to me has still given nothing to the working-class Catholic. I just don't believe the Catholics who do well, the civil servants and so on, they still don't hold positions that make anything change. Because in Northern Ireland in the end the Unionists have a veto – and there isn't any question about that. They have a veto on all movement. So you can be influencing people as much as you like, and you're actually making no difference.'

After a period of involvement in civil rights organisation, and then some years later in the SDLP, Colette now says she does not know if 'the idea of Northern Ireland as solvable by a sovereign government is realistic at all – but I think differently from week to week. Sometimes I look at it hopefully.' She has two teenage girls: she says she feels she should not depress them. 'They're very sure of their Irishness – but it doesn't seem attached to a place at all. It's the language, and music. They don't seem to notice politics.'

CULTURAL IDENTITY

For many Northerners, as for Colette's daughters, Irish culture means language, music, literature, sport: a cultural nationalism that can encompass different political affiliations and none, and which has become more evident as Northern Catholics assert their identity. In a reversal of the old pattern, the growing

interest in Irish culture among some young people, and their
assertiveness have pushed parents into rethinking their own
timidity. 'I notice how much more nationalist I sound now, and
I think it has to do with my daughter,' said a woman in mainly
Protestant Ballymoney, County Antrim. 'She says that her
father and me are far too apologetic about being ourselves –
because we used to warn her not to talk about liking Irish too
much outside the house.'

Names entirely in Irish are more common and less self-
consciously borne nowadays, matters of fact rather than
gestures. One recent issue of the *Ulster Tatler* – long a glossy
journal exclusively chronicling the social doings of a Protestant,
unionist middle class but now rushing to catch up with the
transmuted bourgeoisie – contained an account of a fundraiser
for a new convent, complete with photo of nuns, on another
page the Reverend Ian Paisley, Mrs Paisley and artist daughter
Rhonda smiling side by side with a well-known Irish-speaking
Catholic journalist who had just opened Rhonda's latest exhibition, and a number of photographs of Catholic school dances
includng a smiling young couple whose names were given in
Irish, perfectly spelled and accented. I met the girl in the photo
soon afterwards. 'We gave them in like that partly as a joke,' she
said, 'because you couldn't imagine the *Tatler* printing them,
but both of us use the Irish forms of our names most of the time
anyhow.'

Considerable numbers say they now take a pride in talking
about playing or supporting GAA games – gaelic football, hurl-
ing, camogie – in mixed workplaces or with Protestant friends,
where once they would have disguised their interest. There is
a lingering resentment at the long invisibility of GAA fixtures in
the mass media, matched by considerable pleasure that belated
BBC programming on gaelic football, as on the Irish language,
is done well and has a growing audience. But arrival on the

wider public scene is a haphazard process. Many Catholics still feel that vital elements and concerns in their communal life are either neglected or diminished, usually out of deference to Protestant sensitivities. The conviction has sharpened into disbelieving indignation at the swelling Protestant complaint that Catholics have made steady and unfair gains at Protestant expense. A nun in County Armagh recalled sharply how a BBC religious programme production team sent an advance message before arriving to film a church service, that to ensure the widest possible appeal hymns with no exclusively Catholic connotations should be chosen, and certainly none in Irish. 'The maddening thing was that the producer was a Catholic – they don't all realise yet that you don't have to behave like that any more to get on.'

For much of the past decade, the once staid and ultra-Catholic *Irish News* has struggled to depict a changing community and the consequent shifts in Northern nationalist identity. SDLP policies and even minor pronouncements are still treated with almost invariable respect, but Sinn Féin figures now also receive considerable attention. An editorial when Charles Haughey stepped down as leader of Fianna Fáil caught much of the backwash inside Northern nationalism from the new tides in Southern politics. Under the headline 'Northern nationalists need Fianna Fáil' it read in part: 'Fine Gael and the Labour party are dominated by unionists and crypto-unionists, the Dublin 4 brigade who can't wait to repeal Articles Two and Three and abandon the north to its fate.'

The front page is still liable to be dominated by a large photograph of a smiling bishop or priests surrounded by kneeling people praying beside a 300-year-old Mass rock in County Antrim. But under a young Manchester-Irish editor over the past few years, a series of columns appeared that satirised Catholic piety, including anti-abortion attitudes, and features began to range with some flair over fashion, holidays, the arts, restaurants. The inevitable tensions occasionally surface: after a blizzard of unhappy letters to the editor, three impious journalists were told on the same day that their services were no longer required. One letter-writer summed up what must be considerable disquiet among older readers: 'Forget the tracksuits and the trendy restaurants, tell Britain to get out of Ireland.'

A young reporter who left the *Irish News* to work in a bigger organisation – the BBC – says she disliked many things about the newspaper, but is frustrated by the awareness that it none the less provided a unique service.

'It gave a voice to something that no one else does in the mainstream media, something that's not being aired. The endless saga of discrimination, the cases that come dripping out one after the other: the *Irish News* puts them on the front page, the *Belfast Telegraph* puts them on page fifteen and the BBC doesn't cover them at all. Look at Queen's – three years of cases that show they were complacent beyond belief about the inequality in their own staff, and continued discrimination. That story was nowhere but in the *Irish News*. So Queen's was able to dismiss it and say, "Well, it's only the *Irish News*, the Catholic paper, they're biased." [One Queen's lecturer described a retirement function for a senior Catholic academic, at which the *Irish News* managing director was a guest: 'There was a ring of chill round him from the top university brass.']

'There's the other stuff too: putting it on the record that it's Catholics in north Belfast who've suffered most in the Troubles, listing the deaths. Some people said that was just inflaming hatred – but if it's not reported, how can that be right? The things like GAA games every Sunday with bigger crowds than for any soccer match that's on television, and Clonard novena every year that thousands go to: they might as well not happen for all you see of them on the TV. Local papers do those things, the *Andersonstown News* reports it: but there's no paper other than the *Irish News* that goes all over the North.'

Older people maintain that they read the *Irish News* mainly for the death notices: to see which contemporary has died. Among the traditional piety of more conservative notices and the sickly doggerel foisted upon others, the same bad rhymes repeated, these are glimpses of the multiple strands in contemporary Northern Catholic life, and reminders of the reality of 'culture' for many. Notices for a man shot at work by the UVF declared that he was 'innocent' and 'murdered for his faith'; there followed tributes from relatives and friends in London, Birmingham, Liverpool, 'the Michael Davitt Gaelic Athletic Club, McDermotts football team, the pool hall'.

For some, the revival of cultural Irishness is directly related to republicanism, the two blending into each other. The growth of interest in the Irish language during the Troubles, for example, particularly in west Belfast, has been encouraged by a heightened consciousness of Irishness, and as a matter of policy by Sinn Féin. Prior to the Troubles the language was sustained by a small band of enthusiasts, most of them teachers, who gave their time free or for nominal payments out of school and in holidays. Now parental interest in Derry and Belfast has led to the establishment of nursery classes, several primary schools and a secondary school. Adult beginners' classes spring up regularly ... and as often fade within a short time, according to clear-eyed observers. Republican prisoners learn the language in jail, then try to encourage it in their families. Sinn Féin works at presenting documents and statements with at least some Irish included: Gerry Adams strenuously uses the language on every possible occasion.

'I think it was tainted for a lot of people for some years by association with the Provos, but it's gone beyond that now,' said a senior priest in west Belfast. 'There were people who didn't let their kids learn it who are saying now they're sorry.' The only aspect of living in west Belfast one teenager told me she liked and felt proud of was the Irish school near her home: 'I'll send my kid there when he's old enough,' she said, 'if I can't get out of here before then.' A boy brought up entirely through Irish, who learned English only when he was ten, had another perspective that suggested the diverse currents of thinking in an area where outsiders sometimes imagine uniform beliefs: 'My parents had a sense of being downtrodden as Northern Catholics, and they tackled that by learning Irish – whereas children brought up like me, I see a lot of them who think their identity consists solely of the language, and they see it as a "nicer" identity, more polite, than just being a Catholic in west Belfast. For them it hasn't strengthened any kind of political identity. I think they treat it as a pastime.'

In Derry, Mitchel McLaughlin remembers 'elitist' Irish-language enthusiasts before the Troubles. 'Some used the expression the "lesser Gaels" for those who hadn't got the language, and I still see those people around. I don't know if they have the same influence. For them, there's no development, no life or vibrancy – it's like keeping a dead thing going.'

But he believes that the suppression of Irish by the English in the past, and 'the imposition of another culture' have had long-lasting and damaging effects. 'The fact that we all converse in English doesn't automatically mean we have the same thought processes as English people. We maintained a tenuous contact with our own culture, in the fact that a lot of Gaelic words got built into the form of English, and I have this theory that a lot of the flowery, beautiful use of the English language and the stark contrast with the very brutal and rough use of English is in fact an outworking of the same syndrome: people thinking in their own terms but having to express themselves in a foreign tongue. So what you get is convoluted thought at

times, as well as beautiful use of language – in any group of Irish
people. I think Brian Friel explored that in *Translations*, and I'm
grateful that somebody took it so far. But there is a considerable
amount of useful work to be done there, if people wanted to
understand why some of the divisions in this society are so
intractable and why so many people feel less than whole.'

He is 'frustrated' by Friel, however, by Seamus Heaney and,
to a lesser extent, by his fellow Derryman Seamus Deane. He
thinks all three have opted for a 'mainstream, non-controversial
reflection of Irish society, which devalues us all and certainly
devalues their potential'. The play *Translations* was 'Friel's last
attempt at exploring that particular issue of suppression of who
we are by the colonisers, and then our own suppression of who
we are. Up to then, Friel was right in it, up to his elbows. He
may be frightened off by the subject, by the effect of his exploring those ideas on the conditions of conflict which exist in our
society. He may feel as Yeats and people like that agonised that
he may pour petrol on the flames. I don't think he should take
that amount of responsibility. In a sense he is suppressing what
could be great and lasting literary works. Friel, Heaney and
Deane represent those who you would expect to be in the
vanguard of the anti-revisionist school: they recognise the
challenge which is there, and they haven't the balls for it.'

The irony of this attack – which Mitchel McLaughlin
belatedly recognised – is that these are three writers who have
also been criticised by people he would regard as 'revisionists'.
'That doesn't necessarily mean they're going far enough to
satisfy what I'd be looking for – though that might be more than
they could ever deliver. There's no culture of dialogue and
discourse, and I think they're strategically placed to play a
crucial role in developing that culture. I think they get intimidated by the amount of flak they get. Anyone who is not of the
mainstream of political thought in Ireland is dealt with in this

McCarthyite way, as an extremist.'

A very different point was made by the SDLP veteran BEN CARAHER, a south Armagh man who teaches English and politics in a west Belfast school.

'The idea that gunmen are more pure than politicians runs deep. I remember studying at A levels the novel *Mó Dhá Róisín* [My Two Rosaleens] by Máire [the pen name of Séamus Mac Gríanna]. The narrator and the girl are passing a political meeting in Dublin, before the 1916 Rising. He stops to listen and she drags him on, and she says, "They're only politicians, looking for votes."

'That sort of literature works on you. It's how a political tradition is passed on, almost unconsciously. Looking back, I see the effect. There is this cultural tradition in modern Irish history, of the Pearse figure, the sacrifice. The militarists, the Provos, do think of themselves, because they are prepared to sacrifice their all, that their motives are pure: therefore they are right. They don't have to take account of other people who are in some ways compromisers. They're weak or they're grubby or they're corrupt. Anyway, they're not as good. That tradition is strong – it can't be combated, those people can't be changed in the short term.

'In the long term, it's cultural changes that will alter them: that they are increasingly anachronistic in the world we live in. Society is changing. Just think, the phrase "dying for Ireland". Even when I had no intention of dying for Ireland, or for anything else, being a grubby and corrupt politician, I understood what it meant. It was part of the world I lived in. Now when I hear it, it sounds faintly absurd. Shows you how the cultural make-up has changed – and I don't think that's just me. The vocabulary and thoughts of the past are potent, I im-agine, to a smaller number of people.'

The theme of 'selling-out' that Ben Caraher raised is,

however, still potent, even though some of its force has dissipated as ideas about identity begin to break up and re-form. In my childhood, one of the worst things you could say about another Catholic was that they were 'very British' or 'anti-Irish'. The terms were more or less interchangeable, and I suppose their force depended on the unquestioned identity and cultural distinctiveness of predominantly Catholic areas: south Armagh, parts of mid-Ulster, the Antrim Glens. They generally denoted a lack of interest in or even an expressed dislike for the Irish language, Irish music, dancing, games – if not a declared preference for 'British' games, dancing, culture.

We learned and revered Shakespeare as well as the poetry of Pádraig Pearse ... but to me as a child and even as a young adolescent, it was not entirely clear that Shakespeare as a literary figure was in a different league from the leader of the Easter Rising. Listening to Bernadette McAliskey in mid-1992 taking Pearse's 'Mise Éire' (I am Ireland) as text for a lecture on her own identity, as the start of a campaign intended to pre-empt any alteration of articles Two and Three in the Irish constitution, hearing her hurl the lines

> 'Mo chlann fhéin do dhíol a mháthair
> Uaigní mé ná an cailleach Béara'
>
> (My own children sold their mother
> I am lonelier than the old hag of Beare)

at a Dublin audience, and feeling increasingly chilled by a definition of Irishness that seemed to exclude all but those who like her Devlin ancestors had lived in the hills of Tyrone from a time before history, before Christianity, long long before the coming of the settlers – part of my own unease came from the memory of a *feis* platform and Pearse's rhetoric filling my

eleven-year-old heart with what I imagined to be patriotism.
Who was *I* blaming for 'selling' Ireland?

The Northern Catholic community has never shown much
tolerance of internal dissent or difference: identity may have
been unthinking and unreflective, but its component beliefs
were well-recognised, and mandatory. Those who flout them
publicly have always been made aware of their transgression.
The distaste for independent thought might at first sight seem
ironical, given that Northern Catholics in general traditionally
saw themselves as denied full membership of society and forced
by an alien and alienating state into permanent dissent – a
perception shared across the lines of class and political division
by the better-off and the poor, republican and anti-republican
alike. OLIVER NAPIER, knighted by Queen Elizabeth as the first
and long-serving leader of the non-sectarian but unionist
Alliance Party, is as forthright about old grievances as any
avowed nationalist.

'I don't think there was any Catholic in Northern Ireland
who felt himself to be part of the old Stormont/Unionist state,'
he says. But when Napier began to argue that progress could
only come through agreement to share power in a Northern
Ireland that ensured equality but remained British, the community of the excluded no longer extended to him. Insistence
on pursuing the objective of a united Ireland would inevitaby
inflame unionist Protestant opinion, he said: Catholics should
work with Protestants to build up a new shared Northern identity. 'In the period from 1968 through the early seventies I was
frequently insulted by friends – certainly they upset me.'

Others describe exclusion, isolation, or more mildly, mere
disapproval, for different transgressions against an unspoken
code: what Bishop EDDIE DALY calls, laughingly, an 'identity kit
– I still think there are remnants of that mentality in parts of

Ireland: a Celtic nationalism, the Catholic faith, GAA, Irish music, Irish language, a full package ... I believe we're moving away from that narrow sense of being Irish which is a very false sense of identity and a very offensive sense of Irishness – we're moving, I hope, towards a greater acceptance of difference. However, even recently there was a priest friend I met who said to me, "You were always a soccer follower, you weren't a real Irish person, you know!" He laughed about it then, but I think he betrayed a mentality that would hold unless you had the full package, the official identity kit, you could not be fully Irish.'

In Dr Daly's city of Derry, Sinn Féin councillor MARY NELIS insists on the other hand that she was effectively cast out of Derry's orthodox Catholic society when with two other women she stood wrapped only in a blanket outside the bishop's door to draw attention to the republican prison protest, and to complain that the Church establishment had not supported the protesters. 'I remember this priest came out, I knew him really well, and his face was white with rage. He was furious, he tore into us. Old women coming out of the chapel were shouting things, looking at us desecrating the holy ground.'

Mary Nelis had been alienated from the Church in any case. 'But that was the end – and the first thing I felt was this terrible isolation. If you leave the Church in Derry you're very isolated. I'd left the SDLP too, and I had nothing to do with Sinn Féin then, and now I was in this protest that my mother and everybody thought was mental. That day nearly killed my mother, she wouldn't go out of the house for weeks after it, she didn't want to go into the shop, I disgraced her. It made me a communist, because I was criticising the Church and doing things she just couldn't cope with. I tried to bridge the gulf but I think she died without us being totally reconciled.'

At the other end of the political spectrum, Paddy Devlin and

Gerry Fitt, formerly SDLP chief whip and first party leader
respectively, might as well have slipped off the face of the Northern Catholic world – having labelled both violent republicanism and constitutional nationalism as sectarian in the same
way as unionism. The major difficulty the rebel in Northern
Catholic society has always faced is the impossibility of being
taken at his or her word as an independent agent. On a narrow
political stage, to step outside the tribe is taken to mean going
over to the enemy, whether the form of rebellion actually com-
forts the enemy or not. Mary Nelis found a new niche in
republicanism, and though she believes the Church, like the
SDLP, 'failed' her, she recalls as well that Father Denis Faul con-
tacted her immediately after her first blanket protest to praise
her courage and to get her publicity. It is denial of some facet
of Northern Catholic identity in a way that is deemed to comfort unionism that cannot be forgiven: republicanism, even anti-
clerical republicanism, has always been part of the collective
identity.

But there is confusion. Fault lines are well established in
the identikit: 'leaving the faith' is an increasingly common
phenomenon and nationalism is a shifting concept. Precisely
when public office has become both accessible and thinkable for
the first time, through nominations by both the Irish government and the NIO, it has become more difficult to define what
constitutes an appropriate representative of the Northern
Catholic community. A highly qualified young woman with
Alliance sympathies who sits on a number of public bodies
described recently how she had fallen foul of the elderly SDLP
nominee who chairs the most prestigious of her boards.

'We were at a Saturday afternoon function and it was running
late. He was there with his wife, I was with my daughter, and
we were in a group of mostly unionists. "This is going to keep
on to Mass time," he said. "We'll maybe have to go tomorrow

morning." His wife gave me a beady look, and he picked it up. "What Mass will you be going to yourself?" said he, bold as brass. Just for badness because I knew what he was getting at, I said I didn't think I'd bother. "Well *you'll* surely go anyhow," said he to my daughter, pink in the face. "I don't care if I never set foot in a church again," she said. He sort of flounced away from me. "The next time I'm asked to recommend a woman and a Catholic," he said, "I'll say I can suggest the woman but not the Catholic." The unionists around us were too embarrassed to say anything. I was tempted to ask if he'd say they weren't Protestants if *they* didn't go to church.'

In this case, to someone with little emotional attachment to the idea of a Northern Catholic identity, disapproval meant no more than mild social embarrassment. The question of dissent is at its sharpest, and the threat of being called a traitor most dangerous, inside the tight and traditional sub-world of republicanism, focused by the long-running argument about the necessary conditions for an IRA ceasefire.

'How can we stop, with all the dead – our dead and all the others? If we stop for anything less than a real settlement, people are going to ask what did they all die for. That's a major difficulty for us.' The question posed off the record by a leading IRA man some years ago is unchanged. It is generally believed that if the IRA is to be persuaded to stop, it will only be by other republicans: if they are to achieve an end to the campaign, rather than a vicious split, republicans in general must first be convinced that their action will not be seen as a 'sellout'.

To a considerable degree, there is a distance already between the language of republican statements – measured, cautious, almost bureaucratic – and the rhetoric of people like Bernadette McAliskey and Des Wilson who declaim on the suffering of the 'nationalist people' and make belligerent prophesies about what those people will do if continually thwarted. 'Desi sometimes sounds hysterical,' says a leading Sinn Féiner, 'but you have to remember Desi Wilson hasn't got an organisation to support him – it's very hard to keep a sense of proportion if you're on your own.' A veteran inside observer of the republican world thought it 'remarkable when you think that Bernadette was once seen as modern and radical and daring, and now she sounds terrifically old-fashioned, far more than any Provo'.

There is none the less a degree of recognition that the pitch and tone of those few voices on the wings have become more shrill, as Sinn Féin figures become involved in what increasingly looks like the beginning of a dialogue with Britain, at one remove, about conditions in which there could be an end to an IRA campaign. 'I wouldn't say they're necessarily afraid there's going to be a sellout,' said the Bernadette-watcher. 'But they're outsiders, and they don't know. And the people with no organisations and no responsibility can always afford to be that much more unbending.'

One former supporter says he is now convinced the republican leadership is 'casting around for some way out – they know they're going no place. No one is saying they'll win any more, in public or private. They no longer put forward any positive rationale. Now they're only arguing, well, if we call it off it would be worse. I suppose their problem is they're very afraid of the people on the ground whose motivation is simply frustration and revenge. But I think at some stage they've got to confront that.

'They argue, if we stop, they'll all join the IPLO – but they have to take the risk. There's another problem for them. It's a military organisation. Even the most political of them have a different concept of politics from people involved in conventional, electoral lobbying, where you're conditioned to accept that you may be beaten at times and you then reorganise and come back. Their attitude to politics has been very much – if you don't win, there's no point.'

The assessment that leading republicans are afraid of those in their own movement has become commonplace among many Northern Catholics, like the clear-eyed summary of grassroots motivation as 'simply frustration and revenge'. It is not an assessment that would be made in public without considerable hedging and qualification. The most outspoken Catholic critics of the IRA within the community – clerics, SDLP politicians – habitually take care to point their barbs at the leadership, the 'godfathers', those who 'send others out to kill and be killed', while expressing confidence in the sense and innate virtue of the mass of republican supporters, deluded and misled by an arrogant few.

But no one knows what republicans any longer hope to win. Their own supporters long ago lost their vision of a thirty-two-county republic, in the welter of doubt and change that has swept over the entire Catholic community. Often it sounds as though republicans believe they dare not stop. 'We're not going back into the hole again', said the Belfast IRA man I spoke to, with a child's nightmare turn of phrase.

He added: 'If by some gimmick Britain was able to crush the IRA militarily, in ten to fifteen years my sons and daughters would come back at them. The IRA fifty years ago used Webleys, now it's Kalashnikovs. My kids'll probably use lasers.' He laughs. 'Yes, I can contemplate my kids being involved – I'd have no problem about that. It would be the continuation of an avoidable tragedy, but it's our duty to do all in our power to end the current situation in a fashion and with guarantees and conditions that could produce peace and make it self-sustaining, not to bring about another stand-off. Civil rights: to me, at my age, they just cleared the way. [He was eleven in 1968, when the civil rights marches began.] The only sense I had was of people coming out of the hole, saying that's it, we're not lying down any more. Our community was transformed from the middle sixties, late sixties, beyond all recognition by 1972. What transformed them was the experience of struggle.'

Redefining identity may have taken time to be expressed as such, but in many ways it has been the unspoken exercise all the major elements of the Northern Catholic world and of nationalism have engaged in over the past twenty-five years: Catholic Church, SDLP, republicans, the Southern parties, and opinion-formers. It is inevitably painful and slow. An IRA man sees a crushed people transformed by 'struggle', others see republican violence as having cost their community more than it could ever gain. There is more than a trace of machismo in comparisons between the past and present behaviour of the community: sometimes rhetorical, like the IRA man's insistence that 'we're not lying down any more', occasionally more personal, as in the Derry Sinn Féin leader Mitchel McLaughlin talking about his revulsion from the old Nationalist Party of which his father was a leading local member: 'I had a resentment, which I suppose I transferred to the Nationalist Party from my father, of this generation, and generations before, who had put up with what were manifest injustices and had done nothing about it.'

The argument long ago took on the shape of direct debate, though conducted at arm's length and with pauses often of weeks and months, but for all the attention it gets from many Protestants, and a considerable number of Catholics, it might as well not be happening. 'The day of the nation-state is dead and gone,' says John Hume: 'But I haven't had mine yet,' says Bernadette McAliskey. People talk of their sense of identity now as 'frozen', 'in limbo', 'on pause', 'in flux': they use terms like 'Irishness' and 'nationalism' with personal glosses and often with partial disclaimers. The IRA man was one of many who instantly insisted he was not a nationalist: 'I see the resolution of the national question as the key to the emancipation of the working classes – I'm a socialist, that old word that fell out of vogue.'

Cardinal CAHAL DALY, hammer of republicanism, is as wary of the word 'nationalism', apparently in the main because he sees it as a threat to the proper understanding of Catholicism. He speaks of the importance of the 'universality of the Church rather than a narrow nationalistic understanding', of the Irish Catholic affinity with Europe, and he expresses his own concept of identity in churchman's terms first but with a care to emphasise his Irishness.

'Not in any pious sense, my identity has always been first of all a Christian, Catholic identity – but then I'm an Irish person as well without any sense of a need to rationalise or analyse or justify that, it's what I am . . . Being Irish now, in the context of Europe, doesn't mean being against others but being with others.' He is clear about the relationship between violent republicanism, and violence generally, and notions of identity.

'I ask myself whether it is lack of security in one's sense of identity which drives one to violence or to support for violence: I think it's insecurity, people who feel they've got to assert their identity against, in opposition or enmity to some other identity, just as I sometimes wonder whether the people who are anti-ecumenical, if somehow there is a deep and unconscious insecurity in their own religious identity. Perhaps among some republicans there's a nervous feeling that if they were to cease their armed campaign somehow or other Ireland would lose its sense of national or republican identity – that theirs is the last generation to uphold – that comes from a lack of security in being Irish.'

Cahal Daly is unusual in his willingness to criticise republicans beyond the point of balance: an almost token reference to the insecurity of anti-ecumenicists, in Northern Ireland terms code for Paisleyite fundamentalist Protestants, is followed by a much more direct and damaging imputation of weakness at the heart of republicanism. Similar criticism is more often voiced anonymously: one veteran community worker says, wistfully, that he 'hasn't got the bottle just yet' to say to republicans, 'Will you for Christ's sake stop wallowing in your own self-pity? Freedom doesn't come from the barrel of a gun, it comes from inside you, you've got to free yourself.'

Cahal Daly's suggestions aside, there is little argument that Northern Catholics generally feel more confident in asserting a separate, and Irish, identity, whatever doubts they now have about the nature of Irishness. BRÍD RODGERS measures the change since her arrival in Lurgan thirty years ago from Donegal: 'Moving towards parity of esteem has strengthened people's sense of their own national identity and rights. I think that's only natural: they're no longer prepared to settle for the rhetoric, they want the real thing. And certainly the Anglo-Irish Agreement, whatever you might say about feeling in the South, has made a difference: the simple fact that when Jack Lynch as taoiseach made a statement about the North he got a telegram from Downing Street telling him to mind his own business and now Irish and British ministers are meeting regularly to discuss areas of mutual concerns. I think nationalists know there's no going back.'

But there is no agreement about the shape this strengthened sense of identity is likely to take. ANN, republican, brought up in Ardoyne through the worst early years of the Troubles, is angry at Southern indifference and hostility and says she is 'Northern Irish', but she means in an Irish context: 'Ulster maybe, as in the nine counties, a federal Ireland would suit me grand – it wouldn't matter in a federal state if Protestants dominated Ulster – it would all be Ireland, wouldn't it?' Father DENIS FAUL, like Bríd Rodgers born on the other side of the border, sees a drift towards a Northern identity also, but differently: 'There's a stronger Northern Catholic identity because of the Troubles and the hostility of the South – which the Provos have caused a lot of – and there's an awful loss of the all-Ireland identity.' Like many others he notices the strong everyday ties between many Catholic families and England: television and newspapers but, more important, relatives now settled there, teenagers going to English universities.

Ann's blitheness about possible future Protestant domination is unusual: she lives in Craigavon, near loyalist Portadown. Regional differences in attitudes are often overestimated, but there does seem to be a more laid-back quality about attitudes to the future among those who live in Catholic-majority areas. A Derrywoman talking about identity said briskly that she thought no one now was looking for unity, they wanted equality: and structures linking North and South 'so if they want to grow together well and good – and if they don't, well and good too'. But Derry looks at Northern Ireland from the perspective of the west, where the school population is now three to one Catholic. In even the biggest of Belfast's Catholic ghettos, increased political assurance and the census revelations have scarcely dented the fear of a threatening if now narrow majority. One academic who visits west Belfast every few years was much struck by a glimpse of a street festival recently: 'Little girls reciting the history of the area in a mini-historical pageant, and the main date seemed to be "August 1969, the loyalists came in" – roll of drums, pause.'

The first few years of the Troubles produced a higher rate of violence, and more political experimentation than the subsequent two decades. Republicans, and the SDLP, met loyalist paramilitaries to discuss independence as a solution for Northern Ireland; Unionists, the SDLP and the Alliance Party worked together in the 1974 power-sharing executive; a coalition of Unionists and loyalist paramilitaries brought the executive down; and the IRA called a lengthy, if much-interrupted ceasefire. The SDLP emerged from the 1974 experiment badly shaken and eventually decided it would never again get involved in an administration without the guarantee of an in-built Irish dimension. The IRA emerged from its 1975 cease-fire demoralised – honeycombed by British intelligence, after months during which its members had engaged as freelances in a riot of sectarian killings – and the organisation vowed that next time Britain would have to announce the intent to withdraw before they downed arms. On that platform, the present republican political leadership ousted those who called the ceasefire.

'We don't put down the end position of a united Ireland any more, that was the cynical, traditional Nationalist line – a pretence. They were actually saying, "We know it can't be achieved, but we'll stick it in anyhow, just to show we're not selling out." Well, we've moved the whole community away from that,' says a senior SDLP man, with the confidence his party members now routinely express in their own achieve-ments and in a more realistic Northern Catholic political identity. Sinn Féin leader Gerry Adams as frequently asserts the confidence his supporters now feel in their own identity, and in the distance they have come. But the spokesmen for both main forms of Northern Catholic political expression are well aware that their supporters have long, unforgiving, and disabling memories. The SDLP man also sums up his community's history as a comparatively simple tale of injustice to be righted: 'We were comprehensively shafted back in the twenties, and it's not just going to take a wee bit of unshafting to put right: there will be no internal Northern Ireland settlement, people will not accept an arrangement which doesn't recognise their Irishness in exactly the same way as the Britishness of Unionists.' A woman once involved in politics but now observing from the sidelines has no doubt that on the central issue of where a sense of identity is likely to fetch up, the instinct of politicians is for once

borne out by the drift of academic surveys: 'What John Whyte
calls "the centrist stream" among Catholics, which accepts
the Union while rejecting Unionist domination, has diminished consistently over the last twenty-five years: the Catholic
Alliance vote has become almost negligible, the identity has
changed and become more nationalist.'

Which means? It can seem as if there are as many definitions
and redefinitions as there are Northern Catholics. Mary Nelis,
whose inherited republicanism revived primarily because of her
own family's experience of the Troubles, now says she has
'moved to an international identity rather than an Irish one –
I'd exchange it with the woman struggling in Nicaragua or the
man in Mexico or the woman in Ballymun – I'm acutely aware
of being Irish and I feel good about it, but I meet people from
all over the world whose thinking is the same as mine'.

Mary McAleese, who at eighteen saw a Protestant mob
unhindered by the forces of law and order set fire to houses in
Ardoyne, has no doubts about her own Irishness but knows that
her identity, like that of many others, has been 'tempered' by
experience of the Troubles, of the South, by relationships inside
Northern Ireland and with Britain and Europe. Out of that has
come, she insists, a flexibility about the future and about the
shape government structures should have in order to reflect
identity. Mary McAleese looks at the community she comes
from with a mixture of personal commitment and academic
observation, and with optimism.

'There are new layers of identity overlaying the old – Europe
principally – that offer possibilities for extending the sense of self
beyond Ireland/Britain, Catholic/Protestant. But this is still in
the very early stages. Identity is mutating, and like all things that
touch large tranches of people, it will be slow to take on a final
shape.'

It is the kind of refusal to set parameters that many Catholics see as a healthy way forward – and which maintains in many Protestants a dread about hidden Catholic intentions, the old fear renewed. Northern Catholics have changed, as a community and as individuals. Their assurance, their increased visibility in public life, and above all the dawning awareness of their increased proportion in the population gall Protestants, who ask why these supposedly more politically sophisticated people should continue to support the gunmen and bombers of the IRA. But Catholic confidence is shadowed, difficult to maintain. This was a suppressed community for half a century: ignored by Britain, abandoned in all but rhetoric by their supposed kith and kin in the Republic, accustomed – most damagingly of all – to the idea that they could achieve nothing politically for themselves. The cynicism and suspicion that bred is still there. Awareness of a growing gap between North and South is a challenge to the adventurous few, who look to the development of a new identity – perhaps Northern, perhaps wider – in a future political setting of which at present they glimpse only the outline. The republican response is to insist that the gap between North and South is not real. Many, of all political persuasions and none, see and are frightened by an increased rate of loyalist attack . . . which loyalist paramilitaries themselves explain as a reaction to perceived 'pan-nationalist, pan-Catholic' gain.

Census figures offer consolation to some, who look to the future in the light of assessments, for example, that there is now a Catholic majority among students and probably among the school population too. Others look instead to the loyalist reaction. There is a tension between those who hope Protestant opinion will behave 'like the white supremacists in the southern states of the US and de Klerk in South Africa who said right, OK, we give up, and they flipped over and made a deal'; there are others who fear that instead Protestant opinion will 'go to the last ditch'.

After a long freeze, this is an evolving community, full of doubts and scepticism. Some are willing to work the system, in the hope that it will evolve as they do; many do the best they can and leave all such considerations to the party-political few. Northern Catholics waver between optimism that some day John Hume will manage to convince Sinn Féin that the IRA should stop, and dread that, if they do, Britain will allow Unionists to take control once more and there will be a terrible reckoning.

In the past few years it has become fashionable to suggest that the Northern conflict is now a phoney war for most and 'the Troubles' a phenomenon confined to the deprived and isolated. At the heart of all discussion about identity and how it can be accommodated is a cold and intensely practical consideration: of the number of guns in Northern Ireland, and who holds them. To those who look behind the rhetoric, it is steadily becoming clearer that if and when the shooting stops no one envisages general disarmament. Many agree with the elderly man who said, 'I want the Provos to disband – to give up their arms to the gardaí or the police here – but I wouldn't argue with them if they put some away in the bogs or the hills, just in case. The Catholic community cannot ever leave itself defenceless again.'

INDEX